Internet for Information Management Series

INTERNET
for
Information Services

Internet for Information Management Series

INTERNET
for
Information Services

R. Raman Nair
Former University Librarian
Kerala Agricultural University

Ess Ess Publications

4837/24, Ansari Road, Darya Ganj,
New Delhi-110002
✆ : 3260807, 3201533, Fax : 3274173
E-mail: essess@del3.vsnl.net.in
url:http://www.essessbooks.com

First Published 2002

ISBN : 81-7000-322-9

Price : Rs. 825/-

Published by:

Ess Ess Publications

4837/24, Ansari Road, Darya Ganj,
New Delhi - 110 002
Phone : 3260807; Fax : 3274173
E-mail : essess@del3.vsnl.net.in
url:http://www.essessbooks.com

Laser Typesetting:

Mukesh Graphics

L-2/8, Mangolepuri, New Delhi
Ph. : 7924405

Printed at : Print Line

Content

Preface

Internet is a network of networks and it connects information in individual computers, networks owned by governments, universities and library and information systems small and large like the community information centre at a Chinese village to the Library of Congress the largest library in the world. Internet rivals great inventions of our time. Gutenberg's invention of the printing press took books out of ecclesiastical libraries and placed them in everyone's hands. The telephone system allows people to communicate instantaneously with each other. The Internet is now merging these two technologies. It is bringing people and information together without any intermediaries that are necessitated by traditional media and without primarily one to one synchronous limitations of the telephone system. Internet is new information storage and dissemination mechanism, an electronic virtual worldwide library where time and space has almost no meaning. Internet has made real the democratisation of information.

Internet is transforming the library systems and the way in which we view information sources. The idea of library as a place is being questioned now. Librarians are forced to learn to organise and manage systems that find out and provide access to information kept elsewhere. Personal computers are now usually part of a network of computers and often part of a network of networks spanning the globe

Internet has made profound effects on the way in which we acquire, organize and disseminate information due to the astounding increase in the amount of information available at the Information Superhighway and the diversity of tools we have at our disposal for managing information. The focus of information management has shifted from acquiring to facilitating access and libraries are becoming digital or virtual and are now acting as the central hub of live information infrastructures worldwide. Thousands of online information systems, digital libraries and virtual museums have already come into existence to support research and development. Within the vast plethora of web sites there is valuable information materials, guidance, knowledge and experience from people all over the world; that are very valuable for education and research.

Librarians cannot today afford to be a mere wayside observer of these phenomenal sources of information.

This books forms the second one of the *Internet for Information Management Series* and is intended to give those engaged in managing library and information services awareness about the aspects of Internet. The book discusses the aspects like connectivity requirements, selecting an Internet Service Provider, Networking, TCP/IP and Unix fundamentals, the major Internet tools still dear to the information specialists like the Gopher, Usenet, Telnet, FTP, WAIS, Listserv etc, communication through Internet, World Wide Web, web files and formats, web design tips, DNS, web publishing and publicizing, HTML and many more aspects. The first book in this series *Accessing Information through Internet* covered the basics Librarians and Library users should know for speedily retrieving their information from the net. This book is intended for those who want to use Internet as a tool for providing information services. This is revised version of Internet for Library and Information Services.

Being a companion volume to *Accessing Information through Internet* it is advisible to use this volume along with that as many basic aspects covered in that are not touched by this book. Like the earlier books in the series this being a guide no originality is claimed. Information was freely extracted from the course materials prepared by Center for Library and Information Science (CLIS) of KAU, CIRD and also from many of the books listed in the bibliography. The materials have been class tested during the courses offered at CLIS of KAU. I would like to thank Sri. K.H Hussain of KFRI and Sri. K. Rajasekharan of KILA who contributed to these volumes by source materials and valuable suggestions and also Dr. S. Murali who has prepared the illustrations. Many readers who sent their critical suggestions to cirdindia@yahoo.com also contributed useful information for this volume, which has helped me. My sincere thanks are also due to Centre for Informatics Research and Development for launching this series and Ess Ess publications for the continuous encouragement they give.

I hope that this book can give the basic things librarians must understand and master in order to use Internet for library and information service.

R. Raman Nair

1

Introduction

Internet has made information, any bit of knowledge recorded at any time, kept at any part of the world if it is available in digital media just a click away, and lakhs and lakhs of libraries are now on the side of Information Super Highway and millions of people are joining the rush in the superhighway seeking information from the net.

Internet is a 'network of networks' and is the 'the world's largest network'. But these networks are simply the medium that carries information. The importance of Internet is in the information itself and the sources or the libraries, which it connects. Internet is now a huge source of academic, research and general information. Internet facilitates the sharing of information by millions of people and institutions all over the world. It is like a global library that every one can access at any time. It is a global venue where every one can present their knowledge and information. So Internet is like a library where people and information are connected. Like the library which was the old mechanism that linked information in traditional media and people, here computers which link the information in digital media and people and is called Internet. So Internet is a library that transcends space and media.

Internet was established more than 25 years ago to meet the research needs of the American defense industry. Now it has grown into a huge global network serving universities and libraries, academic researchers, government agencies, and commercial interests, both in the United States and in more than 100 other countries. It is not a person or an organization that runs the Internet, and pays all the costs for its maintenance. There is no Internet Corporation. The Internet exists as a result of the cooperation of thousands of people all over the world, working in all sorts of organizational and computing environments. The Internet never closes down, mostly because of its decentralized structure, and today the Internet is reliable and predictable. Individual servers may close for upgrades or hardware replacements, but the network is always available to you for access without any break.

1. Evolution of Internet

The Advanced Research Projects Agency (ARPA) of the U.S. Department of Defense established ARPA net in 1969. It was an experimental four-computer network, for the research scientists to communicate among themselves. The first link was between a computer at UCLA's Boelter Hall, home of the Computer Science Department, and another computer hundreds of miles away at the Stanford Research Institute. In 1971, ARPA net comprised almost two dozen sites, including MIT and Harvard; by 1974 that number had grown to 62 and by 1981, ARPA net consisted of more than 200 sites. When more and more computers using different operating systems were connected, the need for a common communications protocol became obvious. The theory required that any computer on the net- work should be able to talk to any other computer, as a peer. Fault tolerance was designed in at an early stage so that a message from one computer to another could travel by anyone of many routes rather than always following a single, unvarying, fixed path. The messages passed between two computers may often take different paths, depending on the availability of the connecting links and the level of network traffic at that time.

1.1. Standards

Gradually the communications protocol called TCP /IP (Transmission Control Protocol/Internet Protocol) was developed and in 1983 it became the standard communications protocol on the Internet. The design of TCP /IP was one of the major achievements in the sphere which solved many communications headaches. Even today it is popular. In 1980s, many more computer networks were linked to the Internet. Many of them used Ethernet, and many of them ran one variation or another of the Unix operating system a version, which included IP networking software. In 1983, the military portion of ARPA net was moved onto the MIL net, and ARPA net was officially disbanded in 1990. By the late 1980s, the National Science Foundation's NSF net linked five super- computer centers at major universities. At first ARPA net was tried for communications, but for many reasons this eventually failed. Therefore, NFS net began its own network, based on the IP technology and using 56Kbps, which was considered very fast at the time.

An important aspect of the NSF participation was that it allowed everyone to access the network; however, the NSF had a policy known as "acceptable use," which prohibited most commercial activities unless they involved "scholarly communications and research." This acceptable use policy was thrown away in 1994 when the U.S. government extracted itself from the Internet and passed control of the NSF backbone to commercial companies. By 1995, with most of the government involvement removed, commercial activity started.

1.2. Hypertext and Browsers

Major phase of the history of the Internet Software starts in 1989, when Tim Berners Lee, of European Particle Research Center (CERN) in Switzerland, and his associates invented a way of formatting documents for their easy transmission, display, and printing on almost any kind of network computer. Berners Lee also invented the term World Wide Web to describe the results of his work. Users later shortened this to 'the Web'. The World Wide Web was released for internal use at CERN in 1991, where it was used for publishing scientific research papers and the results of experiments. In 1992, the system and the software were made available to the public.

1.3. HTML and HTTP

The proposal given by Berners Lee consisted of two separate but closely related parts:

- Hypertext Markup Language (HTML) for formatting the documents

- Hypertext Transfer Protocol (HTTP) for transmitting the documents from one computer to another

The HTML format not only make the documents attractive for us to look at or print online, but also it allows these documents to contain hypertext links to other documents on other computers on the Internet. Hypertext is a way of presenting information so that we can look at it in a non-sequential way, regardless of how the original topics were organized by the author of the document. Hypertext was designed to allow the computer to respond to the nonlinear way that humans think and access information. For example consider association, rather than linear arrangement of films, books, or recorded speech.

In a hypertext application, we can browse through the information with a great deal of flexibility. We can choose to follow a different path through the information each time we look at a specific document, that is something we can't do with video or recorded speech.

A hypertext document can contain a hypertext link to any other document or resource on the Internet, and this link is managed by HTTP. When we select a link, the associated document is displayed, even though it may be on a different computer system, thousands of miles away from our location.

1.4 Introducing URL

The computer that requests the document is known as a client, and the computer that makes the document available is known as a server. Put the two together, and we have the fundamentals of the client-server model for distributed computing.

A Universal Resource Locator, or URL, is a basic HTML element, and when embedded in an HTML document, it points directly to another document somewhere on the Internet that can be retrieved by HTTP.

The client software that makes this process happen is called a browser, and the first HTML browsers were text based. They displayed hypertext links followed by a number in brackets. By typing that number, we could follow that link. All this changed with the advent of Mosaic and the other graphical browsers that came later.

1.5 Mosaic and Other Browsers

The web pages are not transmitted all at once, but are built up over several browser transactions to avoid a long wait, as a huge file is downloaded into our system. The text portion of the page is transmitted first, and it contains information about which graphics go where on the page and about where they are located on the server. The browser hides these organizational details from us, and we don't normally see them on our screen.

These processes allow our browser to display the text page quickly and easily so that we have something to look at as the graphics are downloaded. We can read this page, wait for the rest of the graphics to arrive, or jump to another page; the browser simply forgets about loading the graphics and instead starts to display the initial text portion of the new page requested by us.

Marc Andreeson while working at the University of Illinois National Center for Supercomputing Applications (NCSA) wrote Mosaic, which hid all the HTML elements from the viewer and presented a clear, easy-to-read document containing graphics as well as text. Hypertext links to other documents were displayed as highlighted text; all we have to do was click on a link to display the document. Mosaic also lets us add to a list of frequently visited sites and displayed any links we had already visited in a separate color on the screen for our convenience.

In late 1993, NCSA simultaneously released versions of Mosaic for Microsoft Windows, for Unix systems running the X Window System, and for the Apple Macintosh. Within a short while Mosaic became very popular.

Andreeson left NCSA in 1994 and co-found Netscape Communications, creators of the popular Netscape browser. The Netscape browser has been bundled free with all sorts of services from companies such as America Online and CompuServe and is freely available by download from the Netscape Web site. We only have to pay the line charges associated with downloading the files from their site.

A Web browser when it encounters a type of file that it cannot manage, checks to see if there is a helper application, or plug-in, for that file type. Common plug-ins include JPEG viewers, sound players, and animation or video viewers and are available for almost all the popular file types we will encounter on the net.

Now most of the companies including such biggest ones like as IBM and Microsoft, offer browser software based on Mosaic and because they are based on the open standards defined by HTML and HTTP, they work in the same way. If we can use one of them we can use any of them.

1.6 The Web Explodes

It was not any single invention or event that led to the Web taking off in such a dramatic way. But numerous related events, including the following ones have resulted in it.

- easy availability of Internet connections
- removal of restrictions to commercial development of the Internet
- access to powerful graphical browsers such as Mosaic and Netscape
- adoption of many important standards

Every one of these elements combined to fuel the Web explosion. The growth in registered commercial names on the Internet has produced increases in excess of 720 percent, which, taken on a daily basis, means that hundreds of new sites are being added every day. And this figure does not take into account those small businesses that rent space on third-party Web servers, because we don't have to register those sites with any supervising authority.

Recent Internet surveys estimate that there are more than 50 million Internet users today, and of that total, some 25 to 30 million have access to the World Wide Web. Commercial providers such as America Online and CompuServe add new users to this total each and every minute.

Experts put the number of web pages at somewhere about 60 million. Given that an average web page contains about 500 words, or about 7K of text, the total web contents must be somewhere near 500 gigabytes of text, and these numbers are growing at a rate of about 25 percent a month. At this current rate of growth, the web will soon contain more words than the today's Library of Congress, which contains approximately 30 terabytes by the end of 2000.

Some of the most successful web sites, such as those run by Microsoft Corporation that is http: //www. microsoft .com/ or Netscape Communications that is http: //home. netscape .com/, each register several million hits every day. A hit occurs when a user with a web browser opens a file or a graphic from the concerned web page.

2. Internet and Intranet

All this emphasizes on the Internet and the World Wide Web. The availability of free or almost free web browsers has led some computer staffs in the corporate world to look at their internal networks in a new light.

The questions asked most often is, how can we benefit from this explosion in tools and standards and what happens if we implement World Wide Web standards in our department or even the network of our own organization. The answer is an Intranet, an internal company network that uses the Web standards of HTML and HTTP and the TCP /IP communications protocol along with a graphical Web browser to support real business applications and provide departmental, interdepartmental, and organization wide communications solutions.

An Intranet consists of a web server connected to an organization's local area network. The web server contains electronic copies of important company documents, and as information changes over time, these documents are updated on the server. People in the organization access this information using a web browser; thus, they need learn how to use only a single application to access all the organization's information, rather than many applications as in times past. Cost effectiveness is considerable, and information is up to date and available to everyone on demand.

Intranets are used to publish documents ranging from organization's detailed reports, research papers, journals and also policies and procedures manuals, phone listings, training manuals, new job opportunities and even day to day activity information. The old barriers of proprietary hardware and software are easily overcome when we adopt the emerging web standards; web technology is available for almost all leading operating systems and hardware platforms. Programmers can add links to legacy databases that is essential information on mainframe systems that can be considered ancient in computer years so that information can be viewed and updated quickly and easily. Secure servers can isolate sensitive classified information and make it available only to those users in, say the Finance Department. The possible uses for an Intranet are almost endless.

3 Windows NT and Unix

Almost all of the computer systems that originally made up the Internet ran one of the variations of the Unix operating system, and so it was only natural that the early web servers were written to run on Unix; it was simply convenient. But there are few natural advantages to using Unix as a web server, and in fact there are also some very good reasons to avoid using Unix if we possibly can.

Unix has been around for more than 30 years, and many of the security lapses in the operating system and system utilities are well known. But the fact that they are well known does not mean that they have been fixed in all versions and in all installations. Intruders are still exploiting well-known holes in Unix e-mail systems to gain unauthorized access.

Windows NT Server is one of the most stable operating systems around, from any vendor, and the cost of hardware and software is low when compared with the large server hardware appetites usually inherent in Unix. NT Server runs on the Intel series of microprocessors familiar to all PC users, as well as on MIPS RISC, Alpha, and Power PC platforms, and the operating system is licensed to the Apple Computer Corporation. NT Server can also integrate with all the popular network operating systems available today and supports many networking protocols, including TCP /IP, IPX, SNA, and NetBEUI.

3.1. Internet Information Server

Microsoft began shipping the first release of the Internet Information Server, or IIS in 1996, which was later, incorporated into the BackOffice suite of products. We can also download the software free from Microsoft's own World Wide Web site. Internet Information Server is a network file and information server that transmits information in HTML using H1TP over a TCP /IP network. The package also includes a Gopher service for publishing information archives and an FTP service for transmitting and receiving files. We can also find copies of Microsoft's own Web browser, Internet Explorer, for a variety of platforms, including Windows NT, Windows 95, and Windows for Workgroups, Windows 3.1, and the Macintosh in the Windows NT 4 package and at the Microsoft web site.

Most people will undoubtedly use IIS primarily as a web server, providing all the Internet and Intranet services. Microsoft uses IIS running on multiple servers to operate its own web site, one of the busiest web sites in the world.

3.2. Windows NT 4

Microsoft released version 4 of Windows NT Server, in 1996 containing many additional features, including the famous Windows 95 graphical user interface, already familiar to millions of computer users all over the world. Adding the stability and scalability of Windows NT to the power of the Internet Information Server creates a formidable combination with many advantages over a Unix-based Internet server, including:

- World Wide Web, Gopher, and FTP services included in IIS are completely integrated with NT's user accounts and file access permissions. This is not an application that runs "on top" of NT, but as an integrated part of NT.
- Facility to configure our NT Server security in several ways, including physical or protocol isolation, to keep potential intruders at bay.

- Windows NT Server is easy to install, configure, and use. A department full of Unix gurus and C programmers are not needed to establish an Internet presence using NT.
- The security accounts and the tools we use to manage them with IIS are the same tools we use to manage NT security.
- All the software needed to establish an Internet presence is included in the NT package; we won't need to buy other programs later.
- Facility to extend the reach of the Web server using CGI (Common Gateway Interface) scripts or Microsoft's own Internet Server API (ISAPI).
- A large number of database servers are available for the NT plat- form, and vendors are showing a great deal of innovation in this arena.
- Windows NT can be configured either as an Internet server or as an Intranet server Windows NT has an inherent scalability that makes changing system components relatively straightforward. Visitors at our site consume resources in the same way as local users do. We can add memory and hard-disk space to NT Server quickly and easily.

Considering all the above aspects will show that a low-risk, relatively low-cost Internet server running on NT, which is easy to install, configure, and maintain will be suitable for providing our library an exclusive Internet presence.

4. Right Connections

If we want to publish information on the web or get information from the Web, we must obtain a connection to the Internet. There are two parts to this connection. They are the communications link and an Internet Service Provider (ISP). The communications link can be one of many kinds, and it is very important that the connection match our anticipated requirements as closely as possible. On the one hand, we don't want to pay for unused capacity; but on the other, we don't want visitors to our web site to be put off by too many "port unavailable" or "the server is not responding" error messages. Let us discuss now the various types of connections available, as well as the ways in which we can estimate our requirements, and then look at a checklist of questions to be asked of any Internet Service Provider. We need to be well informed to make our own decisions about the level of service we need now and the level of service that we may need in the immediate future. We will also discuss here how we can establish a domain name for our library or organization.

4.1 Types of Connections

As no Internet Corporation is in overall charge of the Internet, the connection and service-level choices can seem overwhelming at first. There is no single individual we can contact to order service; instead, we will find a large number of options offered by the phone companies, ISPs, consultants, and contractors. Each organization must assess its needs and then choose a service accordingly.

The Internet connection we will be having will be via a network interface card or other device in our NT Server computer, and this device, along with the bandwidth of the communications circuit to which it is attached determine the capacity of our web server. Bandwidth is expressed in terms of megabits per second (Mbps), or millions of bits per second, and determines how many simultaneous users our web server can process at one time. Put crudely, the higher the bandwidth, the more users our server will be able to support.

An important aspect to remember throughout here is that the web runs 24 hours a day, 365 day a year, and what may well be a suitable access method for a web browser supporting a single user turns out to be totally inadequate for a major organization like an university supporting a large web-server site with hundreds of simultaneous users.

4.2 Leased Web Space

At any point of time someone in our organization will ask, why do we have to have our own web site instead of just leasing web space from one of these ISPs. There are many answers to these questions, and they all are related to network control and who will be doing that. In the case if we represent a very small library and want to experiment with a web presence on a tiny budget, leasing space can be a good way to start. We have to bear in mind that if we expand our presence to the point where the original site cannot provide adequate levels of support, we will have to move to a new site and change our library URL to reflect this new site. There could be a period of upset as users become accustomed to our new Internet address.

But normally, we will pay for leased space by the megabyte of stored material. Graphics are very popular on most web sites and can consume a lot of hard-disk space. If our application includes large documents that contain multiple graphics, it will be cheaper to run our own site. Other aspects of control that we lose when we lease include server response time. We will be sharing the leased space with other users, and we will have no control over server configuration or management or over the type or frequency of hardware or software upgrades. If one of the other sites on the same service turns out to be very popular, our user's response time may suffer as a consequence.

But the benefits of leasing web space are in the initial cost savings; it is relatively cheap to start a small web site this way. The ISP takes care of all the issues and decisions related to connecting to the Internet; and installing and maintaining the host systems, as well as all the administrative and technical details associated with maintaining the site and keeping it running,

4.3. Dial-Up Connection

Popular and simplest type of connection to the Internet is via a dial-up connection, sometimes called an on-demand connection. This can be through a conventional modem or through a digital system such as Integrated Services Digital Network (ISDN). This type of connection is only available part time, as its name suggests, and is not really suitable for a busy web site that should be available day and night every day.

Leased line, also known as a dedicated circuit, on the other hand, is always available and can be provided by modem, by ISDN, and by many other kinds of communications circuits. These circuits range in bandwidth from 56Kbps to almost 45Mbps; and the cost of the service rises with the available bandwidth.

4.4 SLI P or PPP and Modem

Many Web users will start their explorations using a PC and a dial-up modem connection with a 28.8 Kbps V.34 or higher modem. This number refer to standards defined by the International Telecommunications Union (ITU), a United Nations umbrella organization that develops and standardizes telecommunications worldwide. The ITU also includes the CCITT (Comite Consultatif Internationale de Telephonie et de Telegraphie) and several other related organizations. In popular usage CCITT standards are also referred to as ITU standards.

V.34 Modem: The V.34 CCITT standard defines a 28.8Kbps modem for use over dial-up lines using trellis-encoding techniques and advanced data compression techniques to boost effective data-transfer rates well beyond the nominal 28.8Kbps; when V.42 bis compression is added, theoretical data-transfer rates of up to 115.2Kbps are possible.

SLIP: Serial Line Internet Protocol (SLIP) is used to run the IP protocol over telephone connections using the modems described in the previous paragraphs. SLIP allows us to establish a direct but temporary connection to the Internet, during which our computer appears to the host computer as if it were a port on the host's network. Because it lacks error-correction capabilities, SLIP is slowly being replaced by PPP.

PPP: Point-to-Point Protocol (PPP) is similar to SLIP, in that it allows us to establish a direct but temporary connection to the Internet using a modem and a phone line. PPP also provides router-to-router, host-to-router, and host-to-host connections, as well as an automatic method of assigning an IP address so that mobile users can connect to the network at any point. These modems and protocols are fine for use with web browses, but they are certainly not appropriate for use with a web server, unless we anticipate that we will only ever have two or three simultaneous users. In this kind of low traffic situation, these connections may suffice, but there is little or no extra bandwidth to allow for future expansion.

For most Web servers one of the following options will make much more sense.

4.5 Frame Relay

Frame relay is primarily used in local area networks and in some wide area networks and is offered by most of the Regional Bell Operating Companies and the major carriers such as MCI, and Sprint. Bandwidth is in the range of 56Kbps to 1.544Mbps and is suitable for transmitting data only; it is not suitable for transmitting voice or video, because these require constant transmission capabilities. Frame relay was originally intended as a bearer service for ISDN and is independent of any protocol; therefore, it can transmit packets from TCP /IP, IPX/SPX, and other protocol families. Connections into a frame relay network require a router and a line from the customer site to the carrier's point of entry. After an initial startup cost of somewhere between Rs. 40000 and Rs 2 lakhs a connection will cost us between Rs. 10 000 to 15000 a month.

4.6 ISDN

ISDN is a completely digital service capable of transmitting digitally encoded data, voice, video, and other signals on the same line. ISDN has been popular in developed countries for years; although it is slowly gaining ground in the India, it is still not available in all areas. No special wiring is needed for ISDN; it uses the copper twisted pair wiring of the normal telephone system. ISDN does, however, require a special device to interface between our Web server and the ISDN system. This device is known as a terminal adapter (TA) or as an ISDN modem and can connect normal analog equipment, such as telephones and fax machines, to the ISDN system.

The ISDN Solutions Group, a vendor consortium, has developed a system called ISDN Ordering Codes (IOC) to help simplify ISDN ordering procedures. One group of codes, known as capabilities, is a set of common provisioning profiles, labeled A through S. If our equipment matches one of these profiles, documentation provided by the vendor will tell us to specify that capability when ordering equipment. A second group of codes is equipment-specific, using codes such as Motorola Access 3 to invoke a custom profile for that specific piece of hardware. This ROC system, when used with ISDN service is by far the best way to assemble all the component pieces one will need for his system.

Conventional wisdom says that ordering ISDN is difficult, that we have to be very careful when specifying hardware, and that configuration is painful. It is somewhat true, but now there are dedicated ISDN ordering lines, and most of the newer equipments are flexible enough to work with almost all ISDN lines. In west both Microsoft and Motorola are staging an effort to convert users to ISDN and have posted ISDN specification and ordering forms on their Web sites. Check out Microsoft's site at http://www.microsoft.com/windows/getisdn/ or the Motorola site at http://www.mot .com/isdn/.

ISDN will be available in two forms. First is BRI, or Basic Rate ISDN, which provides 3 data channels. Two are .64Kbps B (or bearer) channels, and the third is a 16Kbps D (or data) channel that carries call-setup and signaling data between our ISDN devices and the phone company. In some areas, the B channels may run at 56Kbps due to limitation in the phone system. On a BRI line, one can make two separate calls to two different locations at the same time, or can combine the two channels to give 128Kbps data-transfer rates. Second form is PRI, or Primary Rate ISDN. It provides twenty-three 64Kbps B channels and one 64Kbps D channel for a total bandwidth of up to 1.544Mbps. In Europe where communications standards are slightly different, PRI consists of either thirty or thirty-one 64Kbps B channels, and one 64Kbps D channel, for a total bandwidth of 2.048Mbps. In most areas, one PRI line is much cheaper than the equivalent number of BRI lines. Each of the B channels operates independently and can carry voice or data.

Prices for ISDN hardware, including ISDN modems, are falling all the time, and connection and line charges are also falling as the services become available in more areas and more popular with users. Normally one ISDN line can be much cheaper than two normal analog phone lines.

Both analog and ISDN phone lines continue to work during a power outage, but our ISDN office equipment will not. Hence we have to install an Uninterruptible Power Supply (UPS) to provide backup power during the inevitable outages.

4.7. Fractional T1, T1, T3, and SMDS

A fractional T1 sometimes abbreviated, as FTI line is a sub channel of a full T1 channel, made available at a correspondingly lower price. Full 1.544Mbps T1 line contains 24 fractional T1 lines, each with a bandwidth of 64Kbps. Users can contract for one or more fractional lines without the need to purchase a complete T1 line, and they can add to and expand their stock of fractional T1 lines at any time. Fractional T1 lines are also made available as packages of 384Kb (6 fractional T1 lines), 512Kbps (8 fractional T1 lines), and 768Kbps (12 fractional T1 lines).

T1: This is a long-distance point-to-point communications circuit that provides 24 channels of 64Kbps, giving a total bandwidth of 1.544Mbps. T1 is one of the main carriers in the U.S. and although it was originally developed to transmit voice, it can also transmit data and images. In Europe and South America, a comparable carrier is designated as El with a bandwidth of 2.048Mbps. Tl services are usually leased on a month-to-month basis and are still quite expensive, especially if they involve two or more phone companies. Installation costs are also high; so Tl services tend to be used for longer-distance links. To connect our local area network to a T1 line, we will need a Channel Service Unit (CSU), which functions as a certified safe electrical circuit, acting as a buffer between our equipment and the public carrier's network. The CSU prevents faulty equipment from affecting the transmission systems and ensures that all signals placed on the line are appropriately timed and formed. Also Data Service Unit (DSU), which connects data terminal equipment (DTE) to the digital communications lines, is essential. The DSU connects to the CSU and converts the local area network signals to T1 signaling formats. Then Multiplexor, which loads multiple channels of voice or data onto the T1b line and the Bridge or router, which provides the actual connection point between our local area network and the T1 system are other requirements. The leased lines such as a T1 circuit have their limitations; they are dedicated lines with a fixed bandwidth. We could, therefore, find ourselves paying for bandwidth that we don't use most of the time, but need very occasionally to accommodate short periods of high- burst traffic. Some newer technologies such as SMDS and ATM may actually be more flexible than a T1 line, but we still need the T1 line to connect to the access point of the service. A T1 connection will cost on the order of Rs. 1 lakh to 2.5 lakhs a month; a fractional T1 will be substantially less.

T3: It is a circuit is a big pipe indeed; equivalent to 28 T1 circuits, it provides a bandwidth of 44.736Mbps and was used originally for transmission between microwave stations. A T3 line can carry 672 channels of 64Kbps and is usually made available over high-speed fiber-optic cable. Almost exclusively AT&T and the regional telephone companies use it, although certain private companies are using T3 with digital microwave or fiber-optic networks. Fractional T3 lines may be available to customers at a lower cost. Two other T-carrier services are T2 and T4. T2 is a long-distance, point-to-point communications service, providing up to 4 T1 channels. T2 offers 96 channels of 64Kbps, for a total bandwidth of 6.3Mbps. T2 service is not available commercially, although it is used within company telephone networks. T4 provides up to 168 T1 channels, or 4032 channels of 64Kbps, for a total bandwidth of 274.176Mbps. There are also T-carrier service referred to as a DS, an abbreviation for digital signal or digital service. DS-0 is equivalent to one 64Kbps circuit, and DS-1 is equivalent to a T1 circuit. Four DS-1 circuits are multiplexed to make equivalent to a T2 circuit, and seven DS-2 circuits are combined to create a DS-3, equivalent to a T3 circuit. Finally, six DS-3 circuits are combined to create a DS-4 circuit, equivalent to a T4 circuit.

SMDS: Switched Multimegabit Data Service known by the

acronym (SMDS) is a connectionless, high-speed wide area network service that can transfer data at rates of between I.544Mbps and 44.736Mbps over T1 and T3 circuits. Bellcore developed SDMS, and full SMDS services will be made generally available in selected metropolitan areas over a several year period. Equipment and installation costs are high, approximately five times those of frame relay.

4.8. ATM, Microwave, and Others

Asynchronous Transfer Mode known by the acronym ATM is also called cell relay in order to distinguish it from frame relay. It is a relatively new, very high-speed digital data transmission circuit capable of data-transfer rates of up to the 2.488 gigabits per second range under experimental conditions. Initial implementations are usually slower, either 155.52Mbps or 622.08Mbps. Companies such as AT&T and Sprint offer ATM, but the adoption rate has been relatively slow. Because of this, several variations in the basic ATM service have emerged in an attempt to get at least some form of ATM into the market. ATM25 and ATM LAN Emulation are two such attempts. Information on related aspects are available at ATM forum in http: //www .atmforum.com/ which can be referred if interested.

Microwave, and Satellite: The microwave and satellite options might be worth considering if we are in a very remote area or if we want to transmit a very large amount of data allover the world. The International Telecommunications Satellite Organization web site at http://www.intelsat.int: 8080/ gives detailed information on this.

SVC versus PVC: Many of the services we have seen above can be obtained in two configurations: that is as an SVC, or Switched Virtual Circuit, or as a PVC, or Permanent Virtual Circuit. There are some differences between the two. An SVC is a connection that is established for a communications session and that is terminated when the session is complete. In this way, a service can provide bandwidth-on-demand as the need for service fluctuates. A different virtual circuit may be established each time a call is made. PVC is a logical circuit established between two locations, since the path is fixed, we can think of PVC as the equivalent of a dedicated line over a packet-switched network.

4.9. Hardware Compatibility Information

Microsoft runs an extensive hardware testing and qualification system for Windows NT, and we can find a list of all the computer systems and peripherals that have been successfully tested, called the Hardware Compatibility List, at several locations. This list includes modems, ISDN, and other communications devices. On the web, we can see the main Microsoft site at: http://www.microsoft.com/BackOffice/ntserver/hcl . We can also get this information by FTP from: ftp.microsoft.com\bussys\winnt\winnt-docs\hcl and in Library 1 of the WINNT forum named GO WINNT or in Library 17 of the MSWIN32 forum called GO MSWIN32, both on CompuServe. Microsoft is constantly qualifying new hardware and adding new material to this list; so it is a very good idea to check one of these sites regularly.

5. Defining Library's Needs

In the previous section, we looked at some of the communications circuits commonly available, including frame relay, ISDN, and T1, as well as some of the rarely available options such as ATM and SMDS. Now we'll look at methods we can use to try to estimate the traffic on our web server. We can then use that number to select a specific communications option.

5.1 Stand Alone Web Server

The quickest and easiest way to establish our presence on the web is by installing a stand-alone web server. It is attached to the Internet via an ISP, but there are no other connections to any of our other networks. This approach simplifies estimating traffic and procuring service, because all we have to do is estimate the amount of traffic we expect from the Internet, and it makes dealing with security issues much easier. The down side of this approach is that we cannot connect our Web site to any other software running on other computers in our organization's computers that may contain a customer database or a mailing list that visitors to our Web site might need to update. For most corporations, a stand-alone web server might be a good place to start, but sooner or later, a corporation will want to connect its web server to information available elsewhere in the organization, and that means adding the Web server to an existing network or net- works.

5.2 Web Server for Existing Network

Once we connect our web server to our existing network, the traffic-estimation problems and security issues become much complex. We must spend much more time carefully estimating the incremental network traffic that we expect the web server to introduce, and we must have adequate hardware in place to ensure that network performance is not degraded for existing users inside the corporation. When we have properly evaluated our needs, we will know whether our site requires a low, medium, or high-speed connection to the Internet. After we connect our corporate network to the outside world via the Internet, security concerns become much more serious. Some network administrators assume as a matter of course that all visitors to their Web sites are potential intruders, and they plan for this right from the very beginning; others actually try to break into their own networks via the Web server, just to see how hard or easy it the process can be.

5.3. Bandwidth Needs

Assessing our bandwidth needs requires an attempt to measure the amount of data that is likely to flow to and from our Web site. Initially, doing so can be difficult. If we are offering something new and unusual on our site, we may see much more traffic than we expect; some popular sites generate lakhs and lakhs of hits a day. We have to talk to other network administrators in the corporation or in similar corporations to get an idea of how they approached estimating their needs, and then understand from them how they were realistic.

5.4. Web Page Size

In case we have already designed our web page, we can calculate the average size of each page in kilobytes. An average web text page is about 500 words, or about 7K, but as soon as we add a graphic or two, we must increase this size estimate. A number somewhere between 30K and 50K is probably a reasonable starting point, so use this number if we have not yet designed any of our web pages. Then, we have to add in a component for any other services we plan to offer on our web page, including e-mail, FTP, or Gopher services. These services will probably attract a lower level of interest, and therefore create less traffic, but we should not forget them or exclude them from the picture. Here are some real numbers to help with this illustration. The following table shows the times it takes to move a 250K file over various communications links.

Link type	*Speed*	*Transfer time*
V.32 Modem	14.4Kbps	2.22 minutes
Frame Relay	56Kbps	34.35 seconds
T1	1.544Mbps	1.24 seconds
T3	44.736Mbps	0.04 seconds

One other useful point of reference we can use to get a handle on our web-related needs is the speed of our own network. Ethernet usually runs at 10Mbps, and Fast Ethernet and its variations run at speeds of up to 100Mbps. we can also relate the data-communication rates with the data transfer rates of other familiar devices we will find in our own office, such as our hard disk systems or SCSI (Small Computer System Interface) hard disk and CDROMs. If we plan to use lots of static Web pages with lots of text, our bandwidth requirements will be very different from those of a site that intends to implement video conferencing and real time audio and video.

5.6 Hit Rates

The next task is to estimate the number of times a day that we think our site will be visited. This is in other words, how many times our site will receive hits each day. This is another quantity that is difficult to estimate, but we can make some sensible assumptions. We will probably see a large number of hits as people discover our new site. Then, as time goes on, we will see the hit rate level off. To get an idea of the traffic all this involves, multiply the hit rate we expect by the average size of our web pages; for example, if we expect a hit rate of 5,000 a day, and our average web page is 25K, our daily server traffic will be on the order of 2500MB of data.

5.7 Keeping Systems Live Day and Night

These calculations can be taken further and we can estimate our average hourly traffic. But we have to remember that the Internet pays no attention to time zones; it is always there, not just for an 8-hour workday, but 24 hours every day. We will certainly see peaks and troughs in our hit rates during any 24-hour period, because when it is night at one region of the world it is morning or evening in another place from were people will access.

5.8 Quantum of Use

The final part in the equation is to estimate how many simultaneous users we want to be able to support. It should be maximum available bandwidth on purpose, as there are many other influencing factors that come into play when we attempt to calculate actual bandwidth rates, including protocol overhead, the speed of intermediate connecting circuits, configuration of intermediate host computer systems, and many others. For these reasons, we will never attain these maximum rates, but we have to start assessing our needs somewhere, and this is a good place. The following is a comparison of maximum bandwidth and maximum number of users for popular Internet connections

Connection Type	*Maximum Bandwidth*	*Maximum Number of Users*
V32 or V42 modem	14.4 Kbps	1 to 3
V.34 modem	28.8 Kbps	1 to 3
Frame relay	56 Kbps	10 to 20
ISDN	128 Kbps	10 to 55
Fractional T1	64 Kbps increments	10 to 20
T1	1.544 Mbps	100 to 500
T3	44 736 Mbps	More than 5,000

If our Web site will be designed primarily to help handle technical, support material, ask the existing technical support staff to understand how many calls a day they get. If our site will offer customer service information, ask the current staff to describe their workload.

5.9. The Website Manager

We should not assume that we could add the responsibilities of looking after a busy, evolving web site to those of our already overburdened network administrator. We need an additional librarian or persons with some Windows NT Server administration, experience who also have Internet and web experience and a good eye for attractive design so that they can help to layout the HTML pages we want our Web server to display. Someone will also have to collect, distribute, and perhaps even reply to any e-mail our site collects. He should also stay up to date on all matters relating to the Internet and the Web as well as all the information sought for from the organization as well as sought by the organization and its scientists and others and are prepared to supply that information or provide instant guidance for accessing it. He should spend some time surfing the web looking for sites and libraries to link to our own site, and should check that links from other sites lead visitors to the right place on our site. Many links lead to dead ends, and nothing repels visitors like repeated error messages.

6. Making the Choice

When we start to choose a communications link, the following principles should be kept in mind.

- We should never consider dial-up links using conventional PC modems with data-transfer rates of 14.4Kbps or 28.8Kbps. These modems are too slow to support a busy web server site.
- Frame relay at 56Kbps is really the minimum data-transfer rate that most sites can manage with, giving access to somewhere between 10 and 20 simultaneous users.
- When we anticipate a moderate use of our Web site, say as many as 40 or 50 users at a time, a Primary Rate ISDN service could well rum out to be the best way to go.
- When we think our Web site will attract a great deal of traffic, somewhere up to 500 users at a time, we can start with a Fractional T1 and then expand as usage grows to a full T1 circuit.
- If we think that our site will be phenomenally busy, with thousands of simultaneous users, we should establish a 44.736Mbps T3 connection right from the start.

The decision whatever may be that we make now may not last for very long, and this will certainly not be the last time we consider our' company's bandwidth needs.

6.1 Future Expansion

We will undoubtedly need to increase both the amount of the hard disk storage on our web server, as our site becomes more popular with both visitors and staff within the corporation, and the bandwidth of our communications link in the fairly immediate future, and certainly within a couple of years. Internet applications will continue to grow in terms of computing and storage needs, as well as in terms of the loads they impose on our communications links. Selecting certain communications options can be expensive when it is time to upgrade our service. We should not put it off. We have to just assume that we will have to upgrade and that we will be upgrading sooner than our current plans indicate. Both ISDN and Fractional T1 services are scalable, and we can work with our service provider to add bandwidth as soon as it becomes obvious that we need a little extra bandwidth.

7. Finding an ISP

Now there are more than 500 ISPs in India. ISPs are consolidating in an attempt to cope with the vastly increased competition from the Telephone department. One of the best places to look for information on ISPs is the Web. We can check those web sites for comprehensive lists of ISPs, and then check out the individual ISP's web pages for details. Some popular cites listing worldwide service provides are http://thelist.com,and http://wings.buffalo.edu/world http:// www. Cyber today. com. cybertoday/isps/. We can also find ISPs listed in the Yellow Pages under Computers, Networking, and many ISPs advertise in the local newspapers. In choosing an ISP, we must decide the relative importance of several interrelated factors. We will examine some of them here.

7.1 Evaluating ISPs

The most important feature of our Internet connection is that it works and that it works all the time. We can check the reliability figures from our ISP, and ask for the names of at least three references. We can also look for references with the same number of comparable systems to the ones we have and in a similar organization. When we get the names, we can call them and ask them to tell us about their worst day and the nature of the problems encountered. Some ISPs offer service guarantees, and others offer rebates based on down time. All networks fail at some point, and the important factor here is how quickly the ISP isolates the problem and how fast it is fixed and the service is restored.

Coping with Power Outages: The most common cause of service loss is one that is not actually under the control of the ISP. It is a power outage at the customer site. A backhoe on a neighboring construction site can bring the best made plans crashing. A power outage will either be transient and very short, resulting in no loss or virtually no loss in service, or it will last days, depending on the severity. A long power outage is also likely to affect our ISP and also other providers in the area.

Circuit Failure Rates: The next most common failure after a power failure is loss of the communications circuit. Again, this can range from a very brief interruption to a total loss in service that lasts for several hours or days. We can ask our ISP what contingency plans are in place to provide an alternative service if the break lasts for longer than expected.

Maintenance Outages: Finally, there are two areas of maintenance to consider. Unscheduled maintenance relates to fixing unexpected hardware or software problems and should amount to less than an hour per occurrence. Scheduled maintenance, on the other hand, is planned well in advance, and our ISP should be able to give us a list of all scheduled and preventive maintenance operations, the length of time they are expected to take, and their potential impact on services.

Assessing Technical Support: Another way to assess an ISP's ability to provide continuing service is to find out when its network operations center is fully staffed. If we expect Internet access 24 hours a day, for 7 days a week, we need to know if we can call the ISP with technical problems outside normal business hours. The support must be there when we need it. ISPs with people on site provide better service than those whose support staff is "on call." If staff is on call during the night, we have to ask about average response time and about how many service outages of what duration take place during the night. We should also check an ISP's policies for staffing the technical support desk during major holidays; again, those ISPs with staff on call tend to provide terrible support during holidays.

We have to ensure that the ISP has an adequate supply of spares on hand to be able to cope quickly with common emergencies associated with hardware failures. To determine if the technical support desk is adequately staffed, we can try calling them at odd hours of the day and night before we sign up for service. This way we can make sure that we can get through to a person who can answer our questions, and not just leave a voice-mail message that may or may not ever be answered.

7.2. Network Connectivity Bottlenecks

If we decide to install a high-performance link to our ISP, we have to be sure that there are no network bottlenecks or bandwidth restrictions within the ISP's network or in the onward connection between the ISP's systems and the rest of the Internet. If we install a T3 connection with a bandwidth of 1.544Mbps, but have to pass through a slower 56Kbps link to get from our ISP to the rest of the Internet, our effective bandwidth to all points on the Internet side of our ISP is only 56Kbps. Also, if we have to pass through a very congested network section, our data will be slowed down. The total performance of the network is a result of the available bandwidth of the path our data travels from end to end. The larger ISPs will have several exit points that connect to the Internet; ask about the speed of all these exit points, and be sure that they are all at least as fast as our connection to the ISP, if not faster. We can use the average round-trip time of data from our network to that of our ISP in an attempt to quantify network performance. The following table lists typical round trip times, in milliseconds (ms), for some popular communications links.

Connection Speed	*Round-trip time*
28.8Kbps	180 ms
56Kbps	45 ms
1.544Mbps	7 ms

We should always keep in mind tomorrow's needs. We have to ask our ISP about its plans for future upgrades. The network technology can be very expensive and it needs very careful planning for efficient existence.

7.3. Security Concerns

When we connect our network to the Internet via an ISP, the whole security picture changes. We have to talk with the ISP about what preventive measures are appropriate and what it is doing to protect us against unwanted intruders.

7.4. Value-Added Services

Most of the ISPs also provide additional information or services. Many can provide activity statistics for our site, and most publish a newsletter. We should see copies of all the reports we will receive as a customer of that service provider.

7.5 Installation and Operational Costs

Any ISP will be able to provide us with information on installation and operating costs, and we should also ask about any charges that might apply in the future if we decide to upgrade our services. High prices do not necessarily mean good service. Typical operating costs for a T1 circuit might run to Rs. 75000 a month; a Basic Rate ISDN connection might cost only less than one tenth of that a month. Communications is an area where we can look forward to declining costs over the years, as the ISP's costs also fall. We had to be sure that we understand exactly what we are getting for us the amount we spend.

7.6 Changing ISP

The world of the ISP is changing from day to day. Competition in the form of the large telephone companies will undoubtedly lead to industry consolidation and a reduction in the number of service providers in any given area. We have to be careful about an ISP who asks us to sign a multi year agreement for services. Changing to another ISP can be a time consuming as well as expensive undertaking; so we have to be sure that we evaluate and understand all the steps along the way. But we should not let this put us off if we feel that our current ISP is not providing the service level we need or that our library and information system will get significant benefits from changing to another provider.

7.7 Information About the ISP

The following can be considered as the important aspects we should evaluate when we consider availing the services of one.

- For how long it has been providing internet services
- What are the services it provide
- Is it giving a service guarantee or a rebate against system outages
- What type of service outages it and how long will last
- How it will inform subscribers that the service is down- by phone or by e-mail
- What kind of network monitoring equipment do it have
- What are their plans to upgrade hardware software, and communications circuits
- When is their operations center staffed and how do they report problems
- Is there any restrictions on how we can use the Internet connection
- To which other networks are it connected and at what speeds
- What security techniques do they use at their site and recommend that we use at ours
- How will they ensure that our data is kept private

Once we have received satisfactory answers to these questions and understand how costs are charged for the service, we will be in a good position to make an informed decision about each ISP we are considering.

8. Domain Name

Now let us look at the steps involved in establishing our domain name. Unfortunately, the term domain is used in several ways depending on the context. In the Internet context here, a domain refers to a collection of network host computers known by the same name. Many ISPs will register a domain name for us as an additional service, but if our ISP doesn't provide this service, it is not difficult to do it our self.

8.1 Domain Name System (DNS)

The Computers work best with numbers, and people work best with names; to bridge this dichotomy, the Domain Name System (DNS), a distributed database, was invented. A domain name maps or translates the actual numeric IP address used for our web server into an easy to remember alphanumeric name. An IP address is a set of 4 numbers separated by periods or decimal points and is sometimes known as a dotted decimal address. Such an address might look like this: 198.15.170.10. By now we will have noticed that we do not access our favorite web site by means of these numbers. A web site has a name, and this dotted decimal address is translated into a name by the DNS. The process of looking up the domain name to derive the IP address is known as name resolution.

But before DNS can do this for us, we must register any name we want to use. A consortium between AT& T and Network Solutions, called Inter NIC (Internet Network Information Center) Registration Services, manages the task of assigning IP addresses and domain names to Internet users. In times past, this service was provided free by the National Science Foundation, but now a charge is levied for most services simply because the demand for domain registrations is so high. Since 1993, the NSF has funded the administration of domain name registration through a cooperative agreement with Network Solutions, and this agreement extends through to 1998. Seven domains were established originally:

. com a commercial organization. Most companies will end up as a part of this domain.

.edu an educational establishment such as a university.

.gov a branch of the U.S. government.

.int an international organization, such as NATO or the United Nations. 54

.mil a branch of the U.S. military.

.net a network organization.

.org a nonprofit organization.

These so called top level domain names are in common use in the United States and the .gov and .mil domains are reserved strictly for use by the government and the military. In other parts of the world, we will find that the final part of a domain address represents the country in which the server is located for example; .jp for Japan, .uk for Great Britain, and .ru for Russia. Here is a quick look at how these domain names are distributed. A 1996 survey yielded a total of 9.4 million host computers on the Internet, an increase of 2.8 million over the July 1995 total. The .com domain is the largest group at more than 2.4 million and has increased its lead over the second largest, .edu (at 1.8 million). Hosts with www in their names are by far the most numerous, and at the time of the survey, 129 countries were connected to the Internet. Of the organizations, no single organization has more than 1.6 percent of the total.

One may think that that most of the new .com sites are in the Pacific Northwest close to Microsoft and other high tech companies. It is not like that. The largest number of registered commercial site names is in San Francisco. The Puget Sound area is actually seventh after Manhattan, San Jose, Boston, Los Angeles, and the Boulder-Denver area. Completing the top ten list are Vancouver in British Columbia, Anaheim in California, and Oakland, also in California.

9. Web Presence

Our domain name should reflect our library or organization; many companies use their own names to capitalize on any name recognition that they already have in the mind of the user. The name we choose will then have a top level domain name type added to the end of it. For example, if our institution is Centre for Agricultural Informatics we might use agriinformatics as our domain name, which would have. org added to the end to become agriinformatics.org

Alternatively, we may choose agri_informatics which would become agri_informatics.org.

It is possible that someone else has already reserved or may even be actively using a domain name that we are interested in using for our company. If this is the case, we can either choose a new name or an unused variation on our original choice, or we can seek legal advice. Responsibility rests with the applicant to ensure that a domain name is not a trademark that already belongs to or is legally protected by someone else. We can contact InterNIC at URL: http://rs.internic.net or by e-mail at: hostmaster@internic .net for information on related matters. If we are not connected to the Internet yet, we can send mail to this address; Network Solutions, InterNIC Registration Services, 505 Huntmar, Park Drive, Herewndon, VA 220070. There are also many agents in India like the one who can be reached through the web site net4domains.com.

InterNIC lets us apply for any domain name we like, regardless of our company name; the only restriction is that the name must be available and not already reserved by someone else. Several names are reserved, but do not appear on any Web sites, at least not yet; like cirdindia the organization that supported this project has reserved name, but it has no web site when we are discussing this. To see if a domain name is available, we can use the InterNIC Who is service at: http://rs.internic.net/cgi-bin/whois. To use the Who is service, we can type our proposed name in the query box, for example, cirdindia.org , and press Enter when we are ready to search the database. When the search is complete, we will find out if anyone has already reserved the name we entered. If no one has registered our chosen name, we will see a message similar to 'Congratulations. cirdindia is available'.

To register our new name, we can go to: http://rs.internic.net/help/domain/new-domain-reg.html as a good starting point. Here we will be guided through the many steps in the process, and we can fill in our application form right here using our favorite web browser. A summary of the steps to be followed will be like this:

- We review the appropriate policies.
- Then determine whether our selected name is already in use.
- Coordinate for primary and secondary DNS service for the name.
- Obtain a Domain Name Registration Template. We fill in information on this screen, and an application is sent to we by e-mail. Complete the application and send it back to InterNIC; otherwise, our domain name will not be registered.
- Review the template.
- Review the most common errors made in the process.
- Then we have to submit the template.

We can also apply to modify, transfer, or delete a domain name, and a help desk is always available if we need to ask a question or two. When we are done, we can track the process of our application, and an invoice will be mailed to us automatically. The whole process can take several weeks, depending on the size of the current backlog. A domain name costs around Rs. 500 per year and some are still free. InterNIC charges about Rs. 2500 a year to maintain an already existing domain name.

2

Networking Basics

Now a days networks control most of the things. For the simple reason that networks are made up of, computers that people always seem to consider complex, it is assumed that networking is too complex for the average person. But in truth it is not like that. Networking is very much like doing other works with computers. By spending a little time learning the basics, getting some practice, and having some patience, networking is relatively simple. Networking like any other specialized skill, has its own terminology. We are not expected to know everything about networking, but as librarians we have to try to familiarize our self with as many of the concepts and terms related to networks that people in a networked or automated library environment would be forced to use. A good knowledge base is one of our best assets for successful networking as well as automating libraries.

If we have ever used a telephone, send a speed post, or purchased a computer from a dealership, we have used a network. Of course, they were not computer networks. They were, respectively, the phone company's switching network, the government's postal services network, and the computer manufacturer's distribution network. And although these networks move phone calls, packages, and computers instead of computer data, they are examples that explain the fundamental purpose of a network. The single most important purpose of any network computer or otherwise is to link similar items together using a set of rules that ensures reliable service.

In the telephone network's case, the rules have to do with

what happens when we dial a phone number based on how many digits we dial. If we dial seven digits, it is a local call; eleven digits is a long distance call. For the postal network the rule is that our package is assigned a registration number that must be recorded each time the package goes through a transfer point. And for the computer dealership, the rule is that there is only one reseller within a given geographical area; all new computers are delivered to that dealer, and that dealership has a direct link to the manufacturer.

1. Uses of Network

The need for networks is a usual question. Why we want to build a network in the library. There are a lot of reasons for building networks, whether they are computer networks or book distribution networks. Computer networks have enhanced significantly the productivity and efficiency of libraries and other organizations and individuals. Computer networks are used to conduct personal and or professional business. They ease transactions at library circulation counters, department stores, banks, reservation counters etc. They enable transfer and exchange data between computers and terminals of users. This data exchange provides for the many computer-based services and functions such as library stock verification, bank teller machines, sales counter terminals, and cheque verification devices, space shuttle guides, bus/rail/air reservations, on line database services, electronic journal access, OPAC catalogues and many other things. Networking of computers permit the sharing of resources and or load of the machines, for example consider another computer, data, information, software, peripheral, etc. They provide high reliability by having alternative sources of supply of files that could be replicated on more than one machine, so that if some hardware is unavailable copies on other could be used. Networking allows a flexible working environment. Users can work on any of the terminals or computers connected through network. Now a days many people carry portable computers and connect into their network through telephones. Networks enable cost efficiency also. Small computers have a much better performance and price ratio than large ones. Large ones are faster and have a huge secondary storage space. Networks consist of powerful personal computers with data kept on one or more shared file server machines. A network with many computers located in a small area is called a Local Area Network (LAN) in contrast with a far-flung Wide Area Network (WAN). WAN is also called long haul network.

Access to remote databases in a network eliminate the necessity of servicing personnel and users in paperless society, as well as minimize circulation of unwanted information. Using a computer network may reduce the amount of traveling, save energy, make home work popular, encourage part-time workers, render office and school redundant, allow shopping through electronic mail, reduce the need for physical proximity, disperse population, etc. Networks can provide a powerful communication medium among widely separated people. Electronic bulletins board and Electronic mail containing digitized voice, still pictures, moving television, video images etc. will be a potential for wide spread network use. The use of networks to enhance human-to-human communication is more important than goals such as improved reliability. However diverse the reasons, they ultimately end to the basic points which we can list as below:

* networks can increase efficiency
* networks can help standardize policies, procedures, and practices among network users
* networks can bring together diverse ideas and issues into a common forum, where they can be addressed in a global fashion rather than in a haphazard, case by case fashion
* networks help ensure that information is redundant; in other words, that it exists in more than one mind (or computer) at a time

Beyond all these there are many other different reasons also for building computer networks. A Librarian may have a bunch of computers at the library; one for him, one for his Reference Assistant, one for his administrative staff, and one at the circulation counter. He wants to hook all the computers together so that they can have a common calendar and email as well as facility for communicating between them. So he networks the computers. Another librarian may have a small library with a couple computers and a single dial-up Internet account. He wants to provide Internet access to all users with a single account. So he networks the computers. And then we have computer hobbyists who want to join together computers just because they can be joined together. Basically, if we have a need to communicate, to share data, to share applications, and want to avoid running from machine to machine with floppy disks, networking offers a lot of benefits.

2. Ways of Networks

Like other networks, computer networks have basic rules that ensure the safe delivery of information instead of telephone calls, speed post letters, or new computers. A basic set of rules for how a computer network should do its job might look something like this:

* information must be delivered reliably without any corruption of data.
* information must be delivered consistently.
* the network should be capable of determining where its information is going.
* multiple computers must be able to identify each other across the network.
* there must be a standard way of naming and identifying the parts of the network.

These rules are simple, but they are the cores of what a computer network does. Networks can be as simple as a file transfer program that runs between two computers on a printer port cable. Networks can also be as complex as the high end banking systems that transfer data on pulses of light in fiber optic cables. Despite this variety, all networks have the same basic goal: To ensure that data is shared quickly, reliably, and accurately.

2.1 Network Constituents

If we were to break a network down into its simplest components, we have two pieces. One is the physical network; the cabling, network cards, computers, and other equipment that the network uses to transmit data. The other is the logical arrangement of these physical pieces; the rules that allow the physical pieces to work together. We will look at both of these broad subdivisions.

3 Physical Networking

It is concerned with the hardware aspect. The physical network is easy to understand because it is easy to see. It is the wiring and network cards and computers and hubs and all the other stuff that allows the network to function. This physical part of networking is all hardware. It is tangible. We can hold it in our hands.

The physical side of the network is, at its simplest, made of wires actually, coaxial cables, which are similar to cable TV wires strung between computers and other network devices. The wires connect to network interface cards, or NICs, installed in computers. NICs handle the computer's interaction with the rest of the network. With these two items, we can create a simple network based on what is called a network bus topology. So it is the physical network configuration that is called a network topology. A network topology is the shape of the physical connectivity of the network. The topology of a network fulfils the following functions.

* provide maximum possible reliability to assure proper receipt of all traffic.
* routes the traffic across the least-cost path within the network between the sending and receiving Data Terminal Equipments (DTE) and
* gives the end-user the best possible response time and through put.

Network reliability refers to the ability to deliver used data correctly from one Data Terminal Equipment (DTE) to another DTE. It entails the ability to recover from errors or lost data in the network including channel in the event of DTE, or DSF failure. Reliability also refers to the maintenance of the system, which includes daily testing, preventive maintenance, relieving faculty or failing components.

The least-cost path between the Application Processors (APs) residing on the DTEs minimizes the actual length of the channel between the components by routing the traffic thorough the fewest number of intermediate components. It also provides the least expensive channel option for a particular application.

The best possible response time and throughput is provided by minimizing, delay between the transmission of the data and the receipt of the data between the DTEs and transmission of the maximum amount of end-user data in a given period.

The more common network topologies are, hierarchical topology (tree), horizontal topology (bus), star topology (hub), ring topology (loop) and mesh topology (complete).

3.1 Hierarchical Topology

The software to control the network is relatively simple and the topology provides a concentration point for control and error resolution. The DTE will be at the highest order if the hierarchy is in control of the network. Root DTE initiates traffic slow among and between the Dates. A distributed aspect to the hierarchical network provides methods for the Branch DTEs to directly control those DTEs below them in the hierarchy. This reduces the workload of the Root.

The hierarchical topology (Tree) presents problems. The root controls all traffic between DTEs thus creating bottlenecks and reliability problems in the event the Root fails. Still, hierarchical topologies are being used as they permit Branch DTEs to be added easily.

The hierarchical topology is also called a vertical network as a tree network.

3.2 Horizontal Topology

The bus permits all stations to receive every transmission. That is a single station broadcasts to multiple stations. The main drawback of a horizontal topology (Bus) is that in the event of a failure of the communications channel, the entire network is lost unless redundant channels are provided. Another problem is in isolating faults and problem solving.

3.3 Star Topology (Hub)

The star network is easy to control. The software is not

complex and the traffic flow is simple. All traffic emanates from the hub of the star, the control site, which is in complete control of the DTEs attached to it and is responsible for routing traffic through it to other components. It is responsible for fault isolation as well, which is simple because the lines can be isolated to identify the problem. However, like the hierarchical structure the star network is subject to problems unless a redundant back up of the hub node provides reliability.

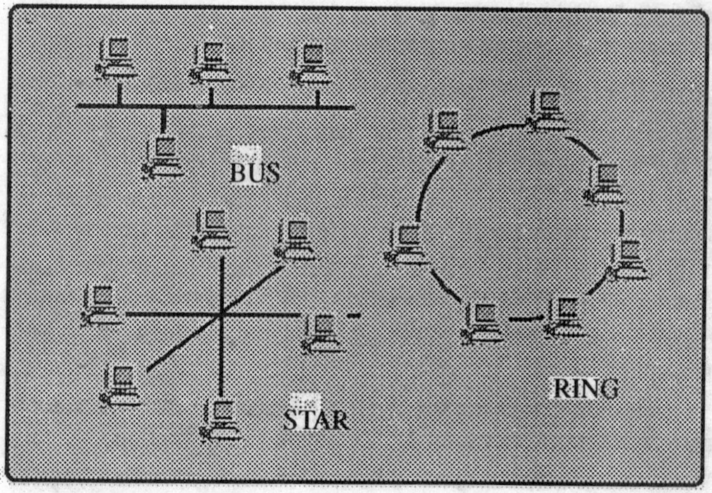

3.4 Ring Topology

In ring topology, the data flows in a circular manner. Generally, data flows in one direction only, with one single station receiving the signal and relying it to the next station in the ring. The logic to implement a ring network is simple. The ring network does have its deficiencies. So either provides back up channels or switches to automatically route data around a failed node to the next node on the ring to prevent the failure from bringing down the entire network.

3.5 Mesh Topology

Mesh topology has multiplicity of paths from the DTEs and DSEs and is immune to bottleneck and failure problems. This approach is a complex and expensive undertaking.

3.6 Network Devices

To get the functionalities described above from our network, we need a host of network devices to connect to each other in specific ways. Without getting into the specifics of how to hook these things together, let us take a look at the basic network devices we will encounter while establishing a network. The first of the devices are computers and printers, neither of which requires a network to function.

* workstation is the computer on which a user does his or her work.
* server is a computer whose resources are shared with other computers.
* network printer is a printer connected to the network so that more than one user can print to it.

Other devices that can be connected to a network mentioned earlier are specific to networks. Without a network, these devices have no function. They are absolutely central to the process of networking. They are Hub or MAU a device that provides the network with a single point of contact for all other devices and Routers and bridges that are devices that move data between networks. Although wiring and cabling do not strictly sound like devices, they actually are very important to the process. Wire has to meet very stringent standards for networking to work and so it is also included in the list of devices.

4. The Logical Network

The logical network is what users see when they are working at their desktops. Logical networks are collections of resources such as hard drive space, printers, and applications our computer would not have access to if it were not connected to a network. Logical networks are not physical. They result from the organization of the physical network. In other words, the logical network is the organization of the hardware that results from networking software. Examples of logical networks include things like network protocols. Network protocols are special ways in which computers have to communicate with each other. They are a lot like a language. If we speak only Hindi and we are talking to someone who speaks only German, chances are that we will not be able to communicate as well as if both of us were speaking the same language. For all their complexity, computer networks work the same way they have to talk the same language, which in networking terminology is called a network protocol. The logical network can include other things as well. In fact, it includes anything that is not hardware. Microsoft's method for organizing the network computers and equipments is called a Domain. Such services offer ways to subdivide networks to make them manageable.

A tremendous number of network related services and software packages fit on the logical side of a network. We have to remember one thing. If it is not part of the physical network, it is part of the logical network.

5. Organizational Concepts of Networks

The hardware and topologies that networks run on are only the beginning of networking. Once we understand the basic technical concepts, it is time to become familiar with the basic organizational concepts of networking: LAN, MAN, and WAN. There are two additional network types; CAN and TAN. All these network types are completely different entities. It is important to remember that all the networks mentioned earlier are private networks. That is: they are used by one organization, even though the networks may be in more than one location. This is an important distinction.

5.1 LAN

Local Area Network, (LAN), is the least complex organizational distinction of computer networks. LAN is nothing more than a group of computers linked through a network that is all at a single site. LANs have the following parameters.

* they occupy one physical location, and one physical location only-hence the word local in the title.
* they can be peer networks (which means that there is no central computer), or they may be client/server networks (which means that a central computer, called a server, has

most of the network's resources and is accessed by clients, or users' computers)

* they have high-speed data transfer rates and all data forms part of the local network.

What really makes a LAN a LAN is high-speed data transfer. LANs usually transmit data at 10 megabits per second. For comparison, Token Ring operates at 4 and 16 megabits per second, and FDDI and Fast Ethernet operate at a blistering 100 megabits per second or more. These data transmission speeds are not expensive when they are part of the local network. Although LANs are the simplest networks, that does not mean they are either necessarily small or simple. LANs can become quite large and complex. It is not uncommon in trade press magazines to read about LANs with hundreds or thousands of users.

5.2 MAN

When LAN has grown to thousands of users, it means that the network has expanded beyond its original location. If the expansion is local that is, within a very small geographical region, such as adjoining buildings, it is not uncommon to split the network into several smaller networks and join them into a Metropolitan Area Network (MAN), using high speed leased telephone lines or special hardware radio, microwave, or laser data transmission units that allows full LAN speed data transfer. MANs often enable users in several local geographical locations to use shared network resources as if they were all part of the same local network. MAN s are all one local network, however; they do not necessarily have to use routers the devices responsible for figuring out which data should stay inside the local network and which data should be passed on to other networks. Router is a device that manages data flows between networks. In a network, a router functions like the direction providing people we find along our route. Routers know the best ways for data to travel to get from point A to B. MANs are the first increase in the level of complexity beyond LANs. A consequence of the high speed phone lines or specialty hardware needed to make a MAN work is the substantially greater cost of a MAN than a LAN

5.3 WAN

When a series of LANs or MANs are too geographically scattered to make linking them at full LAN speeds impractical usually when they are separated by a couple of miles, it's time to build a Wide Area Network, or WAN. Wide Area Networks are geographically scattered LANs or MANs joined together using high-speed phone lines. Access to resources across a WAN is often limited by the speed of the phone line. Some of the most popular digital phone lines have speeds of only 56 kilobits per second. WANs are often built when it is important that all users have the ability to access a common pool of information such as product databases or Automatic Teller Machine bank records. As long as the purpose of the WAN is well defined and limited, the speed restrictions imposed by phone lines are not an issue for network designers. If the quantity of data passing through the high-speed phone line is less than or equal to the capacity of the line, the WAN works fine. Unlike LANs and MANs, WANs almost always use routers. Because most of the traffic in a WAN takes place inside the LANs and MANs that make up the WAN, routers provide an important function. They make sure that the LANs and MANs get only the data intended for them. At times, the distinctions between LANs, MANs, and WANs blur. CANs and TANs are examples of what we get when the distinctions blur between the first three types of networks LANs, MANs, and WANs.

5.4 CAN and TAN

CAN is a Campus Area Network. Typically, a CAN is similar to a MAN but has full network speed bandwidth running between all the LANs on the network. Some CANs are all one network distributed over a limited local area; a college campus, for example. When this happens, bridges or repeaters are used to join the various pieces of the network so that the user does not know whether the server he or she is accessing is across the room or across the campus. Bridge is a device that links different networks together so that they form a single unit. As already mentioned repeater enables networks to communicate reasonably well. It amplifies and cleans up digital signals and forwards them on toward their destination.

CANs tend to be very expensive. Nonetheless, they are very useful in computing intensive organizations such as software companies and universities because they make the network seem simpler and easier to the end users than it may actually be.

TANs are Tiny Area Networks. These are the two to three computer networks people set up in small libraries, homes or other non-business locations. Often, TANs are set up as a convenience for an executive who wants to replicate his or her office computer environment at home or to provide children with exposure to networked computing resources. An University Librarian can connect his computer to that of his Personal Assistant and Administrative officer so that he can correct the communication physical types as well as see the files the office finalized without their physical movement.

6. Structure of Communication Network

In a data communication system there are application processes (AP). AP is the one user application. It consists of software, computer program, terminal, etc. A network site can execute on AP to access another AP and or a database file at another site. The application resides in the Data Terminal Equipment (DTE). DTE is the end user machine which is a computer or terminal like a work station, an automated teller machine, a terminal, a data logger, an email computer, a PC, etc.

A network provides logical and physical communications for the computers and terminals to be connected. The physical channel is used to effect logical communications. Logical means the DTEs are not concerned with the physical aspects of the communication process. An AP need only issue a logical request with identification. In turn, the communication system is responsible for sending the request across the physical channels to another AP.

Network has data communication equipment (DCE). DCE connects the DTEs into the communication line or channel. Earlier, DCEs were strictly communication devices. Today DCEs have incorporated more useful functions and contain APs. Still, the primary function of the DCE remains to provide an interface of the DTE into a communications network.

The interfaces are specified and established through protocols. Protocols are agreements on how communication components and DTEs are to communicate with each other. Several levels of interfaces and protocols are required to support an end-user application.

Communication network consists of two distance components: transmission lines and switching elements. Transmission lines, also called circuits, channels, etc. move bits between machines. The switching elements are specialized computers used to connect two or more transmission lines. These components are the data switching equipments or DSEs.

DCEs and DTEs are connected in one of the two ways. They are connected in a point-to-point configuration in which only two DTEs are on the line or channel. Another approach is called a multidrop or broadcast configuration. In this configuration, more than two devices are connected to the same channel.

6.1 Data Flow and Physical Circuits

The DTEs and DCEs send communications to each other in one of three methods that are; Simplex in which transmission is in one direction only, Half-duplex in which transmission is in both directions but only one direction at a time which is also called two-way alternate (TWA), and Full-duplex in which transmission is simultaneously in both directions which is also called two-way simultaneous (TWS). Simplex transmission is common in television and radio. Terminal-based systems often use half-duplex techniques (Key board terminals and terminals with CRT screens). Full-duplex (duplex) provides for simultaneous two-way transmission without the intervening stop-and-wait aspect of half-duplex.

6.2 Communication Technique

Communications channel is described by its capacity in the number of bits per second transmitted. Abbreviations are bits/S.bps.bs.etc. A bit is simply the representation of the electrical, optical or electromagnetic state of the line. Eight bits usually comprise a character/byte. The typical speeds are 300, 600, 1200, 2400, 4800, 9600, 14400, 19200, 98400, 56000, 64000 bps. The bell system has 1.544, 6.312, 44.736, and 274.176 Mbps. The CCITT recommends 2.048, 8.848, 34.304, 139.264 and 565.148 Mbps. The conventional data processing system with disk files attached to computers operates at about 10 Mbps.

When two computers located close to each other, need to communicate it is often easy for it needs only just running a cable between them. However, when the distances are large, or there are many computers, or the cables would have to pass through a public way the costs of running private cables are usually prohibitive. Consequently, the network designers must rely upon the existing telecommunication facilities.

6.3 Voice Communication

The public telephone network is designed with a goal of transmitting the human voice in a more or less recognizable form. Their suitability for use in computer-to-computer communication is worth devoting some attention. A cable running between two computers can transfer data at speeds 10 to 10 bps. In contrast, a dial up line has a maximum data rate of the order of 10 bps. So, much time and effort have been devoted to bring out how to use dial up lines efficiently.

Voice communications generate analog waveforms, which propagate through the air. The waveform exhibits three primary characteristics; amplitude, frequency, and phase. The amplitude, frequency, or phase can be modulated to transmit information. In amplitude modulation, two different voltage levels are used to represent 0 and 1, respectively. In frequency modulation, two or more different tones are used. In phase modulation, the carrier wave is systematically shifted by different degrees at uniformly spaced intervals. Each phase shift transmits 2 bits of information.

6.4 Digital Analogue Conversion

When a telephone subscriber attached to a digital computer makes a call, the signal emerging from user is an ordinary analog signal. This analog signal is then digitized at the computer by a coder-decoder (codec). The code converts a continuous analog signal into a digital bit stream. A device that accepts a serial stream of bits as input and converts the digital bit stream into a modulated analog signal and produces modulated carrier as output (and vice versa) is called a modulator-demodulator (modem). The modem is inserted between the digital computer and the analog telephone system. The modem is a DEC.

Frequency determines the pitch and sound of a person's voice. A human voice occupies the frequencies of approximately 200 Hz to 15,000 Hz. The human ear can detect frequencies over a broader range, from around 40 Hz to 18,000 Hz. The range of frequencies is called the bandwidth.

The transmission of audio signals at their original frequency preludes more than one voice-grade transmission from occupying the channel. However, the greater bandwidths allow the voice-grade bands to occupy different partoons of the frequency spectrum. Since the voice-grade channels now occupy different frequency spectra the signals can use the same physical media. A multiplexer is a device that accepts input from a collection of lines and outputs the data onto a single output line. The multiplexing schemes are FDM and TDM for human-to-human communications. For computer-to-computer communication circuit switching, message switching, packet switching, and hybrid switching are appropriate.

6.5 Synchronization

Digital transmission is superior to analog transmission. First, it has a very low error rate. Second, is that voice, data, music, images; television, facsimile, video-telephone, etc. can all be multiplexed together. Third, higher data rates are possible.

In order for computers and terminals to communicate, they first need to notify each other that they are able to communicate. Second, once they are communicating, they must provide a method, which keeps both devices aware of the ongoing transmissions. On the first point, a transmitting machine must first send to the receiving machine an indication that it wishes to 'talk' with it. The process is part of a communication protocol and is generally referred to as synchronization. Synchronization provides checkpoints into the data stream, so that if there is a crash, only the data after the last checkpoint have to be repeated.

For transporting a bit Stream from one machine to another various physical media can be used. Some common media are magnetic media, twisted pair, base band coaxial cable, broadband coaxial cable, fiber optics, and line of sight transmission and communication satellites.

7. Our Network and Internet

The last two years have seen an explosion of publicity for the Internet. We can see explosion of web addresses, email addresses, and references to cyberspace that have pervaded the public consciousness. The publicity has been difficult to ignore. Unfortunately, with mass media publicity comes the foolish pronouncements of pundits who do not really understand what the Internet is, what it does, or and most importantly for those building networks how it works. Here we will discuss in very basic terms what ramifications the Internet has for our local network. We should understand how our network exists vis a vis the Internet, which is as we have already seen as sort of the huge network from which all other networks have descended.

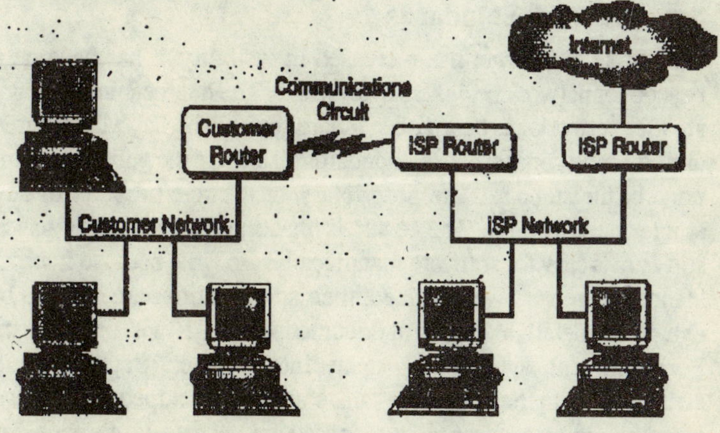

Internet is a series of private computer networks LANs, MANs, and WANs connected to each other. Each individual private network is composed of a series of connected computers within an organization. Each organization takes responsibility for only the computers in its sphere of influence. Typically, the individual networks are connected by special devices called routers that are responsible for figuring out what data should stay inside the local network and what data should be passed on to other networks. If we build a small network, we have a private network. If we connect a router to our network actually, it is more complicated than that, our network could conceivably wind up being part of the Internet.

WAN is all part of a single network and is under one organization's control. By contrast, the only parts of the Internet that can be identified as strictly dedicated to the Internet are the extremely fast also called high bandwidth phone lines that make up what is called the backbone of the Internet. Backbone means a series of very high-speed phone lines ranging from 155 to 622 megabits per second is used to transmit high volumes of traffic. Compare this speed to the speed of our LAN where data moves at 10 megabits per second, and we begin to see why it is called the backbone. New technologies are offering increased speed of over a gigabit per second, which will be useful as more and more people use the Internet.

8. Network Standards

As the Internet has increased in visibility, it has become a beacon for network designers everywhere. The Internet, unlike many smaller networks, is based on standards established by a committee and common consent. These standards all exist in the public domain; none of the standards are proprietary, or the sole property of any single manufacturer. The result is that Internet standards based software is easy for software manufacturers to write because Internet standards are very well defined, their specifications are covered in exhaustive detail in a series of documents called RFCs, or Requests For Comment, available on many Internet sites. Because these standards are in the public domain, software developed using these standards is also cheaper to manufacture. There is no need for software manufacturers to pay royalties on patented or copyrighted ideas.

The best thing about Internet standards, however, is just that they are standards. If we use Internet standard software on our network, it will be much easier to ensure that our computers and applications will be able to interact. In fact, many products from wholly different manufacturers can work with one another if they are standards adherent. When software products adhere to Internet standards, the resulting application cooperation is called interoperability, which essentially means that Part A works with Part B without undue difficulty. And interoperability means a local network functions more smoothly and less expensively than one whose parts do not interoperate.

9. Networks to Internet

Typically, if we build a LAN, MAN, or WAN that is, a private network using Internet standards, we have created an internal Internet, or intranet. Intranets offer a great deal of promise for simplifying the networking of different manufacturers' components; used properly, intranets can reduce costs and simplify life for our end users as well.

If we connect our intranet to the Internet and make provisions for our library users who use our intranet to avail library services we have gone a step beyond an Intranet and created an Extranet. Extranets are essentially intranets that use the Internet as a vehicle; for example libraries to interact with their users, publishes, book sellers and the public. With the proper security precautions, extranets offer tremendous value; they reduce the costs of tying our computer systems to our various departments of our institution or other libraries and potentially expose our services to a huge audience beyond the limits of our campus, state and nation.

3

TCP/IP Basics

Transmission Control Protocol/Internet Protocol is used on the Internet, as well as on many other networks, and Microsoft recognized the importance of this protocol by including TCP /IP support in the Windows NT Server operating system. Before we can put of library on Internet and start services, we need to understand TCP /IP and configure it on our server.

We will discus here TCP /IP family of protocols, and then continue with a description of IP addressing, and conclude with a discussion of how to set up and configure TCP/IP on Windows NT Server. We have attempted to provide here all the essential TCP / IP information we are ever likely to need instead of spreading it through several other parts of this guide. If we are not interested in learning about how TCP /IP works or how to set up Windows NT Server to use TCP /IP, we can safely skip this chapter. But if we are a network administrator with Novell Netware background or if we will be setting up a web server our self, this chapter contains important technical and background information that we will be able to use to make our work smoother.

TCP/IP actually refers to a whole family of protocols, with its name coming from only two of them: the Transmission Control Protocol and the Internet Protocol. There are many more members of the TCP /IP family.

1. Historical Perspective

The TCP /IP protocol was first conceptualized and proposed in 1973, but it was not until 1983 that a standardized version was developed and adopted for wide area use. In that same year, TCP / IP became the official transport mechanism for all connections to ARPAnet, a forerunner of the Internet.

Much of the original work on TCP /IP was done at the University of California at Berkeley: where computer scientists were also working on the Berkeley version of Unix which eventually grew into the Berkeley Software Distribution [BSD] series of Unix releases. TCP /IP was added to the BSD releases, which in turn was made available to universities and other institutions for the cost of a distribution tape. Thus, TCP /IP began to spread in the academic world, laying the foundation for today's explosive growth of the Internet.

During this time, the TCP /IP family continued to evolve and add new members. One of the most important aspects of this growth was the continuing development of the certification and testing program carried out by the U.S. government to ensure that the published standards, which were free, were met. Publication ensured that the developers did not change anything or adds any features specific to their own needs. This open approach has continued to the present day. Use of the TCP /IP family of protocols virtually guarantees a trouble free connection between many hardware and software platforms.

2. Aims of TCP/IP

When the U .S. Department of Defense began to define the TCP /IP network protocols, their design goals included the following:

- should be independent of all hardware and software manufacturers. Even today, this is fundamentally why TCP /IP makes such good sense in the Corporate world; it is not tied to IBM, to Novell, to Microsoft, or to any specific company.
- should have good built in failure recovery. Because TCP /IP was originally a military proposal, the protocol had to have the ability to continue operating even if large parts of the

network suddenly disappeared from view, say after an enemy attack.

- should handle high error rates and still provide completely reliable end-to-end service.
- should be efficient with a very low data overhead. The majority of data packets using the IP protocol have a simple, 20-byte header, which means better performance in comparison with other net- works. A simple protocol translates directly into faster transitions, giving more efficient service.
- should allow the addition of new networks without any service disruptions.

As a result, TCP /IP was developed with two main elements. Each component performs unique and vital functions that allow all the problems involved in moving data between machines over networks to be solved in an elegant and efficient way. We will look at both of them. First, we will see where TCP /IP fits into the broader world of network protocols and particularly how it compares to the theoretical reference model published by the International Standards Organization (ISO) as the Open Systems Interconnection (OSI) model.

2.1 TCP/IP and the OSI

The OSI model divides computer-to-computer communications into seven connected layers. TCP /IP uses 5 layers. Each successively higher layer builds on the functions provided by the layers below. In the OSI model these layers are as listed below:

Application Layer 7: The highest layer, defines the manner in which applications interact with the network, including databases, e-mail, and terminal emulation programs.

Presentation Layer 6: Defines the way in which data is formatted, presented, converted, and encoded.

Session Layer 5: Coordinates communications and maintains the session for as long as it is needed, performing security, logging, and administrative functions.

Transport Layer 4: Defines protocols for structuring messages and supervises the validity of the transmission by doing some - error checking.

Network Layer 3: Defines protocols of data routing to ensure that the information arrives at the correct destination node.

Data Link Layer 2: Validates the integrity of the flow of the data from one node to another by synchronizing blocks of data and controlling the flow of data.

Physical Layer 1: Defines the mechanism for communicating with the transmission medium and the interface hardware.

Although no networking protocol follows this model exactly, most perform all the same functions. In TCP IIP the five layers are as follows:

Application Layer 5 : The highest layer applications such as FTP, Telnet, and others interact through this layer.

Transport Layer 4 : TCP and other protocols add transport data to the data packet.

Internet Layer 3 : Adds IP information to the packet.

Network Interface Layer 2 : Interfaces with the physical layer. .
Physical *Layer 1 :* Defines the mechanism for communicating with the transmission medium and the interface hardware.

Each layer adds its own header and trailer data to the basic data packet and encapsulates the data from the layer above. On the receiving end, this header information is stripped, one layer at a time, until the data arrives at its final destination. Now we can discuss how TCP and IP work together.

3. Transmission Control Protocol

Transmission Control Protocol is the transmission layer of the protocol and serves to ensure reliable, verifiable data exchange between hosts on a network. Transmission Control Protocol breaks data into pieces, wraps it with the information needed to route it to its destination, and reassembles the pieces at the receiving end of the communications link. The wrapped and bundled pieces are called data grams. Transmission Control Protocol puts a header on the data gram that provides the information needed to get the data to its destination. The most important information in the header includes the source and destination port numbers, a sequence number for the data gram, and a checksum.

The source port number and the destination port numbers allow the data to be sent back and forth to the correct process running on each computer. The sequence number allows the data grams to be rebuilt in the correct order in the receiving computer, and the checksum allows the protocol to check whether the data sent is the same as the data received. A checksum totals the contents of a data gram and inserts that number in the header. The receiving computer performs the same calculation, and if the two calculations do not match, an error occurred somewhere along the line, and the data gram is resent.

Once the header is in the data gram, TCP passes the data gram to IP to be routed to its destination.

In addition to the source and destination port numbers, the sequence number, and the checksum, a TCP header contains the following:

Acknowledgment number: Indicates that the data was received successfully. If the data gram is damaged in transit, the receiver throws the data away and does not send an acknowledgment back to the sender. After a predefined time-out expires, the sender retransmits data for which no acknowledgment was received.

Offset: specifies the length of the header.

Reserved: variables set aside for future use.

Flags: indicates that this packet is the end of the data or that the data is urgent.

Window: provides a way to increase packet size, which improves efficiency in data transfers.

Urgent pointer: gives the location of urgent data.

Options: a set of variables reserved for future use or for special options as defined by the user of the protocol.

Padding: ensures that the header ends on a 32bit boundary.

The data in the packet immediately follows this header information.

Transmission Control Protocol communications can be summarized as follows:

- ***Flow control*** allows 2 systems to cooperate in data gram transmission to prevent overflows and lost packets.
- ***Acknowledgment*** lets the sender know that the recipient has received the information.
- ***Sequencing*** ensures that packets arrive in the proper order.
- ***Checksums*** allow easy detection of lost or corrupted packets.
- ***Retransmission*** of lost or corrupted packets is managed in a timely way.

4. Internet Protocol

The Internet Protocol is the network layer portion of TCP / IP, and it actually moves the data from Point A to Point B, which is called routing. Internet Protocol is sometimes described as unreliable because it contains no error detection or recovery code. Internet Protocol is also connectionless; that is, it does not swap control information or handshaking information before establishing an end-to-end connection and starting a transmission.

Internet Protocol must rely on TCP to determine that the data arrived successfully at its destination and retransmit the data if it did not. The only job of IP is to route the data to its destination. In this effort, IP inserts its own header in the data gram once it is received from TCP. The main contents of the IP header are the source and destination addresses, the protocol number, and a checksum. Without this header, intermediate routers between the source and destination commonly called gateways, would not be able to determine where to route the data gram. Now we can have an idea of the fields in the IP header:

Version: Defines the IP version number. Version 4 is the current standard, and values of 5 or 6 indicate that special protocols are being used.

IHL (Internet Header Length): Defines the length of the header information. The header length can vary; the default header is five 32-bit words, and the sixth word is optional

TOS (Type of Service): Indicates the kind or priority of the required service.

Total Length: Specifies the total length of the data gram, which can be a minimum of 576 bytes and a maximum of 65,536 bytes.

Identification: Provides information that the receiving system can use to reassemble fragmented data grams.

Flags: The first flag bit specifies that the data gram not be fragmented and therefore must travel over sub networks that can handle the size without fragmentation; the second flag bit indicates that the data gram is the last of a fragmented packet.

Fragmentation Offset: Indicates the original position the data and is used during reassembly.

Time to Live: Originally, the time in seconds that the data gram could be in transit; if this time was exceeded, the data gram was considered lost. Now interpreted as a hop count and usually set to the default value 32, this number is decremented by each router through which the packet passes.

Protocol: Identifies the protocol type, allowing the use of non TCP IIP protocols. A value of 6 indicates TCP, and a value of 17 indicates UDP.

Header Checksum: An error-checking value that is recalculated at each stopover point, necessary because certain fields change.

TCP Header: The header added by the TCP part of the protocol suite.

The data in the packet immediately follows this header information.

5. Application Protocols

The following applications were built on top of the TCP IIP protocol suite and are available on most implementations:

- Simple Network Management Protocol (SNMP), which allows

network administrators to collect information about the network.

- File Transfer Protocol (FTP), which provides a mechanism for file transfers between computer systems. File Transfer Protocol uses TCP to actually move the files.
- Simple Mail Transfer Protocol (SMTP) allows a simple e-mail service.
- Telnet, which is a terminal emulation package that provides a remote logon over the network.
- TN3270, which is a special version of Telnet specifically designed for use on IBM mainframes using 3270 series terminals and which also provides a remote logon over the network.
- ICMP (Internet Control Message Protocol), which works at the IP network layer level and provides the functions used for network-layer management and control.
- ARP (Address Resolution Protocol), which helps to reference the physical address of a node to its IP address.
- UDP (User Data gram Protocol), which is a transport-layer connectionless protocol that also uses IP to deliver its packets.

5.1. Ports and Sockets Explained

On a TCP/IP network, data travels from a port on the sending computer to a port on the receiving computer. A port is an address that identifies the application associated with the data. The source port number identifies the application that sent the data, and the destination port number identifies the application that receives the data. All ports are assigned unique 16 bit numbers in the range 0 to 32767.

Today, many ports are standardized. Thus, a remote computer can know which port it should connect to for a specific service. For example, all servers that offer Telnet services do so on port 23, and Web Servers normally run on port 80. The TCP/IP protocol uses a modifiable lookup table to determine the correct port for the data type.

In multi-user systems, a program can define a port on the fly if more than one user requires access to the same service at the same time. Such a port is known as a dynamically allocated port and is assigned only when needed, for example, when two remote computers dial into a third computer and simultaneously request Telnet services on that system.

The combination of an IP address and a port number is known as a socket. A socket identifies a single network process in terms of the entire Internet. We may hear or see the words socket and port used as if they were interchangeable terms, but they are not. Two sockets, one on the sending system and one on the receiving host, are needed to define a connection for connection-oriented protocols such as TCP.

Sockets were first developed as a part of the BSD Unix system kernel, in which they allow processes that are not running at the same time or on the same system to exchange information. We can read data from or write data to a socket just as we can do with a file. Socket pairs are bi-directional so that either process can send data to the other.

In the Novell NetWare world, a socket is part of an IPX internet work address and acts as a destination for the IPX data packet. Most socket numbers are allocated dynamically, but a few are associated with specific functions.

6. Benefits of Using TCP/IP

We have by now discussed how TCP and IP are used. Now let us see the major benefits of using TCP /IP over other networking protocols. The following are the major benefits.

- TCP /IP is a routable protocol, which means that it can send data grams over a specific route and thus reduce traffic on other parts of the network.
- TCP /IP has reliable and efficient data-delivery mechanisms.
- TCP /IP is a widely published open standard and is completely independent of any hardware or software manufacturer.
- TCP /IP can send data between different computer systems running completely different operating systems, from small

PCs all the way to mainframes and everything in between.

- TCP /IP is separated from the underlying hardware and will run over Ethernet, Token Ring, or X.25 networks and even over dial- up telephone lines.
- TCP /IP uses a common addressing scheme. Therefore, any sys- tem can address any other system, even in a network as large as the Internet.

Popularity that the TCP /IP family of protocols enjoys today did not arise just because the protocols were there or even because the US Government mandated their use. They are popular because they are robust, solid protocols that solve many of the most difficult networking problems and do so in an elegant and efficient way.

7. I P Addressing

As we saw earlier IP moves data between computers systems in the form of a data gram, and each data gram is delivered to the destination port number that is contained in the data gram header. This destination port number, or address, is a standard 16 bit number that contains enough information to identify the receiving network as well as the specific host on that network for which the data gram is intended. Now we will go over what IP addresses are, why they are so necessary, and how they are used in TCP /IP networking.

7.1 Ethernet Addresses

We may remember that earlier it was mentioned that TCP / IP is independent of the underlying network hardware. If we are running on an Ethernet based network, we have to be careful not to confuse the Ethernet hardware address and the IP address required by TCP /IP. Each Ethernet network card has its own unique hardware address, known as the Media Access Control (MAC) address. This hardware address is predefined and preprogrammed on the network interface card (NIC) by the manufacturer of the board as a unique 48-bit number.

The first three parts of this address are called the OUI (Organizationally Unique Identifier) and are assigned by the Institute of Electrical and Electronics Engineers (IEEE). The manufacturers, who then assign the last three parts of the MAC address, making each assignment unique. We have to remember that the Ethernet address is predetermined and is hard coded onto the network interface card.

7.2 IP Addresses

Transmission Control Protocol/Internet Protocol requires that each host on a TCP /IP network have its own unique IP address. An IP address is a 32-bit number, usually represented as a 4-part number, with each of the 4 parts separated by a period or decimal point. We may also hear this method of representation called dotted decimal or quad decimal. The network address is made up from the higher order bits of the address, and the host address constitutes the rest. In addition, the host part of the address can be divided further to allow for a sub network address, as we will see in a moment. Each individual byte or octet as they are sometimes called can have a usable value from 1 to 254. The term octet is the Internet community's own term for an 8-bit byte and came into common use because some of the early computers attached to the Internet had bytes of more than 8 bits; some of DEC's early systems had bytes of 18-bits.

Some host addresses are reserved for special use. For example, in all network addresses, host numbers 0 and 255 are reserved. An IP host address with all bits set to zero identifies the network itself. So 52.0.0.0 refers to network 52. An IP address with all the bits set is known as a broadcast address. The broadcast address for network 204.176 is 204.176.255.255. A data gram sent to this address is automatically sent to every individual host on the 204.176 network.

InterNIC assigns and regulates IP addresses on the Internet. We can get one directly from the InterNIC, or we can ask our ISP to secure an IP address on our behalf. If we are setting up an Intranet and we don't want to connect to the outside world through the Internet, we don't need an address from InterNIC. Another strategy is to obtain our address from InterNIC and only use it internally until we are ready to connect to the Internet.

7.3 Multihomed Hosts

A host may have more than one IP address, and hosts that do are known as multihomed. Normally, hosts have a single IP address. Today, with the popularity of the World Wide Web and its explosive growth, more and more web servers are becoming multihomed. Multihoming is necessary for several reasons, including the ability to establish virtual web servers.

Virtual web servers allow one single web server to act as if it were actually several web servers. Without the virtual web server capability, a single web server that houses several web sites would have to use URLs that include the web server's domain name.

For example, the CIRD may have a web server whose fully qualified domain name is www .cirdindia.org. Its URL is http : / / www.cird.org. If CIRD decides to host a web site for the KAU whose web server is called kaulis, KAULIS URL might wind up being something like http : //www.cird.org/kaulis. It's easy to associate that the KAULIS identity is with the CIRD identity through the URL, and this may not be acceptable to an orgnization seeking to establish it's own unique identity on the World Wide Web.

If, however, CIRD web server is configured with IIS, which coincidentally makes it a multihomed host, KAULIS can use its own domain name. Thus, its URL is http : //www.kaulis.org, and it now has its own unique identity on the exact same web server as cird. Virtualizing web servers is probably today's most common reason for making a server multihomed.

7.4 Gateways and Routing

Routing is the process of getting our data from Point A to Point B. Routing datagrams is similar to driving a car. Before we drive off to our destination, we determine which roads we will take to get there. And sometimes along the way, we have to change our mind and alter our route.

The IP portion of the TCP /IP protocol inserts a header that contains the source and destination addresses for a datagram. Before the datagram begins its journey, however, IP determines whether it knows the destination. If it does know, IP sends the datagram on its way. If it doesn't know and can't find out, IP sends the datagram to the host's gateway.

Each host on a TCP /IP network has a gateway, an off ramp for datagrams not destined for the local network. They are going somewhere else, and the gateway's job is to forward them to that destination if it knows where it is. Each gateway has a defined set of routing tables that tell the gateway the route to specific destinations.

Because gateways don't know the location of every IP address, they have their own gateways that act just like any TCP /IP host. In the event the first gateway doesn't know the way to the destination, it forwards the datagram to its own gateway. This forwarding, or routing, continues until the datagram reaches its destination. The entire path to the destination is known as the route.

Datagrams intended for the same destination may arrive via different routes. Many variables determine the route. For example, overloaded gateways may not respond in a timely manner or may simply refuse to route traffic and thus time out. That time out causes the sending gateway to seek an alternate route for the datagram. The route can also vary because network links are down or because servers or gateways are down and because of many other factors that we won't get into in this book. Routes can be predefined and made static, and alternate routes can be predefined, providing a maximum probability that our datagrams travel via the shortest and fastest route.

7.5 IP Address Classifications

In the 32bit IP address, the number of bits used to identify the network and the host vary according to the network class of the address. The several classes are as follows:

- Class A is used for very large networks only. The high-order bit in a Class A network is always zero, which leaves 7 bits available to define 127 networks. The remaining 24 bits of the address allow each Class A network to hold as many as 16,777,216 hosts.
- Class B is used for medium-sized networks. The 2 high-order bits are always 10, and the remaining bits are used to

define 16,384 networks, each with as many as 65,535 hosts attached.

- Class C is for smaller networks. The 3 high-order bits are always 110, and the remaining bits are used to define 2,097,152 networks, but each network can have a maximum of only 254 hosts.
- Class D is a special multicast address and cannot be used for networks. The 4 high-order bits are always 1110, and the remaining 28 bits allow access to more than 268 million possible addresses.
- Class E is reserved for experimental purposes. The first 4 bits in the address are always 1111.

Because the bits used to identify the class are combined with the bits that define the network address, we can draw the following conclusions from the size of the first octet, or byte, of the address.

- A value of 126 or less indicates a Class A address. The first octet is the network number, the next three, the host addresses.
- A value of exactly 127 is reserved as a loop back test address. If we send a message to 127.0.0.1, it should get back to we unless something is wrong with your network. Using this number as a j special test address has the unfortunate effect of wasting more, than 24 million possible IP addresses.
- A value from 128 through 191 is a Class B address. The first two octets are the network number, and the last two are the host address.
- A value from 192 through 223 is a Class C address. The first three octets are the network address, and the last octet is the host number.
- A value greater than 223 indicates a reserved address.

7.6 I P Subnets

The IP addressing scheme provides a very flexible solution to the task of addressing thousands of networks, but it is not without problems. The original designers did not imagine the Internet growing as large as it has; at that time, a 32-bit address seemed so large that they quickly divided it into different classes of networks to facilitate routing rather than reserving more bits to manage the growth in network addresses.

An IP subnet modifies the IP address by using host address bits as additional network address bits. In other words, the dividing line between the network address and the host address is moved to the right, creating additional networks, but reducing the number of hosts that can belong to each network. An IP address can be sub netted on an even-byte boundary or on a bit boundary. The solution depends on how we want to manage your address space.

When IP networks are sub netted, they can be routed independently, which allows a much better use of address space and available bandwidth. To subnet an IP network, we define a bit mask known as a subnet mask, in which a bit pattern cancels out unwanted bits so that only the bits of interest remain. The subnet mask is similar in structure to an IP address, in that it has 4 parts, or octets, but now it defines 3 elements (network, subnet, and host) rather than two (network and host). If a bit is on in the mask, that equivalent bit in the address is interpreted as a network bit. If a bit in the mask is off, the bit is part of the host address. The 32-bit value is then converted to dotted decimal notation. A subnet is only known and understood locally; to the rest of the Internet, the address is still interpreted as a standard IP address. The following table shows how this all works for the standard IP address classes.

Default Subnet masks for Standard IP address classes

Class	*Subnet Mask Bit Pattern*	*Subnet Mask*
A	11111111 00000000 00000000 00000000	255.0.0.0
B	11111111 11111111 00000000 00000000	255.255.0.0
C	11111111 11111111 11111111 00000000	255.255.255.0

Sub netting has many advantages, including reducing the size of routing tables, minimizing network traffic, isolating networks from others, maximizing performance, optimizing IP address space, and enhancing the ability to secure a network.

7.7 Internet Host Names

Internet host names are used because they are easier to

remember than long dotted-decimal IP addresses. Host names are typically the name of a device that has a specific IP address and on the Internet is part of what is known as a fully qualified domain name. A fully qualified domain name consists of a host name and a domain name. For example, in the fully qualified domain name www. cird.org, the host name is www, and the domain name is cird.org. It is easier to remember www.microsoft.com than remembering 198.105.232.6.

Several automatic conversion systems are available to translate an IP address into a host name, and HOSTS is one of the simplest. We create a file called HOSTS and enter a line into it for every system, like 198.34.56.25 myserver. com and 198.34.57.03 yourserver.com. We must store this ASCII file on every single workstation; when we make a change, we must change the contents of the HOSTS file on every single workstation. Simple but very difficult inside a network. But if we want to go out to other networks or to the Internet it becomes much more difficult. But there are better solutions to solve this difficulty.

8 Using DNS

The abbreviation DNS stands for Domain Name Service. We use DNS to translate host names and domain names to IP addresses, and vice versa, by means of a standardized lookup table that the network administrator defines and configures. Suppose we are using our browser to surf the Web, and we enter the URL http://www.microsoft.com to bring up the Microsoft home page. Our Web browser then asks the TCP /IP protocol to ask the DNS server for the IP address of www.microsoft.com. When our Web browser receives this address, it connects to the Microsoft Web server and downloads the home page.

DNS is an essential part of any TCP /IP network, simplifying the task of remembering addresses. Wee may recall that humans think best with words, and computers work best with numbers. DNS provides the human a simple way to relate numeric addresses without having to remember them all. We simply remember the host name and domain name instead. DNS Tables are composed of records. Each record is composed of a host name, a record type, and an address. There are several record types, including the address record, the mail exchange record, and the CNAME record. The address record, commonly known as the A record, maps a host name to an IP address. The example below shows the address record for a host called mail in the company. com domain:

mail.company.com. IN A 204.176.47.9

The mail exchange record points to the mail exchanger for a particular host. DNS is structured so that we can actually specify several mail exchangers for one host. This feature provides a higher probability that e-mail will actually arrive at its intended destination. The mail exchangers are listed in order in the record, with a priority code that indicates the order in which the mall exchangers should be accessed by other mail delivery systems.

If the first priority doesn't respond in a given amount of time, the mail delivery system tries the second one, and so on. Here are some sample mail exchange records:

hostname.company.com. IN MX 10 mail.company.com.
hostname.company. com. IN MX 20 mai12.company.com.
hostname.company.com. IN MX 30 mai13.company.com.

In this example, if the first mail exchanger, mail. company. com, does not respond, the second one, mail2 .company. com is tried, and so on.

The CNAME record, or canonical name record, is also commonly known as the alias record and allows hosts to have more than one name. For example, our web server has the host name www, and we want that machine also to have the name ftp so that users can easily FTP in to manage web pages. We can accomplish this with a CNAME record. Assuming we already have an address record established for the host name www, a CNAME record adding ftp as a host name would look something like this:

www.company.com. IN A 204.176.47.2
ftp.company.com. IN CNAME www.company.com.

When we put all these record types together in a file, its called a DNS table, and it might look like this:

mail.company.com.	IN	A	204.176.47.9
mai12.company.com.	IN	A	204.176.47.21
mai13.company.com.	IN	A	204.176.47.89
ourhost.company. com.	IN	MX	10 mail. company. com.
ourhost.company.com.	IN	MX	20 mai12.company.com.
ourhost.company.com.	IN	MX	30 mai13.company.com.
www.company. com.	IN	A	204.176.47.2
ftp.company.com.	IN	CNAME	www.company. com.

We can establish other types of records for specific purposes, but won't go into those in this book. DNS can become very complex very quickly for the novice, and there are many books and guides on the DNS system.

8.1 Using WI NS

WINS, or Windows Internet Naming Service, are an essential part of the Microsoft networking topology. Before we discussion WINS, we need to understand a few new terms including Net BIOS and NetBEUI.

Net BIOS: It is pronounced net-bye-os and is an acronym formed from network basic input/output system, a session layer network protocol originally developed by IBM and Sytek to manage data exchange and network access. NetBIOS provides an API with a consistent set of commands for requesting lower level network services to transmit information from node to node, thus separating the applications from the underlying network operating system. Many vendors provide either their own version of NetBIOs or an emulation of its communications services in their products.

NetBEUI: It is pronounced net-boo-ee and is an acronym formed from NetBIOS Extended User Interface, an implementation and extension of IBM's NetBIOs transport protocol from Microsoft. NetBEUI communicates with the network through Microsoft's NDIs (Network Driver Interface Specification). NetBEUI is shipped with all versions of Microsoft's operating systems today and is generally considered to have a lot of overhead, making it a poor choice for large networks.

WINS is used in conjunction with TCP /IP and maps NetBIOs names to IP addresses. For example, we have a print server on our LAN that we have come to know as Printserver 1. In the past, to print to that server we needed only to remember its name and to select that name from a list. Because TCP /IP is a completely different protocol, it doesn't understand NetBIOs names. It therefore has no way of knowing the location of those servers or their addresses. That is where WINS comes in. When we install TCP /IP on our Windows NT Server, we will probably find that things work a lot better, and more seamlessly, if we also install WINS.

Each time we access a network resource on a Windows NT network using TCP /IP, our system needs to know the host name or IP address. If WINS is installed, we can continue using the NetBIOS names that we have previously used to access the resources because WINS provides the cross-reference from name to address for us.

When we install and configure TCP /IP, we'll see a place to specify the WINS server addresses. These addresses are stored with the configuration, and TCP /IP uses them to query for host names and addresses when necessary. WINS is to DNS in that it cross references host names to addresses. But WINS references NetBIOS names to IP addresses, and DNS references TCP /IP host names to IP addresses.

Another major difference between WINS and DNS is that WINS builds its own reference tables, and we have to configure DNS manually. When a workstation running TCP /IP is booted and attached to the network, it uses the WINS address settings in the TCP /IP configuration to communicate with the WINS server. The workstation gives the WINS server various pieces of information about itself, such as the NetBIOS host name, the actual username logged on to the workstation, and the workstation's IP address. WINS stores information for use on the network and periodically refresh it to maintain accuracy.

The Microsoft DNS Server software currently ships with Windows NT. The value in the Microsoft DNS Server is anew type of DNS record called a WINS record, which allows the DNS server to work in perfect harmony with a WINS server. When a DNS query returns a WINS record, the DNS server then asks the WINS server for the host name address. Thus, we need not build complex DNS tables to establish and configure name resolution on our server; Microsoft DNS relies entirely on WINS to tell it the addresses it needs to resolve. And because WINS builds its tables automatically on the fly, we don't have to edit the DNS tables when addresses change; WINS takes care of this for us.

We can use both WINS and DNS on our network, or we can use one without the other. Our choice is determined by whether our network is connected to the Internet and whether our host addresses are dynamically assigned. When we are connected to the Internet, we must use DNS to resolve host names and addresses because TCP /IP depends on DNS service for address resolution.

9. Configuring TCP/I P with Windows NT

Now we can see how we can configure WindowsNT 4 to use TCP /IP. We should have NT 4 installed in our system so that we will be installing TCP /IP on a machine that will have a TCP/IP host name of www and a domain name of company.com . We have also to assume that this server uses an IP address of 204.176.47.2, a subnet mask of 255.255.255.0, and a default gateway of 204.176.47.1 and that it has only one network card installed. There should also be a WINS server on our network with an IPAddress of 204.176.47.11. To begin installing TCP /IP, we can follow these steps:

- Click on the Start button, select Settings, and then select Control Panel. Windows NT displays a window that contains icons for all installed objects.
- Scroll down until we locate the Network icon and click on it. In the Network dialog box, select the Protocols tab, F and then click on the Add button. Windows NT display the Select Network Protocol dialog box.
- Scroll down the list of available protocols until we see TCP /IP Protocol. Double-click on TCP /IP Protocol, or click on the Add button to add TCP /IP to your network configuration.
- Windows NT displays the TCP /IP Setup dialog box, which

asks if we have a DHCP Server on our network and if we want to use it for dynamic IP address assignment. Because we want a static IP address for your Web server, click on the No button even if we have a DHCP server on your network. Windows NT displays the Windows NT Setup dialog box.

- In the text box, select or enter the drive and path of the Windows NT installation files. These files should be on the CD-ROM from which we installed Windows NT; so we can insert our CD-ROM in the appropriate drive, enter its drive letter in the dialog box, and click on Continue. TCP /IP Setup then copies the necessary files to your hard drive.
- Click on the Close button. Windows NT begins rebuilding the registry entries and bindings for the network. It detects that TCP /IP has not been configured yet and displays the Microsoft TCP /IP Properties dialog box.

Across the top of the Microsoft TCP /IP Properties dialog box we will see five tabs labeled from left to right as follows:

- IP Address
- DNS
- WINS Address
- DHCP Relay
- Routing

Each tab controls the settings associated with a specific aspect of using TCP /IP under Windows NT Server; and in the sections that follow, we'll look at all the settings we can configure on all these tabs. The settings that we use on our system will obviously depend on the configuration of that system and exactly how we intend to use it.

- In the Microsoft TCP /IP Properties dialog box, select the IPAddress tab to bring it to the front. Be sure that our network card is the one displayed in the Adapter list.
- Click on the Specify an IP Address radio button, and fill in the IP Address, Subnet Mask, and Default Gateway text boxes. {If we click on the Advanced button, Windows NT displays

the Advanced IP Addressing dialog box in which we can add other IP addresses and gateways and manage certain aspects of TCP /IP security. Assuming that this host has only one gate- way and one IP address; we won't go into the Advanced IP Addressing dialog box at this time. This aspect of Windows NT TCP/IP security is covered in the External Security and Firewalls chapter.) Now click on the DNStab.

- Windows NT displays the DNS section of the Microsoft TCP /IP Properties dialog box. In the Host Name text box, type www, and in the Domain text box, enter your domain name or the domain name of your ISP. Remember, we're using the domain name company. com for this example installation.
- Now we can click on the Add button beneath the DNS Service Search Order list box. Windows NT displays the TCP /IP DNS Server dialog box. In the DNS Server text box, enter the IP address of our first DNS server, and click on the Add button. Windows NT displays the DNS section of the Microsoft TCP /IP Properties dialog box. Click on the Add button in the Microsoft TCP /IP Properties dialog box to add the IP address of our second DNS server, if we have one. We can specify a maximum of three DNS servers.
- If we specify only a host name in step 9 above, Windows NT displays the Domain Suffix Search Order list box, shown in the lower half of Figure 3.12. This provides a list of domain names for NT Server to use when we specify only a host name in a command. For example, if we want to use the ping command with a host named mail. company. com, we can open a command-line window and enter this command: ping mail

As long as the domain company. com is listed in the Domain Suffix Search Order list box, Windows NT can combine this with our original command, making it equivalent to the complete name, as though we had originally typed: ping mail.company.com

In this example, mail is called the prefix, and company. com is the suffix. To take advantage of this feature, we can enter the name we want to use into the Domain Suffix Search Order list box.

9.1 Installing WI NS

Now that we're finished with the DNS properties, we'll install WINS. To do so, we can follow the steps listed below.

- In the Microsoft TCP /IP Properties dialog box, click on the WINS Address tab. Windows NT displays the WINS Address section.
- In the Primary WINS Server text box, enter the IP address of our WINS server. In the Secondary WINS Server text box, enter the IP address of our secondary WINS server.
- Because we want Windows NT to use DNS to look up hosts and addresses, check the Enable DNS for Windows Resolution checkbox.
- By default, the Enable LMHOSTS Lookup checkbox is checked. In this example installation, we want to rely only on DNS for lookups; so uncheck this box. LMHOSTS Lookup is another method of name resolution. It is quite different from DNS in that it maps IP addresses to Net BIOS computer names, which is similar to the way that WINS operates. So that DHCP can manage IP addresses, it must know which IP addresses it can give out. We give IP this information with a scope, which are simply a range of IP addresses. We use a scope for two reasons that is; we can assign at least one scope to each subnet serviced by our DHCP server and second we might also want to divide a subnet's IP addresses for reasons associated with fault tolerance planning.
- In the Scope ID text box, enter a name for our scope.

Dynamic Host Configuration Protocol, or DHCP, is a service that allows workstations and servers to be assigned IP addresses automatically. The primary reason for using DHCP is to centralize the management of IP addresses. When the DHCP service is used, pools of IP addresses are assigned for distribution to client computers. The address pools are centralized on the DHCP server, allowing all IP addresses on our network to be administered from a single server. It should be apparent that this saves loads of time when changing the IP addresses on our network. Instead of running around to every work station and server and resetting the IP address to anew address, we -simply reset the IP address pool on the DHCP server. The next time the client machines are rebooted, they are assigned new addresses.

DHCP can manage much more than the IP addresses of client computers. It can also assign DNS servers, gateway addresses, subnet I masks, and much more. For purposes of our example installation, we'll assume that no DHCP servers are in use on our network. If we want to look at or change any of the DHCP settings, however, click on the DHCP Relay tab in the Microsoft TCP IIP Properties dialog box. The DCHP Relay agent allows a computer to relay messages from one network to another. Normally, we would have a DHCP server on both networks, but with NT Server, we can install a DHCP Relay agent on any computer on a network, and it will relay messages through the router that connects the two networks to the DHCP Server on the other network.

When we install the DHCP Relay agent, we can accept the default values displayed in the DHCP Relay dialog box or we can set new values for Seconds Threshold, Maximum Hops and DHCP Servers addresses. To specify the address of the DHCP Server to which DHCP messages will be relayed, click on the Add button in the DHCP Relay dialog box to open the DHCP Relay Agent dialog box. Enter the server's IP address in the DHCP Server field, and click on the Add button. To return to the DHCP Relay dialog box without adding the server's IP address, click on the Cancel button. The DHCP Relay agent is installed as an NT service and is enabled automatically.

Finally, to complete our tour of the TCP /IP settings under Windows NT Server, we can click on the Routing tab in the Microsoft TCP /IP Properties dialog box, and we will see the Routing section. Internet Protocol forwarding allows data grams to be forwarded on a multihomed host. In some multihomed hosts, we need data grams to be able to route between the network cards to other parts or segments of the network. If we have more than one network card installed in a server and we want Windows NT to be able to send data grams between them, check the Enable IP Forwarding checkbox in the Routing section of the Microsoft TCP /IP Properties dialog box. Otherwise, leave it unchecked. This setting can also be key in establishing a secure network segment.

Now that we have looked at and configured all the settings in the five sections of the Microsoft TCP /IP Properties dialog box, click on the OK button at the bottom of this dialog box to continue with our original mission, which, if we can still remember, was to configure TCP /IP on Windows NT Server. Windows NT continues the installation process, and, as we have made a significant change to NT's configuration by installing TCP /IP, asks if we want to restart the system. Click on Yes to reboot Windows NT and to load and use the TCP /IP protocol on your system.

All this TCP /IP configuration information is stored in the Windows NT Registry database, along with other hardware-specific information. We can change most of the TCP /IP parameters by using either the Control Panel or the Administrative Tools. Certain parameters, such as Time to Live and the default Type of Service, can only be changed using the Registry Editor. If we change some of these Registry parameters, we may affect the performance of TCP /IP on your system in an adverse way; to find out more, see the regentry.hp file on the Microsoft Windows NT Resource Kit CD-ROM.

9.2. Testing Configuration with Ping

Now that the server has rebooted, we can log on and test your configuration using the ping command. To do so, open the Command Prompt window, and enter this command:

ping 127.0.0.1

The ping command in which ping stands for packet internet groper transmits a special diagnostic packet that is an ICMP echo request to a specific node on network, forcing that node to acknowledge that the packet reached its destination. We will often hear people use ping as a verb; they will say something like, "Ping that workstation to see if it is awake." In this example, which uses the special loop back test IP address, the ping command sends 4 packets to the server itself and shows the turnaround time of the responses. Pinging the server simply ensures that the TCP /IP protocol is actually working at the basic levels.

If there is a problem with our TCP /IP configuration, we may receive time out errors instead of a valid response. In that case, the transmission rate for the packets of data was too long, and the receiving host did not respond. The ping command uses a default time setting that tells ping how long to wait for responses. We can adjust this time setting with a command line switch; however, the default setting is usually sufficient for testing most TCP /IP-based network devices. If the host received none of the 4 packets successfully, a time out error from ping might look something like this:

```
C:\users\default> ping 127.0.0.1
Pinging 127.0.0.1 with 32 bytes of data:
Request time-out.
Request time-out.
Request time-out.
Request time-out.
C:\users\default>-
```

After we ping the special loop back test address, try to ping another host on your network. For example, if we have another host on your network with the IP address of 204.176.47.31, ping that address. Or, if your network has a DNS or a WINS server, ping another machine by name. Additionally, if your network is attached to the Internet and we have set the correct gateway address to your network's Internet gateway, try pinging a popular Web server, such as www.microsoft.com. In any event, when we ping these other machines, the response should be similar to that we receive when we ping our server.

9.3 Remote Access Service

RAS is an acronym for Microsoft's Remote Access Service, an NT Server feature that lets mobile or remote users connect to the main NT Server network by means of a dial-up connection.

Remote users run a RAS client application on their computer and then open a connection to the RAS server using a modem, using an X.25 or using an ISDN connection.

The RAS server, running on NT Server, authenticates the user and services the communications session until it is terminated by the originating user or by the system administrator. Everything that a conventionally connected user can access on the NT server is also available to someone using RAS, given the usual user and account permissions. Windows NT logon and domain security, support for security hosts, data encryption, and callback provide secure access for remote users.

Without RAS, we would have no way to connect NT-based systems, via dial-up connections, and we would simply be stuck using physically wired networks. RAS supports several local-area networking protocols that can be used when establishing a connection between the client and the server, including NetBEUI, IPX/SPX, and TCP IIP. In addition, several other remote-access protocols are also supported, including PPP SLIP, the proprietary Microsoft RAS protocol, and the new Point-to-Point Tunneling Protocol (PPTP).

NT's RAS supports a maximum of 256 remote clients and can be configured to give a remote client access to an entire network or to only the RAS server itself. By means of RAS, Windows NT can provide a range of services to Internet users. We can configure a Windows NT Server system as an ISP, offering dial-up connections to any PPP client. We can configure the ports on a RAS server as:

- Dial Out Only
- Receive Calls Only
- Dial Out and Receive Calls

These settings affect only the specified port; we can configure other ports individually.

Errors and other significant events are stored in the NT Server Event Log, and we can use the Event Viewer to look at the log to determine the cause of any problems. We install and configure RAS using the Control Panel Network option, and we use the Control Panel Services icon to establish startup options. When we install and configure RAS, any protocol already installed on the NT Server such as TCP /IP in our example in the last section is enabled for RAS use automatically on inbound and outbound calls.

Each remote computer connecting to the RAS server by means of PPP is automatically provided with an IP address from the range of addresses set up by the system administrator when configuring RAS. Windows RAS clients can also use pre assigned IP addresses specified in their RAS Phone Books. In this latter case, we have to configure the RAS server to allow a RAS client to request this specific address.

As well as an IP address, a RAS client will also need access to one of the name resolution services we looked at earlier in this chapter. RAS clients attaching to a small network on which IP addresses do not change can use HOSTS or LMHOSTS; on larger systems, RAS clients can use the same WINS and DNS servers that the RAS server uses. The Windows NT RAS server also allows remote RAS clients to share subnet addresses with other computers on the network and thus conserve IP addresses.

9.4 Windows NT Server as Internet Gateway

Each workstation on our network that needs access to the Internet has to either connect itself directly to the Internet or route to the Internet through a gateway. The most cost effective and popular way to connect a LAN to the Internet is by using a gateway that routes the entire LAN.

We can easily configure Windows NT Server as an Internet gate- way. How we go about doing so depends on how we are connecting Windows NT Server to the Internet. One of the most common ways today is ISDN, which provides 56Kbps, 64Kbps, and 128Kbps connections; these connections are significantly faster than a 28.8Kbps modem. RAS and Windows NT treat a modem as they would treat any other network interface. Therefore, with an actual network card to connect the server to the rest of the LAN and with an ISDN modem to connect the server to an Internet Service Provider, we can configure TCP /IP routing to forward data grams, and each workstation on our network can access the Internet by using the Windows NT Server as its gateway.

We can also use Windows NT Server as an Internet gateway if portions of your LAN are connected in different ways. For example, one portion of your LAN might be connected to the Internet via Windows NT Server and RAS, another portion might be connected. With a standalone ISDN router, and still other portions of .our LAN might not have direct access to the Internet. We can configure Windows NT to route to the Internet gateway by placing it on both parts of the network and giving it routes to that destination. Once Windows NT has routes to the Internet gateway, workstations on that portion of the LAN can use the Windows NT router's IP address as their default gateway. Windows NT then forwards workstation traffic destined for the Internet straight to the Internet gateway.

9.5. Two Network protocols in One Server

One of the design goals of the Windows NT server developers was to make the integration of multiple network protocols seamless. As a result, configuring Windows NT with more than one networking protocol is easy, as compared with doing so on other operating systems. Once we have installed TCP /IP, we can install additional networking protocols in essentially the same manner; the only difference is in how we configure the new protocol's parameters.

As an example, let's take a look how to install Novell's IPX/SPX protocol on our Windows NT Server running TCP/IP. The steps can be summarized as follows:

- Select the protocol and load the appropriate files from your original NT Server CD.
- Restart Windows NT Server to install the new protocol.
- Configure the operating parameters that are specific to this new protocol.

To begin, we have to open the Control Panel, and double click on the Network icon. Now we can follow the steps given below:

- In the Network dialog box, click on the Protocols tab. Windows NT displays the TCP/IP protocol in the Network Protocols list box. Now, click on the Add button. The Select Network Protocol dialog box displays a list of the available protocols.

Scroll down the list and find NWLink IPX/SPX Compatible Transport, and double click on it. This is the Windows NT implementation of Novell's IPX/SPX protocol.

- In the Windows NT Setup dialog box, enter the location of our Windows NT installation files in the text box, and click on the Continue button. Setup copies the appropriate files to our hard drive.
- If we installed RAS, the Setup dialog box will ask we if we want to enable IPX/SPX for RAS.
- The protocol list in the Network Protocol list box now includes NWLink NetBIOS Compatible Transport and NWLink IPX/SPX Compatible Transport. Click on the Close button.

NT Server knows that we have not yet loaded or configured the protocol and suggests that we reboot the server so that this can be done. Click on the Restart button to reboot NT Server. Once NT has restarted, open the Control Panel, double-click on the Network icon, and we can follow the rest of the steps below:

- In the Network dialog box, choose the Protocols tab.
- In the Network Protocols list box, select NWLink IPX/PX Compatible Transport. Windows NT displays the NWLink IPX/SPX Properties dialog box.
- In the Adapter text box, enter the name of the network card to which we want the IPX/SPX protocol bound. In the Frame Type text box, we can leave Frame Type set to the default of Auto Detect. If Auto Detect does not work on your network, we can enter an Ethernet Frame Type and Network Number manually. The Network Number is a hexadecimal number used to assign a logical number to a NetWare server. Using the network number allows we easily to uniquely identify a NetWare server on a multi-NetWare server network.

9.6. TCP/IP in Our Intranet

Using TCP /IP on our Intranet has all the advantages of using TCP /IP to connect to the Internet. When using TCP/IP on an Intranet with Windows NT, however, we gain one distinct advantage over using TCP /IP with other types of network operating systems: ease of configuration and use. And here are some other 4 advantages.

Hundreds and hundreds of vendors are creating software for the Windows NT operating system. This increases the likelihood of finding software that does what we need.

Transmission Control Protocol/Internet Protocol is available for almost every operating system in production today. Because TCP /IP is a standardized family of protocols, connecting dissimilar operating systems is a breeze. We can also connect new systems to your older legacy systems in a snap.

9.7. Connecting Windows NT to Novell NetWare

Earlier we discussed installing multiple protocols on Windows NT platforms. The most common instance of this is adding Windows NT to a network composed mainly of Netware servers running IPX/SPX. We can use the Windows NT NWLink IPX/SPX Compatible Transport (NWLink) as a protocol between NT Server systems, to connect NT Workstation computers to NT Server systems, or to add NT Server-based networks to a Novell NetWare network. More than this we can use Gateway Service for NetWare to connect a computer running NT Server to NetWare servers and to create a gateway to other NetWare resources. Doing so allows computers running Microsoft software to access NetWare resources through the gateway.

We have to remember that IPX/SPX is a much more traffic-intensive protocol than TCP /IP, and if we need to connect Windows NT to Novell, we should uninstall Novell's IPX/SPX and convert our entire network to TCP /IP. We'll find that network traffic goes down and network performance goes up. Sites that run databases on Unix, NT Server, or OS/2 may depend on Novell NetWare for print and file services. And when the company decides to add Intranet services, this same network must also support a Web server and Web browsers. The only protocol that can do all this and connect all these disparate systems is TCP /IP.

This move toward TCP /IP has certainly not gone unnoticed by the software developers at the major companies that provide networking operating systems. Novell's NetWare now includes

NetWare/IP, a NetWare Loadable Module (NLM) that almost adds IP to a Novell server. NetWare/IP adds a 40-byte header to an IPX packet; so the protocol is certainly not pure TCP /IP, but Novell has promised to add a real implementation of TCP /IP in the near future. And along with Novell go Apple, IBM, Banyan, and many other companies, all working to improve their TCP /IP offerings.

9.8 Connecting Windows NT to Unix

Connecting Windows NT to a Unix network environment is easy, since TCP /IP is the standard protocol for Unix networks. As it does with any other TCP /IP-based networking systems, Windows NT integrates seamlessly into a Unix networking environment. And these days, the large and growing Unix world includes versions and variations of Unix running on hardware from a PC to a Cray supercomputer; Cray offers Unicos, DEC offers Ultrix, IBM offers AIX, Apple Computing offers A/UX, Silicon Graphics offers Irix, and Hewlett Packard offers HP-UX.

Commercial versions of Unix for the Intel series of processors include SCO Unix, Solaris from Sun Micro systems, UnixWare originally from Novell and now from SCO; free versions of Unix include the Free Software Foundation's GNU Project, FreeBSD, NetBSD, and the ever popular Linux. If our network comprises Apple Macintosh systems, minicomputers, mainframe computers, Unix systems, IBM PCs running Novell, and IBM PC compatible systems running some version of Windows, these computers normally could not communicate. But with TCP /IP installed on each of them, they are all capable of communicating and transferring data back and forth with the greatest of ease. This is simply not possible with any other networking protocol in existence today.

4

Unix Familiarization

There were many different platforms in use in the 1960s. In 1970s, with the advent of a mainframe operating system called Unix, which is a program that coordinates and manages all the computer's functions this began to change. Unix is distributed free of cost by AT&T to educational institutions, because AT&T itself was forbidden to sell software by the government. Because it was free, many institutions tried it. Unix was found to be a powerful and extendible operating system, one that was relatively easy for which to develop programs and applications. It caught on around the world, and is today, in various forms, one of the most popular computer operating systems for mainframes, supercomputers, and even some powerful desktop machines and workstations. Unix was also very portable, or able to be used on a variety of different physical machines. With some changes in the software, Unix could run on many different computers. Unix and a very few other popular operating systems indirectly encouraged standards on the net. Programs for network transmission and reception could be written and ported to other Unix systems with relative ease. This enabled the programmer and user to enjoy some stability and similarity across many systems.

On its own, a computer system is just a collection of metal, silicon, communication equipment and magnetic media. It is the application programs, which make a computer system useful to its users. Application can range from word processing, through writing compilers, to generating new operating systems.

To exploit the communications, data storage, and information processing capabilities of the computer hardware, the application software requires some form of overseer, which can handle the details of managing the hardware resources, accessing the files, and interacting with the users. These supervisory functions are the job of the Operating System.

1. Role of Operating System

Operating systems come in many shapes, sizes and guises. All operating systems have more or less the same function, namely to hold the ring between all the different hardware resources of a computer system in such a way that users can get their work done. After all getting the job done faster or easier, or cheaper is the putative reason for which we use computers.

A computer system generally consists of two parts namely Hardware and Software. "Hardware" means the peripherals of the computer components. "Software" means collection of programs. The main role of an operating system is the communication between the user and computer. Unix is one such operating system. Another one is DOS, which is available in the IBM compatible PCs.

In these days Unix operating system is emerging as the most popular operating system. The Unix operating system is a collection of programs that controls the computer and acts as the link between user and computer. For programmers who have been using Unix for several years now, this comes as no surprise; The Unix system provides an elegant and efficient environment for program development. Dennis Ritchie and Ken Thompson developed Unix at Bell laboratories in the late 1960's.

One of the strongest features of the Unix system is its wide collection of programs. Over 200 basic commands are distributed with the standard operating system. These commands also known as "tools" do every thing from counting the number of lines in a file, to sending electronic mail, to displaying a Calander for any desired year. But the real strength of thc Unix system comes not entirely from this large collection of commands but from the elegance and ease with which these commands can be combined to perform more sophisticated functions.

To further this end, and also to provide a consistent buffer between the user and the guts of the Unix system the shell was developed. The shell is a simply a program that reads in the commands we type and converts them into a form that is more readily understandable by the Unix system. It also includes some fundamental programming constructs that let us make decisions, loop and store values in variables. It also offers an interpreted programming language called SHELL Programming Language, in which programs can be written modified and debugged quickly and easily.

2. FEATURES OF UNIX

UNIX is preferred over other operating systems because of its simplicity, popularity, design, and organization and functioning. Some features are given below:

Portability: The Unix system can be placed in different machines in an easy way. The Unix system on every machine appears to be the same. Thus a program written on one machine can be put onto another machine and executed there without any difficulty.

Background Processing: In this processing, a user can execute more than one job simultaneously. This increases productivity of more jobs for different users.

Hierarchical File System: With the hierarchy provided by the file system, a user can organize the information in a structured fashion which make it easy to store and access information or handling data.

Command Interpreter: Unix interprets various commands typed by the user and executes them. In addition to this it acts as a programming language, so that a user can store a number of commands to be executed in a command file and execute all of them by giving the name of the file.

Time Sharing: A multi-user environment that allows user to share the computer's resources with other users without sacrificing productivity. This technique is called Time Sharing. The Unix system interacts between users on a rotating basis so quickly that it appears to be interacting with all users simultaneously.

Security: It protects one user from another. No user is allowed to see the information manipulated by another user.

Communication Facilities: Unix system provides facilities to communicate with other users. Now a days computer are interlinked through telephonic lines or through other ways of signaling. Technically we say that networks are built up for communication.

Utilities: Unix provides a large collection of useful programs that are already written by different people. Many times it is observed that a number of applications need to do the same thing.

2.1 Structure of Unix

The Unix Operating Systems consists of three parts, namely Kernel, Shell and the file system. The kernel is that part of the system which performs the actual computer and memory management activities that allocate resources and maintain proper control. The shell is the command interpreter. The file system is the organizing structure for data.

2.3 MS-DOS and Unix

The main features Unix systems have over MS-DOS are as follows:

Shell Programming Language: Facilities for writing programs in a true programming language capable of handling string and numeric relation ships.

Multitasking: Running more than one program at the same time.

Multi-user: Many users accessing the same computer and operating system at the same time.

Larger Memory: For all practical purposes, the Unix system can use any amount of installed memory to run the programs.

Compatibility: The Unix system can run on many different kinds of systems mainframe, minicomputers and personal computer providing an integrated environment. MS-DOS only runs on PCs.

Commands: Unix systems features additional user-level commands- approximately more than 300 commands depending on version that provide the basic tools for everything from simple memos to complicated database.

Full ASCII Text Editors: The Vi and ed text editors are available.

Communication: Users can communicate with each other using the system's electronic mail utilities.

3. Entering and Quitting

Before we can start using Unix, our system manager must create our own account or one common to all. This will involve assigning a user name and a password, after which we can try logging in. Our terminal should show the following message

host1 (depending upon our sitting terminal)

Welcome to (Unix system)

Host1! login:

We can type our user name and press <Return>. Then it will ask our password. We have to type our password. If we have been able to complete the login procedure without any error Unix will print a prompt usually a $ symbol to indicate that the system is ready to accept our commands. Otherwise once again it will show login.

When we have finished working with the Unix system, we can logout or logoff simply by typing, "exit" or ctrl-d when we see the $ sign. Then the indication that we have logged off is a new request for a login

Example: $ exit <Return>

host1!login:

4. Files and Directories

Unix System knows about three kinds of files: They are directories, ordinary file and special files.

A directory is a file containing information about other files and directories. A directory "contained" within another directory is called a sub directory. The sub directories can themselves contain files and more directories.

An ordinary file is simply a container into which we can put the data. The most important thing about a file is that it has a name by which we can refer to it. It is the container that has the name, not the data in the container. By using the container's name, commands work on the whole collection of data contained therein. The contents of a file can be displayed, files can be copied, they can be removed from file system, or they can be moved around in the file system.

Unix system knows about certain kinds of peripheral devices on the system. These take the form of magnetic disks, magnetic tapes, terminals, communication lines, and all sorts of other things. Every different kind of device has piece of system V called a "driver" which is responsible for communicating with that device. Somewhere deep inside the system there is tables that point to the different device drivers. All devices are treated just like files. These files are called special files.

4.1 Listing Directory Contents

The ls command is a request to the system to 'list the contents of a directory'. If no directory is specified on the ls command line, we can get a list of files in the current directory, which is one we are looking in . For example: $ ls <Return>

The above example shows what are the files contained in the current directory.

Example: $ l <Return>

In this example it shows full details of fields in a file display as given below:

drwxrwxrwx1 raman group 112 jan10 10:40 monil

-rwx——— 1 mohan other 200 jan20 11:15 moni2

-rw-r—r— 1 root group 120 mar15 12:00 msk11

drw-rw-rw-2 francis group 220 jun17 09:50 aaa11

drwx———1 root group 100 jul19 11:00 abcde

The very first column in the file field tell us that whether it is a ordinary file (-) or directory (d). The remainder of the field (rwxrwxrwx) tells us about permissions on that file. The second column tells us the number of links to the file. The third column shows the owner of the directory or file. The fourth column shows the group of users that the owner is part of. The fifth column shows the size of the file in bytes. The sixth column shows the date and time. Seventh column shows is the actual name of the file or directory.

4.2 Wild Card Characters

The Asterisk: One very powerful feature of the Unix system that is actually handled by the shell is file name substitution. Let's say our current directory has these files in it.

$ 1s <Enter>

francis1francis2francis3francis4

Suppose we want to print their contents at the terminal. We could take advantage of the fact that the "cat" command allows us to specify more than one file name at a time. When this is done, the contents of the files are displayed one after another.

$ cat francis francis1 francis2 francis3 francis4 <Enter>

But also we can type

$ cat francis*

In the above example the francis* matches any file name that begins with francis. All such file name matched is substituted on the command line. The * is not limited to the end of a filename; it can be used at the beginning or in the middle as well.

4.3 Matching Single Characters:

The asterisk (*) matches zero or more characters, meaning that x* will match the file x as well as character. So **cat ?** will print all files with one character names, just as **cat x?** will print all files with two character names beginning with x.

```
    $ a
    aa
    aax
    alice
    b
    bb
    bbc
    cc
$ echo? <Enter>
    abc
$ echo a? <Enter>
    aa
$ echo ?? <Enter>
    aa bb cc
$ echo ??* <Enter>
    aa aax alice bb cc
```

In the last example, the ?? matches two characters and the * matches zero or more up to the end.

Another way to match a single character is to give a list of the characters to use in the match inside square brackets [ ]. For example [abc] matches one letter a,b,or c.

5. Input/Output Redirection

Most Unix system commands take input from our terminal

and send the resulting output back to our terminal. A command normally reads its input from a place called **standard input** which happens to be our terminal by default. Similarly a command normally writes its output to **standard output** which is also our terminal by default.

standard input —> command ——> standard output

Suppose we are creating a file through keyboard in our had disk.

For example

$ cat> raman

Now the cursor will come on the nextline. Then we can type

This is a book (Enter)

This is a cat (Enter)

This is a rat (Enter)

This is a pen (Enter)

Press ctrl-d, then our file will be saved in the name of raman then if we want to see the contents of a file we can give the following command

$ cat raman

In the above example our output is redirected to the file raman

Just as the output of a command can be redirected to a file so can the input of a command be redirected from a file. The greater than character > is used for output redirection. The less than character < is used to redirect the input of a command. Of course only commands that normally take their input from standard input can have their input redirected from a file in this manner.

In order to redirect the input of a command, we can type the < character followed by the name of the file that the input is read from, so for example $ raman <francis <Enter>. In this case our input is redirected to the name of the file francis.

5.1 Home Directory and Path Names

The Unix system always associates each user of the system with a particular directory. When we log in to the system, we are placed automatically in to a directory called our home directory.

Assume that our home directory is called raman and that this directory is actually a subdirectory of a directory called usrl is shown below

$ pwd <Enter>

/usrl/raman

Whenever we are "inside" a particular directory called our current working directory, the files contained within that directory are immediately accessible. If we wish to access a file from another directory, then we can either first issue a command to "change" to the appropriate directory and then access the particular file, or we can specify the particular field by its path name.

A path name enables us to uniquely identify a particular file to the unix system. In the specification of a path name successive directories along the path are separated by the slash character/. A path name that begins with a slash character is known as a full path name, since it specifies a complete path from the root so for example, the path name/usrl/guest identifies the directory guest contained under the directory usrl. Similarly the path name /usrl/guest/ documents references the directory documents as contained in the directory guest under usrl.

5.2 Pipes

A pipe can be made between any two programs provided the first program writes its output to the standard output, and the second program reads its input from standard input. The Unix system allows us to effectively "connect" two commands together. This connection is known as a pipe and it enables us to take the output from one command and feed it directly in to the input of another command. A pipe is effected by the character/ which is placed between the two command. So to make a pipe between the ls and wc/l commands we can simply type

$ ls/wc-l

The output indicates the current directory contains how many files. It is also possible to form a pipeline consisting of more than two programs, with the output of one program feeding into the input of the next.

6. Some Basic Commands

Displaying the date and time: The date command tells the system to print the date and time. $ date <Enter>. The current date and time will be displayed. The date command is also used to set current date and time. The format for specifying date is mmddhhmmyy. The above example for the date Jun 15, 1992 time 3 p.m.

Displaying Calendars: $ cal <Enter>. A calendar for the current month, the preceeding and the preceeding months will be printed. A calendar for a specified month and year may be printed by specifying the month and year as in the example; $ cal 7 1998 <Enter> A calendar for an entire year may be printed by specifying only the year, the example is $ cal 1998 <Enter>

Echoing Characters: The echo command prints or echoes at the terminal whatever else we happen to type on the line. $ echo I am learning Unix <Enter>. I am learning Unix.

Displaying Banners: The banner command prints in large letters, character strings supplied as command line arguments. $ banner "kumar" <Enter>

7. Working with Files and Directories

For Listing files we can use the ls Command. To see what files we have stored in our directory, we can type the ls command $ ls <Enter>

For listing the files page wise $ ls/pg <Enter>

For listing the files in column wise $ lc <Enter>

For listing the files in the long format $ l <Enter>

For creating the files in a hard disk we can do the following.

To create a file we will use the "cat" command and redirect the out put to a file. $ cat >francis <Enter>

Then the cursor will come in the next line. Type the following message

I am learning Unix Operating System <Enter>

I am attending a training program for Electronic Library Management at KAU.

(KAU) <Enter>

press <ctrl>-d

The text typed in is saved as file "francis"

For displaying the contents of a file we can examine the contents of a file by using the "cat" command. The argument to cat is the name of the file whose contents we wish to examine is $ cat francis <Enter>

For copying the files let us create duplicate copies of files francis $ cp francis francis1 <Enter>

Execution of this command causes the file named francis to be copied in to a file named francis.

A file can be renamed with "mv" command. The arguments to the mv command follow the same format as the cp command $ mv francis francis2 <Enter>. The file francis renamed as francis2. Now we can see the contents of a file francis2 use "cat" command $ cat francis2 <Enter>

A file can be removed with "rm" command. $ rm francis <Enter>. The file francis removed from the directory.

7.1 Working with Directories

Displaying working directory: The pwd command is used to help us "get out bearings" by telling us the name of our current working directory. $ pwd <Enter> /usrl/guest. It shows the current working directory is guest.

Making directories: To create a directory, the mkdir command must be used. $ mkdir raman <Enter>. It creates a directory in the name of raman in the current directory.

Changing the directories: We can change our current working directory by using the cd command. This command takes as its arguments the name of the directory we wish to change to $ cd raman <Enter> Here it changes the directory to raman.

Removing the directories: We can remove a directory with the rmdir command. The stipulation involved in removing a directory is that no files be contained in the directory. $ rmdir raman <Enter>

Moving files between directories: The mv command can be used to rename a file. However when the two arguments to this command refer different directories, then the file is actually moved from the first directory the second directory. For example mv/usrl/ raman/ francis /usrl/ guest/<Enter>. The above example in the raman directory contains the francis file and it moved in to the guest directory.

8. Ownership and Protection

Unix System provides a means to assign permissions for files and directories, so that the range of users who can access those files and directories is constrained. Here we will discuss the ideas behind access rights to files and directories.

Every file or directory anyone creates on the system has an owner, usually the person who created the file or directory in the first place. The owner of a file or directory can then assign various permissions (or protections) allowing or prohibiting access to that directory or file.

For every file and every directory in the file system there are three classes of users who may have access to it.

Owner: The owner is the user who initially created it.

Group: Several users can be combined into a user group and so there is a group ownership associated with each file and directory.

Others: All other users of the system.

For every file and every directory on the system there will be three types of permission namely read, write and execution.

Read(r): A user who has read permission for a file can look at the contents of that file.

Write(w): A user who has write permission for a file can change the contents of the file.

Execute(x): A user who has execute permission for a file can use that filename as a Unix System V command.

8.1 Changing Permissions

By combining the three types of permissions and three types

of users we can come up with a total of nine sets of permissions. The nine permissions are collectively known as the "mode" of the file or directory. The command chmod changes the mode of a file or directory. A mode is constructed by adding togethei the actal values representing access permissions where

0 = no access

4 = read permission

2 = write permission

1 = execure permission

$ chmod 700 francis <Enter>; Here the owner can read, write and execute the file francis.

8.2 Text Manipulation

Printing a file: The lp command

lp is the command to route files to the printer and is used this way.

lp francis <Enter>

Here francis is the file name. In the next line it shows request id is prl-182 (l file). If the printer is on, the out put is printed.

Cancel a print a file the cancel command can be used. If we request a print out of a file, then decide we don't want it, we can use cancel to remove the request.

$ cancel prl-182 <Enter>

Counting things in a file

The we command counts the number of lines, words and characters in a file. We can count what is in our "raman" file with a wc command like this:

$ wc raman <Enter>

10 30 200 raman

The first number is the number of lines in the file. The second number is the number of words in the file. The third number is the number of characters in the file, finally, wc display the name of the file it counted.

8.3 Formatting the Floppy

Formatting the floppy means to prepare the floppy to store information. In Unix Operating System the formatting of floppy is as shown below:

$ format /dev/rfd096ds15 <Enter>

$ format /dev/rfd048ds9 <Enter> $ format <Enter>

8.4 Dumping and Extracting the Files:

A useful command for dumping files to floppy is the tar command. Tar dump files on to a specified device in a special format, with headers and checksums. Let us assume that we have a floppy disk device and we have to dump all the files in a directory to that floppy

$ tar cvf /dev/fd0 * <Enter>

After completing we want to see what are the files that are dumped in the floppy. The command is

$ tar tcf /dev/fd0 <Enter>

Now let us assume that we want to extract the files from floppy to our hard disk. The command is

$ tar xvf /dev/fd0 * <Enter>

9. Selected Unix Commands

at	: execute commands at a later time
Example	: $ at 23 filename <Enter>runs the commands at 23 hours (11 p.m.)
banner	: prints large letters or make posters
Example	: $ banner "kumar" <Enter>
bc	: invokes calculator
Example	: $ be <Enter>
cal	: prints calendar
Example	: $ cal 1992 <Enter> it shows only the month July 1992
cancel	: cancel to print a file

Example	: $ cancel prl-200 <Enter>
cat	: concatenate and print files
Example	: $ cat kumar <Enter> it shows the contents of the file kumar
ee	: c language compiler
Example	: $ cc filename <Enter>
cd	: changes the current directory
Example	: $ cd monil <Enter>it changes the current directory to monil directory
chgrp	: hange group of a file or directory
Example	: $ chgrp name filename <Enter>
chmod	: change mode of a file or directory
Example	: $ chmod mode filname <Enter>
chown	: change owner of a file or directory
Example	: $ chown name filename <Enter>
clear	: to clear the screen
Example	: $ clear <Enter>
cp	: makes a duplicate file
Example	: $ cp file1 file2 <Enter> it makes duplicate file 1 to file2
date	: it shows date and time
Example	: $ date <Enter>
dcmbasic	: basic compiler
Example	: $ dcmbasic filename <Enter>
dcmfortran	: fortran compiler
Example	: $ dcmfortran filename <Enter>
diskep	: makes a duplicate floppy
Example	: $ diskep <Enter>
dosdir	: list of files in the floppy
Exampl	: $ dosdir a: <Enter>
doscp	: copies the files from dos to unix

Example	: $ doscp a:filename. <Enter>
dosformat	: formatting the floppy in dos under unix environment
Example	: $ dosformat /dev/fd048ds9 <Enter>
echo	: print arguments
Example	: $ echo "arguments" <Enter>
find	: finds designated files and acts upon them
Example	: $ find-name filename <Enter> it shows files named 'filename'
format	: formatting the floppy in Unix environment
Example	: $ format /dev/rfd048ds9 <Enter> $ format /dev/rfd096ds15 <Enter>
head	: print first lines of a file (default=10)
Example	: head (options) filename <Enter> give option for no. of lines
kill	: terminate jobs
Example	: $ kill-9 job number or process ID option-9 for sure killing of a process
i	: list contents of a directory
Example	: $1 <Enter>
ic	: list name of files in a directory in column wise
Example	: $lc <Enter>
is	: list name of files only
Example	: $ ls <Enter>
in	: make file links
Example	: $ In file1 file2 <Enter>
ip	: print a file in the printer
Example	: $ lp filename <Enter> option-n for no. of copies
ipstat	: print file status information
Example	: $ lpstat <Enter>
mkdir	: make a directory

Example	: $ mkdir kumar <Enter>
more	: print files one screen at a time
Example	: $ filename more <Enter>
mv	: move or rename the file
Example	: $ mv file1 file2 <Enter> it rename the file1 file2
pg	: files scanning one screen at a time
Example	: 1/pg <Enter>
pwd	: print working directory
Example	: $ pwd <Enter>
rm	: removing the files
Example	: $ rm (option) filename <Enter> option-i interactive deletion of files
rmdir	: removing the directory
Example	: $ rmdir kumar <Enter>
sort	: sort or merge files
Example	: $ sort (options) filename <Enter>
tail	: prints the last part of the file (default=10)
Example	: $ tail (options) filename <Enter>
tar	: tape archives of files
Example	: $ tar cvf/dev/fd048ds9 filename it copies from hard disk to floppy $tar xvf/dev/fd096ds15 filename it copies from floppy to hard disk $ tar tvf/dev/fd048ds9 <Enter>
tty	: get's the terminal name
Example	: $tty <Enter>
uname	: prints the name of the current system
Example	: $ uname <Enter>
vi	: visual ASCII text editor
Example	: $ vi filename <Enter>
write	: write message to another user
Eample	: $ write login name <Enter>

wall : write message to all users

Example : $ wall <Enter> This command only applicable for super user

wc : characters, word and line counts in a file

Example : $ wc <Enter>

5

Gopher for Information Search

Gopher is a menu-driven interface that allows users to access the large number of varied resources on the Internet without requiring users to know computer commands. With Gopher, accessing information on the Internet can be as easy as making a selection on a menu. No matter where we are on the Internet Gopher allows us to locate, see, and retrieve information from throughout the Internet as if it were a single set of directories and menus on our computer. Anyone can make use of the resources available on the Internet by using this programme.

Internet is a powerful communication tool, which allows people to cooperate over distances. It brings together communities and creates opportunities for collaborative work. Internet is also a repository of vast storehouses of digital information. Computers are, after all, tireless beings that will answer our questions quickly and at any time. So we can entrust huge databases of information to them and allow them to serve people's requests for the information. Especially if the information is to be publicly available, this offers unlimited facilities and Gopher is a tool that enables this.

For decades before the web came into existence the principal tools for using the net other than for email and newsgroups were Telnet and FTP and, in the final pre web years, Gopher. None of these three tools are as easy or fun as the web, and also so much is available on the web these days that most newcomers to the Internet never bother. Connor Sexton writes, "I remember when my using of Internet before five years through gopher with my dad on my old 486. I remember how cool it was to know that this information was out there on another computer, being accessed by other people. There was a wealth of information so overwhelming I did not know what to do with it. As a young child, I was highly fascinated by Space, and I asked my dad to type in 'How to be and Astronaut' and I got an essay on that topic. I was so happy; I was amazed at what was happening. Today, I use the Internet and witness the horrible commercialization of a wonderful place. The far-reaching hands of capitalism leave no stone unturned. I am willing to help you pull this together in any way I can. I would love to see the reinstatement of Gopher." Earlier most of the things used to be accessible only through the tools FTP, Gopher and Telnet. But now they reside on web pages. But not everything. Most of their domain has yet to be brought into the web. So these tools remain an important part of our Internet toolset even now. To use all that the Internet has to offer, we must be familiar with these powerful tools also, which are easier to use than we might think them to be. Even than we do not need much technical expertise to use them.

Gopher was the first real attempt for making the Internet easier to use, and it worked but not as well as the web, which was developed hot on Gopher's heels. A team of programmers at the University of Minnesota developed Gopher in 1991. It allowed campus computer users to quickly gain access to information available on their campus network. Within a year, it became popular both as a means of making information available and for accessing information. Within two years, there were more than a thousand registered Gopher servers, computer sites where information is made available through the use of Gopher.

The menu choices in a Gopher server include text files, graphic images, and sounds. These resources may reside in our computer or in a completely different system, located anywhere else in the world. Gopher Space, the term used to refer to all the menus and information accessible through the use of Gopher, is a tree-like structure: There is a root server or menu/from which you start, and as you go up the tree into the structure, branches or other menus will shoot off in every direction. This will be well organized by subject matter, which will make search easy.

Depending on the computer system we are using to access Gopher, we may or may not be able to display or utilize retrieved information. For example, we cannot display a graphic image or play audio files unless the equipment we are using has the capability to access them.

Gopher servers are mainly two types. They are the Campus Wide Information System (CWIS) and the general audience information system. CWIS generally contain information of interest to the students, faculty, and staff of a university or an organization. In addition to campus related information, such as campus events and course information, it often contains pointers to other Gopher sites, including general audience information servers or Gopher available information of particular interest to the campus community. A general audience information server is devoted to providing specific kinds of information that will be of use to large groups of people.

1. Working of Gopher

Functioning of Gopher systems can be explained like this. It is based on what is called client/server architecture. There will be Gopher client program and Gopher server program. The Gopher server program runs on those host computers that are Gopher servers or information providers. A user runs the Gopher client program to access information on the Gopher server. The client program takes the user's keystrokes, displays menus, retrieves and displays documents, and performs all the works that do not require the machine on the far side of the network. The server program waits for clients to ask it about menus and documents. Whenever it is asked about any such item, it provides it for the client.

Sometimes we may find that certain documents or menus take a long time to show upon screen, or refuse to show up at all. This is because, as we wander through Gopher Space, we will probably talk to several different servers, even though we are using the same client. Sometimes these servers are extremely popular, or have a slow network connection, or perhaps have simply gone down. In the face of these difficulties, one can always back up and try a different approach to the same information. In Gopher Space, many ways lead to the same information.

Gopher space is a term that collectively describes all the Gopher servers in the world and the information they contain. All the Gopher servers are interconnected and so clicking a menu item on a menu displayed by one Gopher server may display a new menu or file that is stored on another Gopher server. Gopher Space is friendly. There are some basic steps we need to know to enter it. They are how to start Gopher; how to specify the Gopher server we want to access; how to navigate through the Gopher menus; how to make a selection; and how to quit.

2. Exploring the Net with Gopher

In Windows Gopher clients are available. It takes the flavor of the Windows on which it is running. For example, to run the program, we have to double click on the icon of the Gopher client. To make a selection, we have to click with the mouse, or to close a menu, click on the close box on the upper left corner. On a window, client working with the Gopher is like doing anything else on Windows. Anything that we can do on one Gopher client, we can do on another.

Gopher host menu that is displayed depends on how the client software was installed. If our site is running a Gopher server, the menu displayed by the client will most likely be the menu from that server. Otherwise, it will present the main menu from another server, which will provide a good starting place from which we can find information.

The default setting for Gopher clients is to generally display the menu from the University of Minnesota because it was developed at that University. We will find the similarity in all Gopher menus.

Gopher introduced the idea that we could explore online information by navigating through an organized index of menu items, links, in effect. We can explore all the information stored on Gopher servers the world over most of which are in colleges and universities; by clicking our way through the menus and links in Gopher space. As on an FTP server, all the online information accessible through Gopher is organized like a table of contents or index.

We generally begin at a high level directory. When we click an item in that directory, another more specific subdirectory of choices appears. We continue clicking down through the menu structure until we reach our goal, which is usually a document that displays to show us the information to which our choices have led.

Also like FTP, an icon that indicates what the link leads to when viewed through a web browser or graphical Gopher client precedes each item in a Gopher menu. Items flagged by folder icons lead to other Gopher menus, items flagged by page icons lead to documents, and so on.

3. Netscape Navigator and Internet Explorer

Most web browsers can act as FTP clients. But again, all versions of Netscape Navigator and Internet Explorer can also be used as Gopher clients. So we probably already have our Gopher client ready to go.

In case we had not already guessed, we can access Gopher space through a web browser by entering a Gopher URL in the address box. A Gopher URL begins with the prefix gopher:// followed by a server address. This URL stuff gets pretty obvious after awhile.

Unlike a real FTP client, a real Gopher client offers no advantage over using our web browser for Gopher. Just in case we use a browser that does not do Gopher, we have to note that Gopher client programs are available for any system. Our ISP can probably set us up with a Gopher client from among the programs it offers to subscribers. We may also find a Gopher client on our own, by exploring Yahoo!s directory of Gopher clients at www. yahoo.com/ Computers _and _Internet/Internet/Gopher/Software

3.2 Exploring Gopher space

As told earlier Gopher was developed at the University of Minnesota. Gopher borrows its name from the university's mascot, although the name also implies that we use it to "burrow" or to 'go for' information. So the University of Minnesota Gopher some times known affectionately as "Mother Gopher" is a great place to begin exploring. Let us begin by following steps given below that can be used by a novice. First we have to begin in the browser, online and on any page.

* In our address box, enter the URL: gopher:// gopher.micro.umn.edu/ to display the top level directory on Mother Gopher. Now The top-level menu at Mother Gopher will appear, showing a menu of links leading to other menus.
* Click the top choice, information About Gopher. Another menu appears. At the top of the menu is a link to a document about Gopher (About Gopher).
* Click About Gopher. A document introducing us to Gopher opens.
* Click Back once. The document closes, and we return to the menu.
* Click Back again. We return to the top menu.
* Now check out another great Gopher called Gopher Jewels at University of Southern California. Enter the URL: gopher:/ /cwis.usc.edu/
* On the menu that appears, choose Other Gophers and Information Resources.

* On the next menu, choose Gopher Jewels. A menu of fun and interesting Gophers appears.

4. Gopher Through Unix

At first we have to run a Gopher client program. The client program may reside on a personal computer, a workstation, or on a mainframe. Here, a Gopher client on a Unix computer is used. First we have to find out if the Gopher client is available on the Unix computer we are using. For this we have to connect to our Unix host by typing gopher and pressing Enter. Unix is case sensitive. Hence this must be typed in lowercase. If there is a Gopher client, a Gopher menu similar to the one shown below will come.

Root gopher server: gopher. <name of server>

1. About this Gopher Server/
2. General Campus Information/
3. Departmental Information/
4. Library Resources/
5. Directories of People, Services, Etc./
6. Campus News and Events/
7. Interesting Information/
8. New Things in Gopher (2/25/94)/
9. Other Gopher and Information Servers/
10. Help Searching this Gopher Space
11. Search this Gopher Space <?>

If the message "gopher: command not found" appears, then the Gopher client software is not available on our host computer. Then we have to connect with a computer that runs a Gopher client. For this we have to type telnet consultant.micro.umn.edu and press Enter. Then a screen with details similar to that provided below will appear.

Trying 134.84.132.4 ...

Connected to hafnhaf,micro.umn.edu.

Escape character is ^]'

AIX telnet (hafnhaf)

Notice : this system is very heavily used. For better performance, you should install and run a gopher client on your own system.

Gopher clients are available for anonymous ftp from boombox.micro.umn.edu

To run gopher on this system log in as "gopher"

(C) Copyrights by IBM and by others 1982, 1998.

log in:

The instructions on the screen tell us that if we want to run Gopher on this computer, use the name "gopher" to login. At the login: prompt, we have to type gopher and press Enter. Then the message TERM=vt(100) is displayed. We have to press Enter again and the Gopher screen similar to the following will come.

Internet Gopher Information Client

Root gopher server: hafnhaf.micro.umn.edu

1. Information About Gopher/
2. Computer Information/
3. Internet file server (ftp) sites/
4. Fun & Games/
5. Libraries/
6. Mailing Lists/
7. News/
8. Other Gopher and Information Servers/
9. Phone Books/
10. Search Gopher Titles at the University of Minnesota <?>
11. Search lots of places at the U of M <?>
12. Campus Information/Press ? for Help, q to quit

As we can see at the bottom of screens in Gopher menus when we access Gopher from a unix client, there is a menu option to quit. We can close the session by typing q and then confirming by pressing Enter.

4.1 Accessing Gopher

Gopher clients generally allow us to connect directly to

Gophers other than our local Gopher which is already present by the client software by specifying the name of the desired Gopher computer. On a Unix computer, we type gopher and the address of the computer to which we want to connect. In addition, we may or may not need to specify the port. The port refers to a specific communication channel on which the destination Gopher server is waiting for requests similar to a phone extension. 70 is the standard port, but sometimes a Gopher server uses a non-standard port number. The Gopher server at University of Minnesota has the address gopher.micro.umn.edu, and it is on port 70. If we have a Gopher client, we can type gopher gopher.micro.umn.edu 70 and press Enter. The University of Minnesota root menu appears, as shown earlier.

5. The Gopher Menu

Type of information provided is mostly relevant to the campus itself or collections of information available elsewhere on the Internet. What we accessed is the root gopher server - a place where we can start the search for information. The appearance of the menu and the way in which we make selections will depend on the platform we are using. Nevertheless, the idea is that we start from the root menu, follow the structure by making menu selections, and eventually end up with the information for which we are looking. There are search tools available to assist us in getting to the resource without getting lost in Gopher Space.

In the menu, there are ways in which the type of selection is indicated. In the Unix platform, symbols that follow menu options indicate type of selection. In the Minnesota root menu we have seen entries that end with/and <?>. The forward slash indicates a directory that leads to another menu, and <?> indicates a searchable index that assists us in finding resources. The following shows the symbols and their meanings. Binary, text, sound, or a graphic file would be the documents we will be searching for.

Selection type	**Explanation**
-no symbol-	*text to be viewed or the same as"."* the information is for display only.
	a file (text or some other format) In case of text file, it can be displayed by nearly every kind of computer. The text is not formatted as it may be on a word processor. The file can be displayed on the screen, then saved, e-mailed to our self, or printed.
/	*a directory (further menu options)* when we select this item, another menu is displayed.
<?>	*a searchable index* a collection of documents that have been fully indexed by every word contained in them. When we select this menu item, we are asked for a word on which to search the index.
<tel>	*launches a Telnet session to a remote site* when we make this selection we will leave the Gopher program to access a remote computer system. The Gopher client will present a warning as well as information on how to get into and out of the system to which we have telnetted.
<cso>	*a directory search service* will display names, phone numbers, e-mail, and mailing address of the person for whom we are looking.
<Bin>	*a binary file.* binary code cannot be viewed. It can be saved.
<Picture>	*a graphics file* pictures in various formats, such as GIF or JPEG. Not all clients can handle this information.
<)	*digitized sound* not all clients can handle this information.

5.1 Browsing Gopher Space

During browsing through Gopher Space, we make a selection and see what options are displayed next, make another selection and see what happens, and so on, until we find the piece of information of interest to us. We discover the menus and directories that someone else has thoughtfully designed to present information. Unlike other Internet tools, when we use Gopher, we gain a certain sense of places within the Internet: From the University of Minnesota Gopher, we can choose "Other Gopher and Information Services," then "North America," and so on. There is logic and organization to individual menu structures used in Gopher, but for the most part we are exploring the links that connect Gophers and their information stores.

The best way to become familiar with Gopher is to use it for knowing how Gopher can be used to get information for a specific research task. We will use the browse method to find the Gopher at Willamette University.

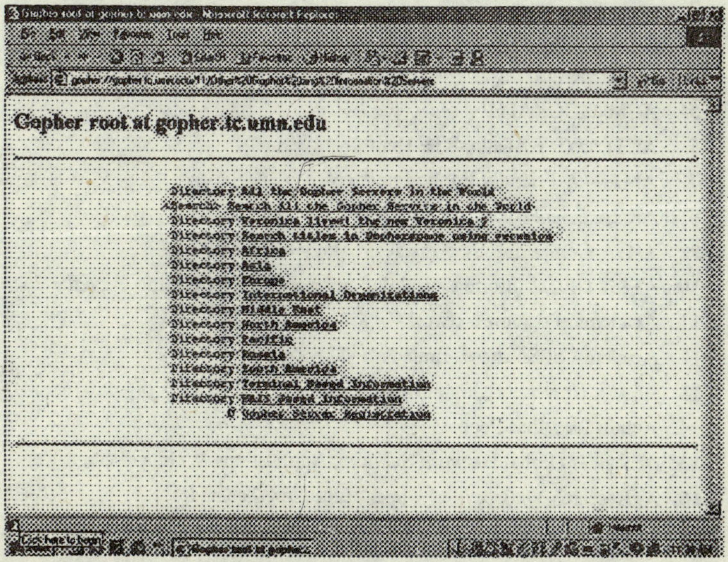

University of Minneso to Gopher

In Gopher screen forward arrow "—>" before option 1 is the pointer. To make a selection, we can use down ward and upward arrow and press Enter. We can also make a selection by typing the option number and pressing Enter. The bottom of the screen shows other available commands. The specific commands displayed will change depending on where we are in the Gopher. We can select the Other Gopher and Information Servers/option by using downward arrow or typing 9 and pressing enter. Now the Other Gopher and Information Servers menu will come. So we have opened a menu and moved further into Gopher Space. The screen now displays a list of Gophers or information servers that we can access, by geographic location or type of server. We can select and open the first menu item; All the Gopher Servers in the World. After some times a new menu will appear. It will be similar to the following.

Internet Gopher Information Client

All the Gopher Servers in the World

1. Search Gopher space using Veronica/
2. /
3. Academe this Week (Chronicle of Higher Education)
4. ACM SIGDA/
5. ACM SIGGRAPH/
6. ACTLab (UT Austin, RTF Dept)/
7. AMI — A Friendly Public Interface/
8. AREA Science Park, Trieste, (IT)/
9. ARPA Computing Systems Technology office (CSTO)/
10. AT&T Global Information Solutions (formerly NCR) Info Server/
11. Academic Position Network/
12. Academy of Sciences, Bratislava (Slovakia)/
13. Acadia University Gopher/
14. Action for Blind People/
15. Advant is Global Network Services, Applications & Outsourcing/
16. AgResearch Wallaceville, Upper Hutt, New Zealand/
17. Agricultural Genome Gopher/Press ? for Help. Q to quit P1/86

The list contains all officially announced Gopher hosts in

the world. In the UNIX platform as shown above we see the word "Page:" at the bottom right corner followed by two numbers separated by a slash. The number is the number of screens in the menu; the first is the presently viewing. The above screen will show that there are 97 screens of All the Gopher Servers in the World. Undoubtedly, by the time we use this book, the number will have increased. If there are 18 items on a screen, that's over 1,400 Gophers.

For viewing other pages in the menu, we can use the arrow keys to move "—>" down the screen off the end or press Space bar. A new menu, starting with the next number at the left, will appear. To see the previous page we can use upward arrow to move back up a screen. If we want to go back to the previous menu we can type u for up. To get help we can type? Then a help screen with a list of commands will come.

The menu is organized by geographical location. Hence, there will be no problem in locating the Gopher at a University. For this we can select the geographical option from the Other Gopher and Information Servers Menu. We will see a menu listing countries or territories that have Gopher servers officially announced. The country we search will be one of them, we can select the country/ option. The country menu will appear, listing all the states alphabetically.

We want a State, and for this we can advance pages on the menu screen by Pressing Space bar and can select the state. A menu of those regions Gophers will open. From there we can find and select the specific University Gopher. The main menu of the university Gopher, as was shown earlier will come up. So we have navigated through an ocean of information to reach a particular library, which was our aim.

5.2 Bookmarks

It is easy to get lost in Gopher Space. It will be very difficult to retrace the route that brought us to useful information or a library. There are methods to keep track of these places, so that finding them again is easy. Bookmarks are used for that. They are the method by which the client allows us to mark useful spots for later reference. We can add any type of item to our bookmark list, including directories or the results of searches. We can easily add whole categories of information. Our bookmark list will appear as a Gopher menu, and we can select items from it just as we would select items from any Gopher menu.

To make a bookmark, we have to make a selection on a menu, then type a for add bookmark. A dialogue box will appear with the title of the Gopher item for which we are making a bookmark in the text field. We can use Backspace and type to edit the title of this bookmark to whatever is meaningful for later selection. We can then press [Enter] when we have made changes.

If we want to see the bookmarks, we can type v for view bookmarks. We should see a new Gopher menu, with the first item being the bookmark selection we have just created. If we select it we will be transported directly to the desired selection. We could store all kinds of bookmarks of the Gopher items that we use most often. This bookmark menu is just like any other Gopher menu; we can select different items just as if they were in their original menus. By adding, using and deleting bookmarks we customize our information structure and presentation. To delete a bookmark we can position the pointer on the bookmark we wish to delete and press d for delete:

6. Campus Wide Information Systems

Gophers are used in many Campus Wide Information Systems (CWIS). Many colleges and universities have adopted Gopher as a tool to disseminate information about the institution. Several menu options exist for the purpose of publicizing campus information. If we are looking for information about a college or a university, we can go through the All the Gophers in the World option to see if there is a CWIS for that university or research institute. CWISs usually include a directory of faculty, staff, and students and a phone book, and lists of their e-mail addresses. If we are looking for e-mail address of someone at a particular institution, again we can locate the Gopher and see if such a directory service is provided by it.

7. Subject Trees

We can browse through Gopher Space or just explore it by selecting the items on the menu that look interesting and reach the special place of our interest. If we don't want to just browse, but go directly to out information we want we can do that also. Many Gophers are organized in such a way as to make it easier for us to go to resources on a specific topic. Although it is true that all Gopher menus are organized by subject, some sites have put on menus and organizations that make locating resources on the Internet easier. Such sites have a subject tree. We will find these on options using a variety of names like subject resources, study carrels, Internet resources by Subject etc. Arrangement of resources by some subject scheme is there purpose.

Many university libraries have already launched gopher servers. It we select Library resources option from the main menu of university Gopher we will get a menu as follows.

Internet Gopher Information Client

Library Resources

1. About This Library Gopher
2. Library Online Catalog <TEL>
3. Library Information/
4. Topical Resources/
5. The Internet Reviews Archive
6. Electronic Books and Journals/
7. Reference Desk/
8. Library of Congress Catalog and Gopher/
9. Other Library Gophers and Catalogs/
10. Search this Gopher Space README
11. Search this Gopher Space <?>
12. Local Menu of Veronica Servers/

University Library Gopher menus will list directories of different Internet services, analogous to what we would find in a library. Hatfield Library Online Catalogue connects us to the online catalogue of the library to search its book collection. The Reference

Desk contains resources that are often-used or general reference information, such as dictionaries, index and the like.

The menu lists different Internet services. The Library online catalogue option connects us to the online catalogue of the library to search the book collection. Reference desk contains reference information, dictionaries, indexes and other reference tools. The Other Library Gophers and Catalogues and Library of Congress Catalogue and Gopher give access to other library and information systems for perusing their online catalogues and accessing books and other resources not to be found at the institution itself. Topical Resources option is the subject tree of this Gopher, where resources are organized by subject. Here, we can search the Topical Resources menu for natural science. If we select Topical Resources; a menu similar to the one shown below will appear.

Internet Gopher Information Client

Topical Resources

1. About the Topical Resources Readme!
2. Applied Sciences/
3. Fine Arts/
4. History/
5. Internet Guides and Help/
6. Languages and Literature/
7. Law and Politics/
8. Management and Business Economics/
9. Mathematics/
10. Medicine/
11. Natural Sciences/
12. Philosophy and Religious Studies/
13. Social Sciences/
14. Use VERONICA to search All Gopher space/
15. Search this Gopher Space <?>
16. Search this Gopher Space Readme.

We can see in this an example of a subject scheme: the designers of this Gopher have attempted to classify information by subject. Initial options are very general, leading to more specific categories, such as Psychology, Sociology, and Education.

7.1 Well-constructed Subject Trees

Here is a list of Gophers with good subject trees that we can try. To connect directly the address is specified.

Gopher Jewels at University of Southern California	cwis.usc.edu.
North Carolina State University	dewey.lib.ncsu.edu 70
University of Durham (UK)	delphi.dur.ac.uk
University of California, Irvine	peg.cwis.uci.edu 7000
Kent State University	refmac.kent.edu
United States Department of Education	gopher.ed.gov

When we select Natural Sciences option the menu will again offer further options. The option leads us to other resources on the Internet that relate to natural Sciences. By selecting options at different levels according to our requirement we will reach our specified document. Then the document is displayed on the screen. Once we locate a document of interest, we can view it on the screen, mail the document to a valid e-mail address, or save the document as a file on our local computer. When we save the document as a file on our local computer, we have to know how to access it, whether it be to print, edit, or move download it to our personal computer.

8. Using Search Tools

In Gopher sites subject trees serve as "table of contents". We can browse specific subject areas to find general information on the topic. If we are looking in a book for specific information but don't know exactly where it might be located we will use an index. We can do the same thing in Gopher space also. University of Nevada, had released a program that would search through Gopher Space and index all the titles, which it saw. It is named Veronica, an acronym for Very Easy Rodent-Oriented Net-wide Index to Computerized Archives. This programme has two portions: One half combs the network, maintaining an index of all titles of all documents on most Gopher servers. The other half of Veronica takes requests on keywords and returns a menu of document titles or menu titles that contain those keywords within. For this we have to find a Veronica server. We can back up menus by pressing u, until we find and select Other Gopher and Information Servers, as shown below.

Other Gopher and Information Servers

1. All the Gopher Servers in the World/
2. Search titles in Gopher space using veronica/
3. Africa/
4. Asia/
5. Europe/
6. International Organizations/
7. Middle East/
8. North America/
9. Pacific/
10. South America/
11. Terminal Based Information/
12. WAIS Based Information/

In this menu the second option is Vernonica. We have to select Search titles in Gopher Space using veronica. A menu similar to the one shown below will appear.

Search titles in Gopher space using veronica

1.
2. FAQ: Frequently-Asked Questions about veronica (1993/08/23)
3. How to compose veronica queries (NEW June 24) READ ME!!
4. Search Gopher Directory Titles at PSINet <?>
5. Search Gopher Directory Titles at SUNET <?>
6. Search Gopher Directory Titles at University of Cologne <?>
7. Search gopher space at PSINet <?>
8. Search gopher space at SUNET <?>
9. Search gopher space at University of Cologne <?>

First choices are help items. "Search Gopher Space at..."

will accept keywords we enter to search all Gopher item titles that the Veronica server knows about. This includes directory, file, search tools, sound file, or telnet session. If our keywords match any item, it will get returned to us. "Search Gopher Directory Titles at..." will accept keywords to search only title of directories in Gopher Space. It ignores all other items in Gopher space.

Options within each category list different servers that are different computers that are running the Veronica index program. For a trial we can select search Gopher Space at ... option. A dialogue box will appear, prompting us for keywords. If we are looking for more information on bio diversity, we can type bio diversity and press Enter. There will be a brief pause. During this time, Gopher client will assure that it is "Searching..." with a rotating bar in the far right lower corner on the unix client. Then a new menu will appear.

The screen will be full of options. The entire menu itself will be inordinately long: the Unix client announces in the lower right corner how many screens of options there are. The information located will include; reviews of books or other documents, brief references or annotations to documents not present, files that were listed but were accessible only on-site and some actual documents that dealt directly with bio diversity.

A vast majority will be irrelevant to our needs. The reviews and annotations might give pointers to further resources, and a small percentage would contain useful information. We need to sort through all the selection, but there's too much. This is where the "Search Gopher Directories at... "Veronica comes in. If we try the same search with a directory-searching Veronica, we won't necessarily get fewer returns, but will gain another advantage. Our findings will consist of directories only, and a directory will contain a collection of relevant information, providing better organization to the otherwise unorganized list of sources. For this we have to go back up to the previous menu and search titles in Gopher space using veronica. We can select Search Gopher Directories at... option, and enter the word bio diversity. We will get a menu of returns, all directories. Depending on the site we select, we may or may not retrieve entries. If we can't connect or find any matches, we should try some other server.

Veronica searches only titles, and it has no way of knowing the content or subject of a particular file in its index. Indeed, we have no way of knowing what words are more commonly used to refer to what subjects. We have to be careful when using Veronica. We should have a list of synonyms and words related to the target in mind when we use it; have to skip irrelevant returns immediately and we should not spend time chasing something that doesn't appear to be there. Although the file names are often descriptive, we shouldn't expect too much of them. We can exit Gopher by typing q and confirming. Then we can disconnect from our Unix host also.

9. Boolean Logic

Veronica supports Boolean operators; AND, OR, and NOT. We can place these words between keywords to expand or limit the scope of our search. When we type in more than one word for Veronica to search for, if we don't put an AND, OR, or NOT between the words, Veronica assumes AND. We can put ORs and NOTs between words.

If we perform a Veronica directory title search for "forest rain" or "forest and rain", it finds all resources that have both "forest" and "rain" in the titles. We can limit the search to title entries with both keywords. If we perform a Veronica search for "forest or rain", Veronica finds those titles that contain either "forest" or "rain" or both. Now, if we perform a Veronica search for "forest not rain", it finds those title entries that contain only "forest", but never with the word "rain".

We can link together keywords with more than one Boolean operator, and we can use parentheses to separate distinct units: Searching for "(mountains and hills not peaks or valleys") would return titles with both "mountains" and "hills" only if those titles do not have either "peak" or "valley".

We can define very specific searches with Booleans and parentheses. But as far as Veronica is concerned, it usually takes more time to compose a complex search of several keywords than to type in two or three keywords. If we provide clear and concise keywords we can save time and also retrieve maximum relevant information. The following is a list of gopher sites that may be of interest to librarians.

Resource	**Address**
Scholarly Electronic Conferences	gopher.usask.ca 70
United Nations	nyworkl.undp.org
Electronic Newsstand	gopher.internet.com
Coalition for Networked Information	gopher.cni.org
World Health Organization	gopher.who.ch
The Internet Society	ietf.CNRI.Reston.Va.US
MARVEL Library ofCongress	Gopher marvel.loc.gov
National Science'Foundation Gopher	stis.nsf.gov

9.1 An Index Machine

For library and information workers Gopher is a very useful tool for finding information resources on the Internet. We can search and navigate a vast area without needing to know where exactly we are going. Any librarian can build a Gopher for other people to use. We cannot believe that the information in Gopher space is up-to-date or accurate. Gophers range from those that focus on particular subjects for example ecology or government information to large collections of various subject resources to informational Gophers for college and university campuses. Some Gophers are updated frequently with new information and others are never updated.

6

Usenet for Current News

If we are in the press clippings section of the library every day we have to scan dozens of newspapers covering regional, national and international news. We have to mark or cut the articles on the subjects mandatory to our institute. Usenet enables us to cover more news than all the newspapers that an institution acquire can cover. Also it helps us to limit our scanning to the news on subjects of our interest, so that our time is also saved.

We can read these newspapers and also write to their editors or reply to them. We can even start a new topic of discussion. Usenet is a collection of thousands of topically organized news groups in which we can both discover and express ourselves on topical information. Usenet is known also as news groups, net news, or plain news. But it is not the same as a newspaper. At a newspaper, an editor generally controls what reporters write. Our news group site can, for a fee, pick up news feed from a commercial service or newspaper. But users write the vast majority of news groups on the Internet discussing topics that interest them. This doesn't stop people from referring to the information that gets distributed via Usenet as "articles". Sometimes there is a moderator or someone who reviews the articles before they are distributed and keeps users in line. But most groups function as an open forum on a topic. The topics of discussion can range from space science to bio fertilisers or the Vedic rituals and their scientific basis. It is a good place for browsing for any who has general subject interest or who requires current news on a selected field.

Listservs also serve these purposes, and we can even read some listerv lists via Usenet. The difference is that with a listserv, all postings, or submissions, are sent directly to our mailbox and if we don't delete our mail, they accumulate. In news groups, we can wander into the news group discussion when we have time. Just as with listservs and mailing lists, we can subscribe and un subscribe to news groups. However, unlike with mailing lists, if we don't read the articles, they'll just disappear after some time.

As this is not E-mail, we have to learn how to use additional software. As with most Internet tools, there are several newsreader software packages from which we can choose. On Unix systems, the most common is r n, which is a very basic newsreader program. A newsreader program helps us to keep track of the news items we have already seen and displays new items that have arrived since our last session. The program even displays new news groups that have been formed and asks if we are interested in them. More sophisticate newsreader programs, such as trn and tin, can support threads. Threads allow us to read news items in order within a topic, based on what appears as the subject line of the article. While news groups organize articles loosely by subject threads further organize topics by collecting all articles in that group with the same specific subject field.

1. Functioning of Newsgroups

Any one can start a news group on any topic of interest. There are some news groups that are moderated. But in general news groups are forums where almost anything goes. In fact, there is no guarantee that articles of a news group will even stay on the supposed subject of the group. There is no person or organization to control or regulate news groups. At each site news is received through news feeds. A person known as the news administrator, or a group is responsible for what news groups a site receives and how the news feed is operated. A site may choose to restrict the flow of news to receive every conceivable news group. Administrator also decides how long to keep news items. This depends on things such as the amount of local space available to store the news group articles and the amount of traffic on the particular news group. A new article may be stored for just a few days or up to months. If we don't look a news group for sometime we will miss many topics of discussion, which are of interest to us.

Thousands of newsgroups are there, and new ones appear every day. They do not necessarily contain news as we usually think of it. Newsgroup articles are not the same kind of articles that we might find in newspaper. These are discussion groups, classified as announcements, and just plain old bulletin-board services. But the topics are divided by groups. We can select one of interest to us. Group names are often three or more words long, separated by periods. The first word provides a very general description of the group, and each following words becomes more and more specific. Unlike listservs, the name does not reflect from where the newsgroup originates. For example, the newsgroup named sci.bio.ecology stands for a science group, focusing on biology, with an emphasis for ecology. We could reasonably expect to find discussions of the effect of deforestation on climate in this newsgroup. Some schools have newsgroups for different topics on campus, and will be have their own local hierarchy.

2. Using News Groups

When we know how to use an email program, we know almost everything we need to know to use newsgroups. Reading a message, composing a new message, and replying are all similar in an email program and a newsreader. Where a newsreader differs, of course is that it retrieves messages from, and posts messages to, Internet newsgroups, sometimes known as discussion groups or Usenet. The newsgroups and their messages are stored on a family of servers called news servers or NNTP servers. Sending message to a new group is known as posting, because we are publishing the message in public forum, just as if we had posted a paper note on a bulletin board.

Our ISP or online service has a news server we are authorized to use for reading and contributing to newsgroups. Access to one news server is all we need. The messages sent to any news server on the Internet are automatically copied at regular intervals to all news servers. On any news server, we can open any news group and read any current message posted to that newsgroup, no matter which news server the message was originally posted to. That is why a newsgroup on an ISP's server in New York has messages on it from folks in India, Sree Lanka and Japan.

Before we can open newsgroups and display their messages, we must configure our newsreader to contact our ISP's news server, and we must download the complete list of newsgroups from the server. In general, all news servers carry the same newsgroups and current messages, but not exactly. First, a few ISPs or online services do not carry all newsgroups, omitting those they deem potentially offensive to their customers, such as sex oriented groups. A few ISPs carry only newsgroups specifically requested, by their subscribers, instead of all 40,000 and more existing news groups. Some ISPs' servers carry special newsgroups of local interest that is not copied to other news servers. The only other difference between them is that it takes a day or so for a message posted to one server to be copied to all the others. At any given time, a new message may be on some servers, but not yet on others.

Finally, no news server keeps messages forever. After a set number of days, a newsgroup message is automatically deleted from the server. Each server has its own schedule for removing these old expired messages. So a message that has been deleted from one server may remain on others.

3. Configuring Newsreader

As with other types of clients, many different newsreaders are available. In the popular Internet suites, the programs are called Collabra and Outlook Express. In Netscape Communicator, we can open Collabra from within the Navigator browser by choosing Communicator > Collabra Discussion Groups. In Internet Explorer it's the same program we use for email. We simply click our news server's name near the bottom of the folder list to shift Outlook Express into newsgroup mode. Choosing the server changes the toolbar buttons and menu choice, to those we need for newsgroups. We can open Outlook Express directly in newsgroup mode by choosing Go > News from within the browser.

If we don't already have a newsreader we may apply the file finding techniques discussed earlier to search for one or browse a directory of newsreaders on yahoo at www.yahoo.com/ Computers _and_Internet/Software/Internet/Usenet/

The newsreader programs have a configuration dialog box on which we enter the information required for communicating with our ISP's news server. That dialog box always requires the address of our ISP's news server. If our newsreader is not part of a suite and thus cannot copy configuration information from the email component, the configuration dialog box also requires our email address and full name.

The configuration dialog box can be found in Collabra and Outlook Express by the methods gven here. For Collabra, by choosing Edit > Preferences to open the Preferences dialog box. In the list of Categories, choose Mail & Groups. Complete the configuration settings in the Mail & Groups category's Groups Server subcategory. For Outlook Express, by completing the News dialog boxes of the Connection Wizard. If we choose our news server folder in Outlook Express without having configured first, the Connection Wizard opens automatically.

4. Downloading the Newsgroups List

After our newsreader knows how to contact the server, we must download the complete list of newsgroups, which usually takes just a few minutes. If we open some news readers including Collabra and Outlook Express without first having downloaded, a prompt appears, asking whether we want to download the list.

If our browser does not prompt us to find a button or menu item for downloading the line in Collabra, click the Subscribe button on the tool bar. On the dialog box that appears, click the Get Groups button. In Outlook Express, click the name of your news server, then choose Tools > Newsgroups. In the dialog box that appears, click Reset List.

The list of newsgroups changes periodically, adding new groups and removing others. Collabra, Outlook Express, and some other newsreaders detect automatically when the list changes and display a prompt, asking whether we want to update our list. If our newsreader does not detect changes in the list, it is smart to download the full list again once a month or so, to keep current.

5. Subscribing to Newsgroups

After the list has been downloaded to our computer, we can find and subscribe to any newsgroups we want. While exploring web pages devoted to topics that interest us, we will probably come across the names of related newsgroups. But newsgroups are easy to find, with or without a web page's help.

Unlike mailing lists, we are not required to subscribe to a newsgroup to use it. All subscribing really does is add the group to an easy access list in our newsreader, to make visiting it convenient. Most people have a small list of groups they visit often, so subscribing makes sense. In most newsreaders, however, we can pick a newsgroup out of the full list, or enter the group's name in a dialog box to open the list without subscribing.

Newsgroups are perhaps the one Internet activity where names are a reliable indicator of content. Newsgroups are organized under a system of names and categories. The leftmost portion of the name shows the top-level category in which the group exists; each portion further to the right more narrowly determines the subject of the group. For example, the top-level category recreational newsgroups, are those dedicated to a recreational rather than professional discussion of their topics. So the hypothetical newsgroup name rec.sports.basketball.womens indicates that the discussion focuses on a recreational interest in women's basketball. Thousands of recreational groups exist, many recreational sports groups, several rec. sports. basketball groups, and so on.

5.1 Some Newsgroups

alt — alternative newsgroups, in which the most free wheeling conversations are accepted.

biz — business newsgroups and ads.

comp — computer topics, including use, purchase, and programming

de — technical, recreational, and social discussions in German k12 for students in Kindergarten through 12th grade, or discussions about that group in net.

misc miscellaneous contains news groups that don't fit under other headings.

news news groups about news groups, news. new users. For questions might a good place.

rec recreational groups, including pastimes and sports groups

sci science topics ranging from the every simple to the very serious

5.2 Subscribing Groups in Collabra

To subscribe to and open groups in Collabra,the following steps can be used.

* First we have to open Collabra, and display the newsgroup list. It appears automatically right after we download the full list, but we can redisplay it at any time by clicking the Subscribe button.
* In the All Groups tab, display the group's name in the Discussion Group box. There are several ways to do this:
    - If we know the exact name of the group we want to subscribe to, type the name in the box.
    - Use the list to scroll to the group name, and then click it. In the list, the groups are presented alphabetically and also organized by category; display a category's subcategories or groups by clicking the plus sign (+) that precedes it.
    - Click the Search for a Group tab, and enter a search term to locate group names containing the term. Click the name of the group we want to subscribe to.
* When the name of the group we want to subscribe to appear in the Discussion Group box, click the Subscribe button to subscribe to it. We can then select another group to subscribe to or click OK to close the dialog box.
* In the Message Center, which appears whenever we open Collabra, our subscribed newsgroups are listed like subfolders

under our news server name. If we do not see newsgroups listed under our server, click the plus sign (+) to the left of the server name to display them.

* To open a newsgroup, double click its name in the list.

5.3 Subscribing Groups in Outlook Express

To subscribe to and open groups in Outlook Express, the following steps can be used.

* First we have to display the newsgroup list. It appears automatically right after we download the full list, but we can redisplay it at any time by choosing Tools > Newsgroups.
* The list dialog box has three tabs: All, Subscribed, and New. Choose the All tab to display the full list.
* To find a newsgroup, we can scroll down the alphabetical list. To locate a group about a particular topic, type a word related to that topic in the box at the top of the dialog box; Outlook Express narrows the list to groups whose names include that word.
* When we see in the list the name of a group we want to subscribe to, click it to select it.
* Click the Subscribe button to subscribe to the selected newsgroup. We can now select and subscribe to another group, or click OK to close the dialog box.
* The name of our news server appears near the bottom of Outlook Express's folder list, along the left side of the window. Click it, and our subscribed newsgroups appear in the main pane. To open a newsgroup and display its current message list, click it.

6. Reading Newsgroup Messages

After we open and display a newsgroup's message list, reading messages is just like reading email messages in an email client. In Collabra or Outlook Express, we can single click an item in the list to display it in the preview pane or double click it to display the message in its own window.

The message lists we see in an email program generally show messages that have been copied to our computer. But the messages in the list we see when we open a newsgroup is not on our computer but they are on the news server. All that has been copied to our computer are the message headers, to make up the list. When we display any particular message, that message is then copied to our computer. Because the messages are not copied until we request them, we must stay online while working with newsgroups. Some newsreaders support offline news reading. We can configure them to automatically download messages from newsgroups so that we can read them later, offline. In Outlook Express, we can download all messages from a newsgroup by choosing Tools > Download All.

Important tricky part of the ways to read news messages is organizing the list in a way that works for us. Most newsreaders permit us to arrange the messages in myriad ways alphabetically by subject, by author, by date, and so on. The options for sorting the message list in Collabra, Outlook Express, and most other newsreaders appear on the View menu. The most useful sorting, however, is by thread.

In a newsgroup, a thread is one particular conversation a message and all replies to that message and replies to those replies, and so on. In effect, threads group messages by subject. Two messages can have the same subject but not the same thread, if neither is a reply to the other or a reply to a reply to the other. If we sort messages by thread, and then by subject, we will get all threads on a given subject grouped together. When we sort messages by thread, we can follow the flow of the conversation by clicking our way, in order, through the messages to see how the discussion has progressed. In most newsreaders, when threads sort messages, the replies to a message do not appear automatically in the list; instead, a plus sign (+) appears next to the message's listing, to indicate that there are sub messages, replies to that message. To display the replies, we have to click the plus sign.

7. COMPOSING AND REPLYING TO MESSAGES

We compose and reply to messages in a newsreader exactly

as we do in an email program. The only differences are in the message header, because instead of addressing a message to a person, we are addressing it to a newsgroup. The only other important difference between sending email and newsgroup messages is the terminology we see applied on buttons and menu items. In email, we click Send to send a message. In a newsreader, it is either Send' or Post. In email, we click Reply to reply to a message; in a newsreader, it is either Reply or Respond.

The easiest way to deal with that difference is to start in the right place. For example, when we want to compose a new message not a reply and post it on a newsgroup, we have to begin by opening that newsgroup, and then click our newsreader's button for composing a new message. It is New Message in Collabra and Compose Message in Outlook Express. When the message window opens, we can see that it is preaddressed to the currently open newsgroup.

When replying, open the message to which we want to reply; then click the Reply or Respond button on the message window in which that message appears. In the message window that opens, the message is preaddressed to the appropriate newsgroup, the subject line is correctly phrased to add the reply to the same thread as the original message, and the original message is quoted in the message area. We can just add our comments, and edit the quote as necessary.

After completing a new message or reply, we have to send the message by clicking the button or menu, item labeled Send or Post. When we choose to reply, most newsreaders provide the option of replying to the newsgroup or sending an email reply directly to the author of the message we are replying to. The email option is handy when our reply is really intended only for the author, not the whole group. As in a mailing list we have to follow our netiquette when posting to a newsgroup, and resist using smileys and shorthand.

8. Finding and Reading Messages

Many web browsers can display newsgroup messages. Note, however, that we cannot use web browser to contribute to a newsgroup, so we will still need a newsreader to really get in newsgroups. A web browser's display capability comes in handy when a search tool turns up a newsgroup message. Newsgroup messages show up in a search tool's hot list as links. If our browser displays news group messages, clicking one of those links displays the message. In some suit the news reader and the browser are linked so that clicking a link that leads to a newsgroup automatically opens the newsreader to display the message.

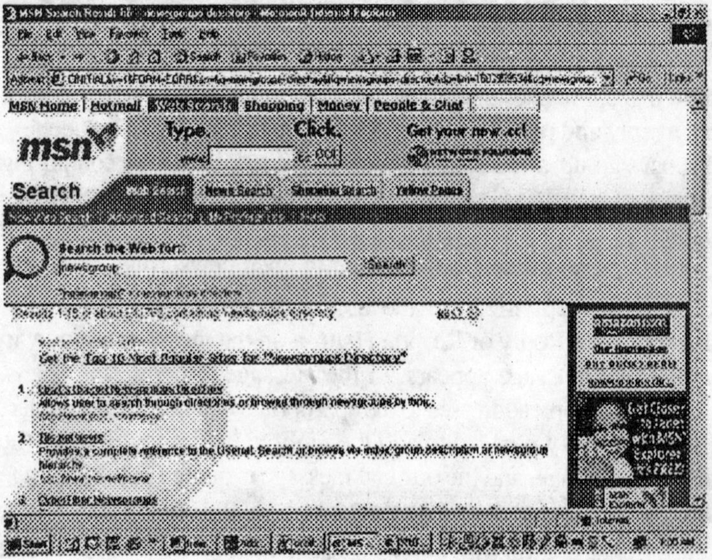

Figure 13.1

Alta Vista is among the search tools that can find newsgroup messages. We will use AltaVista to locate a message and then display that message in our browser. To find and display a newsgroup message in our browser we can follow the steps given below.

- First we have to open our web browser, and go to Alta Vista at altavista.digital.com.
- Drop down the small list labeled Search, right above the search term box
- From the list, choose Usenet to instruct AltaVista to find newsgroup messages instead of web pages.

* In the search term box, type a term for a topic we are interested in. Let us type Woodpecker.
* Click Search. The hit list appears, showing links to newsgroup messages. Observe that the link is also the subject of the message; to the right of the link appears the name of the group on which the message was posted.

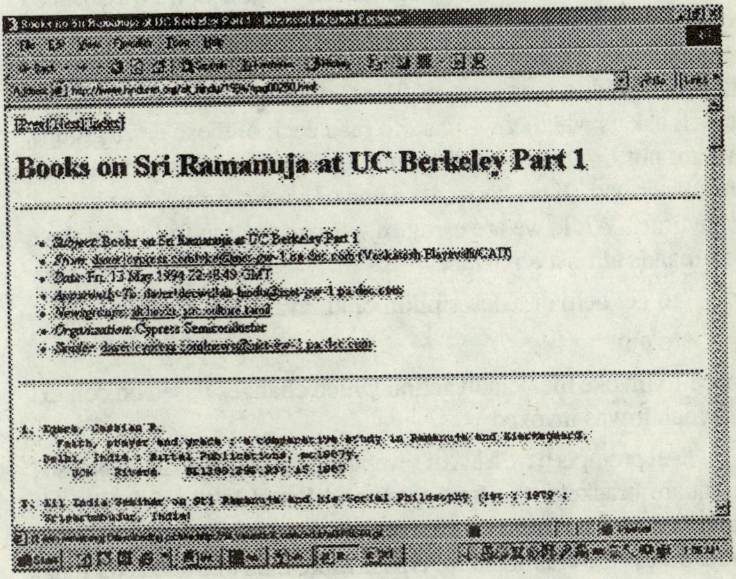

Figure 13.2

9. Using the News Groups Through Unix

To read news groups in Unix we must have a newsreader program installed in our computer. Newsreaders exist for nearly all-major computer platforms. One of the common newsreaders is rn for the UNIX platform, and we will use it for our examples. Regardless of the newsreader we are using, the concepts presented here will be the same everywhere. To read news groups, we need to know to start the newsreader program, to select and subscribe to a news group, to select an article view, to respond to an article, and to quit newsreader.

To start a newsreader program first we have to login to the unix computer. Then type rn and press Enter at the system prompt. What is displayed when we start rn the first time depends on how the program was installed by the news administrator. The program may have been installed so that the first time we run rn, we automatically get subscribed to certain news group and we can subscribe to additional ones later. News groups to which we have already subscribed appear in a special file, called .newsrc associated with our user account. Each time we run rn, it automatically displays the names of the news groups we are subscribed to in the order they are listed in our .newsrc. Then, starting at the top of the list, rn will ask us whether we want to read each of these news groups. We are not limited to reading only the news groups to which we are subscribed. If we know the name of a news group, we can read it anytime. While we are using rn, we can use the following three commands almost anywhere.

h to get help or a description of all available commands

q to quit

space to invoke the default action which changes based on context in which it was invoked

All prompts have a list of several plausible commands enclosed in square brackets; the first command listed is the default. All input is done in cbreak mode, which means we should not press Enter unless the command we type is more than one character long.

When we get a prompt asking if we want to subscribe to different news groups, we will have to answer yes or no to each one before we can go further. The easiest way to do this is to type N (upper case). This tells rn that we don't want to subscribe to any of the new newsgroups that it is offering. To quit we have to type q. Depending on where we are in rn, we may have to type q several times. Then we will return to the system prompt.

9.1 Finding Newsgroups

We can get a complete list of all news groups that we are not subscribed to by typing news groups at the system prompt and pressing Enter. The list can be very long. The rn program allows us to browse or search for news group names using the look command. Science groups have sci as the first word in their names.

Start rn.

A screen similar to the following will be displayed.

	% rn
Unread news in de.sci.misc	8 articles
Unread news in alt. Consciousness	5 articles
Unread news in sci.bio.ecology	21 articles
etc.	
8 unread articles in de.sci.misc read now?	[ynq]

Rn operates on three levels: the news group selection level, the article selection level, and the paging level. Each level has its own set of commands and its own help menu. We are at the news group selection level. Here we can do things like select a news group to read, subscribe and un subscribe to news groups, and search for news groups. Now we can search for news groups on our topic. We can type 1 sci and press [Enter]. Then a screen similar to the one below is displayed.

```
Completely unsubscribed newsgroups:
Alt.folklore.science
alt.sci.ohysics.acoustics
alt.sci.physics.new-theories
alt.sci.sociology
de.sci.medizin
rec.arts.sf.science
sci
sci.aeronautics
sci.anthropology
sci.aquaria
—More—
```

In the list of news groups sci is there in the name. But it is not necessarily as the first word. When we see "—More—" on the screen, we can press Space bar to display the next screen, or type q to stop displaying the list.

—> Press [Space bar]. In fact, keep on pressing [Space bar] until we can see the message [Type return to continue].

—> Press [Enter]

—> Keep on pressing [Space bar] until we return to the newsgroup selection level, which looked like this: = 8 unread articles in de.sci.misc—read now" [ynq]

From news group names, we can see that there is no way to tell the content of each news group. We can search again using a more specific word;

9.2. Subscribing to News Group

We can subscribe to a news group named <news group name> by typing g (for go to) <news group name> at the news group selection level. To subscribe to news group in aeronautic.

At the news group selection level, type sci. aeronautic and press [Enter].

The message similar to *Newsgroup sci. aeronatics not in newsic- subscribe? [ynYN is displayed.*]

If we have already subscribed to the news group, this would take us to that news group and allow us to read the articles. If we have not subscribed, this will allow us to get subscribed. If rn asks where to put the news group in our .newsrc, we can press space bar to put it at the bottom of the list. If we have not subscribed to this group we have to Type y. Rn will respond with the question, "Put news group where? Here we can Press [Space bar]. This will take us to the news group selection level, and we can read articles in that news group.

9.3. Reading the News

Rn operates on three levels: the news group selection level, the article selection level, and the paging level. Each level has its own set of commands and its own help menu. If we don't want to read those articles that already have been posted and we want to read only new postings as they arrive, we can press c (lowercase) to "catch up" on all articles. This marks all earlier as read.

To help the new readers, most news groups have a list of Frequently Asked Questions. FAQs, as they are called, are usually posted to the group once in every three to four weeks so that new users can find them.

9.4 Newsgroup Selection Level

The prompt looks like this at the news group selection level.

******** 17 unread articles in de.sci.misc—read now? [ynq]

The options displayed here are:

y yes, read te articles in this news group (default)

n no, go to the next news group listed in .newsrc

q quit, leave rn

The first page of the first article will be displayed on the screen if we select y. Oiher options not listed include:

c Catch-up - mark all unread articles in this news group as read

p go to the previous news group

l go to the first news group

^ go to the first newsgroup with unread news

By typing y, we can advance to the article selection level.

9.5 Article Selection Level

Unread articles are displayed At the article selection level, in the order in which articles have arrived at our site by rn. At this level, we are not asked whether we want to read an article before the article is displayed. But we are shown the first page of the article and asked if we want to continue. The normal article selection prompt comes at the end of the article. The prompt at the end of an article will be: End of articl 126 (of 170)—what next? [npq]. The options displayed are:

n go to next unread article

p go to previous unread article

q quit this newsgroup;

Other options at this level include:

= for a list of article numbers and corresponding subject lines

<an article#> display that article

m mark the current article as still unread

w<filename> save to <filename> in the News directory within our home directory.

9.6 Paging Level

As we read through a long article one that is more than one screen, we get a prompt that looks like: —More— (22%). 22 indicate what percentage of the article we have read so far. Our options are as follows:

[Spacebar] display the next page

q quit reading the article and return to the article selection level

9.7 Responding to an Article

After reading an article if we really want to respond, we can send a private e-mail message to that person. We can do this without leaving rn by typing r (lowercase) just after we read the article. This will initiate e-mail to that person. If we type R (uppercase) instead, it will not just prepare the e-mail, but will also quote the article text so that you have a reference. If we do quote the article text, we have to trim it down so that only the relevant parts are included. When we finish composing the message, we are asked if we want to "send, abort, edit, or list". We have to type s and press Enter to send.

9.8 Unsubscribing to Newsgroup

Un subscribing means that it is not displayed to us when we enter rn. To re-subscribe, all we need to do is to type g and the name of the news group. We have to type u to unsubscribe to a news group when we are asked if we want to read the articles in a news group. In fact, if we want to un subscribe to all news groups to which we are currently subscribing, we have to type a capital U. Then we have to quit the newsreader program, and disconnect from the UNIX system.

9.9. Tool for Staying Informed

If the web is like a library, newsgroups are like our coffee shops and celebration parties. The information we get from the former is generally more reliable and complete. The information we get from the latter; is usually more personal, immediate, and fun. Perhaps the best way to stay informed about any topic is to make sure we frequent both related web pages and related newsgroups, and use what we learn in both.

7

Telnet and Electronic Libraries

At the initial years of the development of Internet its most powerful tools libraries frequently used were Telnet and FTP. Now along with other old tools Telnet is also called hacker's tool because it was also primitive instrument of the earliest Internet users. Still this tool is important because many things a library may require from other libraries are accessible only through Telnet. So, for the librarians this tool is still important.

In Gopher and World Wide Web we have to navigate within their menus to go to places we want to get connected to. Some times we need to connect directly to remote resources without the aid of a menu to explore areas we find interesting. This is done using Telnet program. Telnet works like a telephone allowing us to "call" another machine, and interact with whatever or whomever is on the other end. This opens up a whole world of opportunity to run programs and search databases that are on computers all over the world. There is a great variety of resources available to us via Telnet, ranging from simply accessing and using the computing power of another machine, to the online catalogues of hundreds of libraries, to the information services for which we must pay.

Once we log to another machine, it will be more than likely that displays and commands are different from what we are used to on our machine. By paying attention to what is happening on the screen and following clues for help and instructions, we can successfully use remote computers. Even if the remote system doesn't provide much help, Telnet has the ability to "hang up" on that remote computer. But we cannot just telnet to any computer system we see on the Internet. Some require that we have a valid user account on their system. Some will let us connect for a specific purpose only.

1. Functioning of Telnet

In the way in which we address an e-mail message to a user at a particular host computer, a Telnet session connects us with a specific host computer with a unique name, called a domain name. The address scheme for sending e-mail to a specific computer is similar to the naming scheme for computers to which we could telnet. There are lakhs and lakhs of sites that can be accessed via Telnet. There are rich and detailed databases to search. There are also many types of publications like reference books, journals, films, sound recordings and the like available online. Which are fascinating and incredibly addictive.

A domain name is several short words separated by periods: the last word tells what kind of organization or geographical location runs the computer for example, .com,.edu, .gov, .org, or .au. The second-to-last generally abbreviates the name of the organization or company; additional worlds give names of sub domains, if they exist; and finally the left-most word is the name of the computer. In addition to this name, each Internet host has a unique number, called the IP address four numbers, each less than 256, separated by dots, which is synonymous with the domain name. Since domain names are easier to remember than the IP address, people generally refer to a computer by its domain name. We can use any of them in telnetting.

2. Using Remote Computers

Using any web server is like using any other FTP servers, news servers, and Gopher servers. Telnet, however, is the exception to the rule. Using Telnet, we access another computer out there on the Internet known to Telnet as a remote computer and use that computer as if we were there, as if we were using a terminal that was connected directly to that computer. For example, many libraries have a computerized card catalog system those visitors to the library use from terminals or computers located at the library. If the library has configured the card catalog to support access via Telnet, we can use our Internet connection to enable the use of the card catalog system from thousands of miles away. What we will see on our screen is exactly what we will see if we went to the library in person and used one of the card catalog terminals.

The trick with Telnet is that all the computers we access work differently. Each has its own procedures for logging on, navigating menus, and more. In fact, accessing a remote computer through Telnet is the easy part. Getting logged on to that computer, and then figuring out how to operate it, is the challenge with Telnet.

Actually, the term log on is not so new. We have been logging on to the Internet entering our username and password. We must also log on or log in, or sign in, or sign on; it is all the same thing to most remote computers we access through Telnet, either using a private name and password we have been given for using that system or by entering a guest or visitor username and password. When we start a Telnet session from a web link, instructions near the link usually describe what we need to know to log on. Some helpful Telnet systems actually tell us the guest username and password when we arrive.

2.1 Getting a Telnet Client

The web browser doubles as a Telnet client. We have no other choice. We can only use Telnet through a real Telnet client. Windows 98 has a built in Telnet client. Even better, most Windows based web browsers know how to open the Telnet client automatically, as a helper program when we click a link leading to a Telnet server. Although we must operate the remote computer through our Telnet client, we can navigate to the server and begin our Telnet session from within our browser.

2.2 Visiting the Library of Congress

The U.S. Library of Congress has a wonderful web site.. But the whole card catalog Of Congress Information System has not yet been added to the web. It remains accessible only through Telnet. We can try to access it. The following steps will be helpful for doing that.

* First we have to go to the Library of Congress web page at www.loc.gov
* Then we have to click the link to Search The Catalogs.
* On the page that appears, scroll down to the Command Search portion.
* Click the link TELNET to LOCIS. Telnet client opens, and the main menu of the LOCIS catalog opens. Observe that a number precedes each menu item. To choose an item, we can type its number and then press Enter. We have to note that Telnet systems do not support our mouse, trackball, or other pointing device. We do everything in a Telnet session with our keyboard.
* Now we have to press the menu number ment for opening the catalogue, and then Enter, to open the Catalog menu.
* On the Catalog menu, type 12 (for Return to LOCIS MENU Screen), and press Enter. We return to the main menu.
* Type 12 and press Enter again to log off LOCIS. Then close our Telnet client.

This shows that Telnet session is very easy. We have to simply choose our menu items, follow any instructions we see onscreen, and we will never go wrong.

3. Entering and Quitting through Unix

Basic things to be known to begin are; how to start the Telnet program; how to enter the address of the place to which we want to go and how to close the program. The concept is the same, as we have seen in Windows environment.

Here let us consider a sample situation. One of our library members has read all the books by Herman Hesse available in our collection. He has enjoyed that and wants to know what other books written by Hesse had already been translated into English and what books are available on life of Hesse. If we had to track literature by and on Hesse surely Telnet can help us. Many library catalogues and large bibliographic databases are available via Telnet for use. First we have to connect to a UNIX host. From the system prompt we have to type telnet and press Enter. Then we will see a telnet>prompt. To start a Telnet session, we have to type open <host.address> and press Enter, where <host.address> is the domain name or the IP address of the system to which we want to connect. The domain name for this example is dra.com (192.65.218.43). Type open dra.com and press Enter. A screen similar to the following is displayed.

Data Research Associates, Inc. Guest Access

Select a command option from the following list. Enter the code between the <> characters and press the (RETURN) key after entering the command.

<A>uthor	to find authors, composers, performers, illustrators, conferences, and corporate authors.
<T>itle	to find a work by title, or generic title.
<E>xit	to log off
<N>ext page	to do other types of searches

Enter our command or search below and press the (return) key.>>

At times we are not able to telnet to a site that we know was there yesterday. There are a number of causes for this, and usually we can't do anything about it. Here are some common messages and possible causes. Unknown host, spelling not correct, name changed, connection refused machine busy, rebooting unreachable. Site network trouble, power failure etc can be some of the reasons listed. . If we see a "connection refused" or "all port in use" message, it could mean that the remote machine is too busy to answer our call right now and that we should try again later. Sometimes names and addresses change without warning, or a machine may be down, and we can connect. This is a fact of life on the Internet, as it is with the telephone, and we have to look elsewhere for the information we need.

Most problems are temporary. If they persist for more than a day, we have to contact our local computer support staff to see if they can determine the cause.

As seen above the system gives us a menu option to disconnect (<ex>it). However, there are many systems for which disconnect method are not the same. If we are at a spot where we can type a command, one of the following commands logoff, logout, quit, bye, exit may disconnect our system. If none of this works we have to try pressing [Ctrl] (hold down the Control key and press the right bracket key).

After at disconnecting from the remote computer, we will either return to the local system prompt or the Telnet prompt. If we see a telnet> prompt, we have to quit and press Enter to exit the session. Type ex and press Enter. Then the system prompt is displayed. If the telnet> prompt appears we have to type quit and press Enter. Thus we have completed a simple Telnet session.

4. Searching a Book

We can now try searching that system. When connecting to remote databases, it is very important that we at least read the screens presented to us to be able to use the database. We may also find it useful to read the help information that is available. Some systems are easier to use than others, but it is always wise to read any information. That comes on the screen about the system when using it. We can do a sample search connecting to the dra.com database again. We are looking for more books by Herman Hesse. Type A for an author search and press Enter. The author search screen, is displayed.

4.1 Author Search

Enter the author, composer, performer, corporate author, or conference we want to find and then press the (return) key.

Hints:

Enter the author's last name first, followed by their first name.

Only enter as many characters of the name as we know. Proper capitalization and punctuation are not required.

For example:

Twain, Mark

Digital Equipment Corporation

Computers in Libraries Conference

For a shortcut, we can also enter the search in one command.

A=King Stephen

Type <??> and press (RETURN) for more help.

Enter Author:

We are now presented with a screen and several examples. Here is why it is important to read the screen when connecting to remote systems. Although we may have never used the system before, we can often determine what we need to do next by looking at the screen. In this case, to find books by Herman Hesse type "Hesse, Herman" at the enter author prompt.

If we make a mistake while typing, we can use backspace and correct our entry. If we end up somewhere we didn't intend, typing st should return us to the main menu, and pressing [Ctrl] will usually end the session.

We can type Hesse, Herman and press [Enter]. The screen, similar to the one shown below will be displayed.

Your search: A=Hesse, Herman

LINE #	# of Titles	Authors
1	12	Hesse, Herman
2	1	Hesse, Herman

Enter: Line # (1,2,3, etc.) to see works associated with our search.

<N>ext screen	<B>ackup
<P>revious screen	<ST>art over
<LIM>it search	<EX>it

\>> Enter <?> for HELP.

This screen displays two sets of books. The first set contains 12 titles. To display the set, enter the line number. Right now, if we want to see the first set we have to type 1 and press Enter. A list similar to the following is displayed.

Your search: A=Hesse, Herman

Line #	Author	Title	Date
1	Hesse Herman	Glassbead Game	1989

```
2    Hesse Herman    Klingsters Last Summer    1920
3    Hesse Herman    Knulp                     1908
4    Hesse Herman    My belief                 1904
5    Hesse Herman    Peter Camenzind           1954
6    Hesse Herman    Prodigy                   1906
7    Hesse Herman    Rossalde                  1914
8    Hesse Herman    Siddhartha                1922
9    Hesse Herman    Steppenwolf               1927
10   Hesse Herman    Stories of Five Decades   1954
11   Hesse Herman    Strange News from         1919
12   Hesse Herman
Enter: Line #  (1,2,3, etc.) to see more information.
<N>ext screen                    <B>ackup
<P>revious screen                <ST>art over
(Up arrow) previous commands     <EX>it          >>
Enter <?> for HELP.
```

We can see that Hesse has written several books. We could then decide if we want to try to obtain one of these books through our local library or bookseller. Now we have to exit and there is a menu option on the screen to disconnect. To exit we have to type ex and press Enter. Then we return to the local system prompt or the Telnet prompt, where we have to type quit.

5. User Names

Remote machines can sometimes give us very clear instructions. They can also be complex and confusing. We have to use help or command to navigate the system to which we have connected. Most Telnet sites are large warehouses of information. When we connect to a remote machine, we will often be greeted by a prompt - login: Sometimes we will know the correct way to login, and sometimes we won't. Sometimes we can guess the login name to use because it will closely match the service we are trying to reach. For example, if we are trying to reach a library catalogue, we can try the login name "library". If we are trying to tenet to a Gopher, we can try logging in as "gopher". Often we can find a login name in the same place in which we found the address. Some systems also require a password so that outside users cannot access them without an account. If we know the correct login name and are prompted for a password we have to make sure that we have entered the name correctly. On many systems, the words "LIBRARY" and "library" are considered different - that is, it matters whether we type text in upper or lower case characters.

5.1 Terminal Emulation

In Gopher; Telnet sessions were often listed. These were the menu items with <tel> or with an icon of a terminal. When choosing these items from a Gopher a dialogue box will pop up to give login information such as "Use the account brouser" to login in". Other question often asked upon logging in is to identify terminal type. Just as with a telephone, we can end up calling someone who does not speak our language. We may notice this as garbled characters appear on our screen. Fortunately, many systems will offer us a choice of terminal types. We may be presented with a list such as the following.

What kind of Terminal are you using?

V> VT 100

A> CCII PC

C> TANDEM

D> TV1910

We may usually be using vt100. If upon choosing that option, if strange things happen, our terminal emulation may be different. We may need to specify the port number also. A port number is similar to a phone extension number. If we can see any reference to a port number we probably don't need one. However, if we do see an additional number, or port number, we can simply add it to our Telnet command.

6. Telnet Addresses

We should know how to find out the Telnet addresses. On the Internet there are groups, which have taken charge of compiling vast database of Telnet addresses including the addresses of most of the Internet-accessible library catalogues. The program, written by Peter Scott of the University of Saskatchewan, is called Hytelnet. By telnet ting to Hytelnet servers we can access it. Two such server addresses: access. usask.ca(128.233.3.1) and login: hytelnet which is the home site of Hytelnet and info.ccit.arizona.edu (129.196.76.201) and login: hytelnet.

The best way to use Hytelnet is to have it installed on our local system. We can try typing "hytelnet" at our system prompt to see if it is available to us. If not, we may want to ask that it be installed on our system. Hytelnet is a very good place to start to get an idea of what types of information and resources are available. The database is frequently updated as new services become available. As with any database, we have to read the help screens to get an idea of the search capabilities offered by it.

7. Connecting to Hytelenet

To connect to Hytelnet database we have to Enter telnet access.usask.ca. If we encounter any problem at this site, we can try the other server, info.ccit.arizona.edu. Then we will see a display similar to the following:

```
Trying 12.233.3.1 ...
Connected to access.usask.ca.
Escape character is '^]'.
ULTRIX V4.3 (Rev.44) (access.usask.ca)
login:
```

We can login as the user hytelnet. After a while, a screen similar to the following is displayed.

```
Welcome to HYTELNET   Last Update: December 10, 1998
What is HYTELNET?              <WHATIS>
Library catalogs               <SITES1>
Other resources                <SUTES2>
Help files for catalogues      <OP000>
Catalogue interfaces           <SYS000>
Internet Glossary              <GLOSSARY>
```

Telnet tips <TELNET>

Telnet/TN3270 escape keys <ESCAPE.KEY>

Key-stroke commands <HELP>

Up/Down arrows MOVE Left/Right arrows SELECT? for HELP anytime

m returns here i searches the index q quits

Hytelnet 6.6 was written by Peter Scott E-mail address: aa375@freenet.carleton.ca

Unix and UMS software by Earl Fogel

We can read the screen to see what types of information are available. We can search the index by typing "i". Since we have already looked at a library catalogue, let's select Other resources <sites2>. We have to press upward arrow or downward arrow until <sites2> is highlighted, then press Enter. A screen with the following information will come.

7.1 Other Telnet-accessible resources:

<ARC000>	Archie: Archive Server Listing Service
<CWI000>	Campus-wide Information systems
<FUL000>	Databases and bibliographies
<DIS000>	Distributed File Servers (Gopher/WAIS/WWW)
<BOOKS>	Electronic books
<FEE000>	Fee-Based Services
<FRE000>	Free-Nets & Community Computing Systems
<BBS000>	General Bulletin Boards
<HYT000>	Hytelenet On-line versions
<MAS000>	NASA databases
<NET000>	Network Information Services
<DIR000>	Who is/White Pages/Directory Services
<OTH000>	Miscellaneous resources

We can see many types of resources available via Telnet. If we are interested in literature, we can choose the <fulooo> Databases and bibliographies. Again, press upward or downward arrow until <sites2> is highlighted, then press Enter. A screen with to the following information will come.

7.2. Databases and Bibliographies

<FUL041	ABSEES: American Bibliography of Slavic & East European Studies
<FUL031	Bank of England Quarterly Bulletin Time Series Data
<FUL001	BLAISE-LINE (British Library's On-Line Service)
<FUL002	British Library Document Supply Centre
<FUL055	CARL System Database Gateway
<FUL046	Coalition for Networked Information Server
<FUL004	CONSER database (journal/serial/periodical indexes)
<FUL005	Constitutional Documents (USA)
<FUL007	Dartmouth Dante Project
<FUL024	Earth Images Catalogue LEDA
<EUL025	Earth observation satellite data inventory service
<FUL033	Einstein On-Line Sergvice
<FUL049	Electronic Periodic Table of the Elements
<FUL008	Environmental Education Database
<FUL009	ERIC (Educational Resources Information Centre Documents)
<FUL048	Eureka Example screens (Research libraries Group)
<FUL044	EX-USSR data files press space for more

This menu contains many diverse items, covering many diverse topics. To browse the menu. Spacebar will take us down a page, and [-] will take us backup. We can get help with any of the Hytelnet functions by pressing [?].

8. Retrieving Full Texts

In our quest for literature on Herman Hesse, let's take a look at <FUL055> CARL System Database gateway by selecting it. We will come upon a menu similar to the one shown below.

CARL System Database Gateway

Telent Database Carl.Org or 192.54.81.76

Select 5 for vt100

Welcome to the Carl System Database

CARL Systems, Inc. is proud to present our Shopping List of Databases.

Many of the databases included require a password. If you would like to look at one of these restricted databases, please contact CARL Systems, Inc. at database@carl.org or 303/758-3030. If you have already been given a password to a database, please enter your password when prompted. There are a number of library catalogues and free databases available, please feel free to look around.

1. UnCover (Article Access and Delivery)
2. Information Access Company Databases (including Business Index, Magazine Index and others)
3. Grolier's Academic American Encyclopedia
4. Facts on File
5. H.W. Wilson Databases (including Library Literature) Press space for more

According to the screen as displayed above we are to telnet to data base.carl.org or 192.43.81.76 to connect to the CARL System Database Gateway. It also tells us to select 5 for VT100 when asked about the emulation. We can press Enter to start the Telnet connection. The prompt TELNET Database.carl.orga Proceed (y/n)? is displayed at the bottom of the screen. We can Type y and press [Enter]. Then we will get a screen similar to the following.

Welcome to the Carl corporation Network and Uncover

CARL Corporation presents here the Shopping List of Databases. Many of the databases included require a password. If you would like to look at one of these restricted databases, please contact CARL Corporation at database@carl.org or 303/758-3030. If you have already been given a password to a database, please enter your password when prompted. There are a number of library catalogs and free databases available, please feel free to look around.

UnCover (Article Access and Delivery)

Information Access Company Databases (including Business Index, Magazine Index and others)

1. Grolier's Academic American Encyclopedia
2. Facts on File
3. H.W. Wilson Databases (including Library Literature)
4. UMI Databases (including ABI/Inform)
5. Other Information and Article Databases (including Journal Graphics, Choice and others)
6. CARL Systems Library Catalogs

You may enter //exit at any time to leave this system.

Enter the number of your choice, and press the <RETURN> key >>

This is the opening screen for the system at CARL (The Colorado Alliance Research Libraries). The message on screen describes restrictions and cost involved in using this service. It also tells that if we want to leave at any time we can type//EXIT. We can use the UnCover option, which is an open free access journal article index with free, full text delivery options. For this we have to Type 1 and press Enter. For the next three screens, we are informed of the access options for UnCover we just want to browse through for now, so we can ignore these options. We have to press [Enter] several times, until we reach the UnCover welcome message similar to the one shown below.

Welcome to UnCover The Article Access and Delivery Solution

UnCover contains records describing journals and their contents. Over 4000 current citations are added daily. UnCover offers you the opportunity to order fax copies of articles from this database. Type? For details.

For information about a new service, UnCover Complete, type ?C

Enter N	for Name search
W	for Word search
B	to Browse by journal title
QS	for Quick Search information
S	to Stop or Switch to another database

Type the letter for the kind of search you want, and end each line you type by pressing <return>

Selected database: UnCover

Enter Command (? For help) >>

We can do word search here as we wish to get articles and books on Hesse. If we use author search we will retrieve books by Herman Hesse. To search by word we have to press W and Enter. Then a screen similar to the following is displayed.

Selected Database: UnCover

Remember — Words can be words from the title, or from subtitles, or abstracts that appear on the Table of Contents page for each journal.

A WORD search will also often return NAMES of people who are discussed or referred to in the articles.

You may also supply the name of a journal in your search in order to limit your results to that publication. . for example

German Literature

Philosopher

Unesco Courier

Enter word or words (no more than one line, please)

separated by spaces and press <RETURN>.

Again, the instructions on the screen tell us how to enter words for search. We can type Herman Hesse and press Enter. A screen similar to the following is displayed. We can see the number of citations that we have retrieved.

Working.920

HESSE Items UnCover

Hess + HERMAN 17 Items

Herman + Hesse 17 Items UnCover

You may make your search more specific (and reduce the size of the list) by adding another word to your search. The result will be items in your current list that also contain the new word.

To ADD a new word, enter it,

<D>ISPLAY to see the current list, or

<Q>UIT for a new search:

New Words:

We can Press Enter to continue. We are asked if we wish to limit our search or add more terms. If we do not wish to limit our search, we can choose D for display to see the titles. We can type D and press [Enter]. A list of articles, of and on Herman as follows Hesse will be displayed. We can now see a list of titles of journal articles on and by Hesse and the names and volume and issue numbers of the journals in which the articles appeared. We can see the rest of the list pressing the Enter key.

9. Charges for Services

The articles are listed in reverse chronological order. We may to take note of when articles began appearing in this database.

Online information often does not cover older material. We may want to check print index of older resources. Selecting a line number will display the full citation of an article. We can select an article that looks interesting to us, say, 1. We can type 1 and press [Enter]. Detailed information as shown, below is displayed.

Titles(s): Nobel Lecture 1946 Herman Hesse.

Summary:

In: World literature today. Wint 1946 v 28 n 1, Page : 20

SICI Code: 0196-3570(199421)68:1L.5:NL1m;1-

This article may be available in your library, at no cost to you. To have it faxed from UnCover, the following charges apply:

Service Charge: 9.50

Fax Surcharge: .00

Copyright Fee: 3.00

more follows — press <RETURN> (Q to quit)

This gives us the information we need to get the article from our library, or if we want to purchase the article from CARL, that information is also given. These articles can help us in writing our paper on Herman Hesse. This article will give us a bibliography also, which may be useful. Now we can leave this database. As per the instructions given earlier we have to type //Exit to leave the system or use Telnet escape key. We can exit the database and disconnect from our local system.

9.1. Doors to Houses of Knowledge

While on windows based browsers many Gopher links also lead to Telnet sessions. An icon that looks like a computer terminal precedes a link that leads to Telnet. If we are browsing Gopher from within our web browser, clicking the link generally opens the Telnet client our web browser is configured to open. FTP, Gopher, and Telnet are a little difficult than web browsing, but we will only use them now and then, when no web page offers what we need. It is nice to have the keys to different doors, so that we will always have a place to go.

8

FTP for Document Retrieval

Internet is like a vast ocean of people and information. Telnet can take us to other places. There are various tools to help us find information. There are tools to help us navigate around. File Transfer Protocol (FTP) provides facilities for files to be transferred between computers on the Internet. It provides a way to connect to another computer on the Internet, and put files on the other computer, or get files from the other computer back to our own system. We can transfer any type of file using FTP. We can find computer programs like DOS, Unix etc. electronic texts, archives of mailing lists, graphic images and audio and video and transfer them. Number of files available from FTP is so large that we will spend hours and hours simply sitting through archive after archive. But to use FTP to retrieve a file, the name and the location of the file we want should be known to us.

FTP was one of the important tools of the Internet earlier. Most of the things used to be accessible only through the tools of FTP are now available on web pages. But when we consider library applications of Internet it is not true. Millions of files related to library contents have yet to be brought into the web. So these tools remain an important part of Internet toolset in libraries even now. Librarians have to be familiar with this tool also.

1. Functioning of FTP

FTP was used largely to obtain software from the Internet

as well as transmitting huge quantum of digitised data, mainly books and other library documents. . The first thing to be aware of is that we will probably need to use the command binary at the ftp> prompt. If we don't issue this command when downloading something that is not simply text such as a software program, it is possible that important information might be accidentally lost. Once we have typed binary, we can then safely get files.

When we have retrieved software, we still find that it is usually compressed. Software is often compressed to save space during transfer, but we must then uncompress it to make it useful. To uncompress it, we need compression software. Listed below are the file extensions that indicate what kind of compression has been used on a file, as well as what software package we can use to un compress that file. We have to be aware that more than one kind of compression can be used on a file, which can result in several extensions, such as .zip, .zoo, .arf. These software packages also can be retrieved through FTP when required.

Extension	*Package*
z	unpack, on most Unix machine
Z	un compress, on most Unix machine
.zip	PkUnzip, for IBM PCs
.zoo	Zoo, for IMB PCs
.arj	Arj, for IBM PCs

If we are FTPing software for a Macintosh or an IBM PC from a Unix host, we will need to get the software from the Unix machine to our machine. If we are using a modem to connect, we will need to use software such as Kermit or Send Zmodem to transfer the files. If our own machine is directly on the network, we may be able to use FTP to transfer it to our machine.

FTP uses the client/server model as like most of the other Internet tools. Through the use of client software, we can connect to remote FTP servers and request files be sent from them. FTP will take care of moving the file across the network and dealing with different kinds of computers and operating systems on the Internet. So, even though one machine might be using Unix and another might be using MS-DOS, it makes no difference while using FTP to transfer the document. The retrieved document is placed on the machine that has the client software running. That means when we use a DOS computer to access a Unix computer that runs FTP, the retrieved file is placed on the Unix computer, not on our DOS computer.

FTP often presents a less friendly interface, especially the client software made for Unix. We must have some understanding of the directory structure of Unix, or, how the files are stored on a Unix computer, in order to make effective use of it. However, some of the newer clients for the Microsoft Windows and even for Unix are changing this traditional drawback by adopting the flavour and feel of user friendliness these platforms are incorporating.

2. Downloading Files with FTP

We now know how files can be downloaded from the web. Some files that we may want are stored not on web servers, but on FTP servers. FTP stands for File Transfer Protocol, but we really do not need to know that. Everybody uses just the abbreviation. Still, the name says it all: FTP is for transferring files between computers. The files stored on FTP servers are waiting to be downloaded by an FTP client, a program on our computer that communicates with FTP servers through the Internet.

Almost all the FTP servers are password protected to limit access to only authorized users. If an FTP server is password protected, we are prompted to enter a username and password when we access the server. If we do not have the correct username and password, we cannot use the server. Many FTP servers are called anonymous FTP servers, because they require no username and password at all, or they display instructions that enable us to enter a guest username and password usually our email address to use the server. When we access an anonymous FTP server through our web browser, we often do not have to log on even with a guest password, because our browser automatically completes the log on with our email address, if required.

Types of files we can download from FTP servers are the

same as those we can download from web pages like; .exe, .doc, .zip, and so on, and are subject to the same issues and considerations such as whether a particular file can run on our type of computer. We have already discussed about the types of file elsewhere.

3. Understanding FTP Addresses

Like accessing other servers, we access an FTP server by entering its address. FTP server addresses are made up of parts separated by periods just like web addresses, and often but not always begin with ftp. For example, ftp.microsoft.com, ftp.mcp.com are FTP server addresses:

Files for downloading are stored in particular directories on FTP servers, just as web page files are stored in particular web server directories. The FTP address can point directly to a file or directory. For example, the address ftp.mcp.com/samples/doc.txt points directly to a file called doc. txt, in a directory called samples, on a server called ftp.mcp.com.

4. Downloading with Navigator and Explorer

Many web browsers, as pointed out earlier are multipurpose clients. At the very least, any web browser can act as a web client, communicating with web servers. Many web clients including all versions of Netscape Navigator and Internet Explorer can double as FTP clients and triple as Gopher clients. If we have such a browser, we do not need a separate FTP client for downloading files from FTP servers.

From a browser, we may use FTP by entering an FTP URL in the address box, just as we would enter a web page URL. We have to remember that the URL of a web page begins with http:// even though we do not have to type that part in many browsers. An FTP URL is made up of ftp:// followed by the FTP server address. For example, the URLs for the FTP addresses shown in the preceding section are ftp://ftp.microsoft.com, ftp://ftp.mcp.com, ftp://ftp.mcp.com/samples /doc.txt If our web browser allows us to omit the http:// prefix when entering a web page URL, it probably also lets us omit the ftp://prefix in an FTP. This feature, however, does not work as reliably with FTP URLs as it does with web URLs.

When entering an FTP URL in any web browser, we have to always include the complete ftp:// prefix.

We can download a file either by entering the complete FTP address of the file, or by entering the address of the FTP server and then browsing through its directories to locate and select the file. When we view FTP directories through a browser, every directory name is a link. Click a directory name, and the contents of that directory appear. Whichever way we get to an FTP file, after we select it, the download proceeds exactly like a regular web download.

Most web browsers do FTP and so, we will often come across links in web pages that are FTP links. They point either to an FTP server or directory, or to a specific file on the server. In particular, the hits turned up by file searches often include links to files that reside on FTP servers. If the link points to a file, clicking the link starts the download, just like any download. We may not even know we are doing an FTP download, unless we look closely at the download status message. If the link points to an FTP server or directory, we will need to browse through the directory listings to find and select a file.

4.1 Getting an FTP File

We can use our browser to get an FTP file, by following the steps listed below. For this begin in the browser, online.

* In Our address box, we have to enter the URL ftp://ftp.microsoft.com to display the toplevel directory on Microsoft's anonymous FTP server. Then the directory will appear, showing folders and documents on Microsoft's FTP server. Each item in the list is a link. In many browsers, folder icons, indicating that they lead to directory listings, although other links show icons that represent the type of file the link downloads such as a page for a document file, may precede the links.
* Click any link preceded by a folder icon or labeled as a "Directory." A new directory listing appears.
* Click back to return to the top directory. In a browser, we move down through the FTP directory structure by clicking

links, and back up by clicking our Back button.

* Find the link for list .zip. This file contains a complete index to the Microsoft FTP server, in a compressed ZIP file.
* Click the link. A download commences, exactly as it would if we had begun downloading a ZIP file from a web page.
* Now we can continue downloading the file or cancel the download.

Due to a number of technical reasons, downloading a file from an FTP server often takes less time than downloading a file of the same size from a web server even when we run the FTP download from a web browser. If we know we can acquire the same file from a web server or an FTP server, we may cut the download time by choosing the FTP server, especially if it is a big file say larger than 1 MB.

5. Using FTP Client

To many who surf the Internet, the FTP capabilities of a web browser are all the FTP power they need. But FTP can do more than just download a file. Using FTP, we can send files and upload them to an FTP server so that others can download them, and control our uploading and downloading to a fine degree such as downloading a whole family of files in one operation. Such advanced FTP functions typically requires a real FTP client, not a web browser posing as one.

We may think, why we need to upload a file. One usual purpose is publishing a web page. After we create a web page on our computer, we must upload it to a web server to make it accessible to others. However, we may not need to learn how to do an FTP upload to upload a web page. Many web-authoring programs now include an easy to use facility that takes care of the uploading for us.

Windows 98 has its own built in FTP clients, but these remain true to FTP heritage as a hacker's tool. To use these clients, we must learn to use a family of FTP commands. Most casual Internet users do not use FTP often enough to justify learning to use these utilitarian FTP clients. A better choice is an easy to use graphical

FTP client, which combines the simplicity of a web browser with the full power of FTP.

A popular choice for Windows, WS_FTP which we can get from www.ipswitch.com which displays the directory of the FTP site we have accessed on the right side of the window and our computers hard disk directory on the left. To download a file, we can drag it from the right to the left. To upload, we drag a file from the left of our hard disk to the right, which is the FTP server. We have to remember that URLs are used only in web browsers. When accessing an FTP server through a real FTP client, we do not enter an FTP URL such as ftp:// ftp.microsoft.com; but only the FTP address itself such as ftp.microsoft.com.

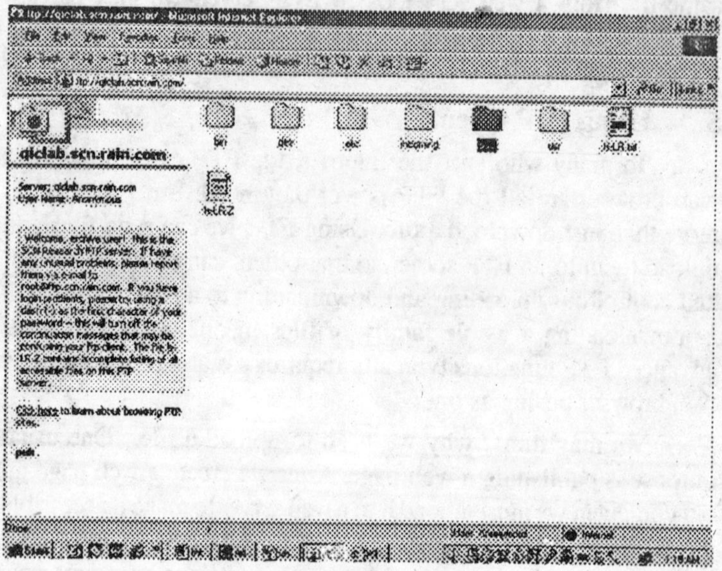

Directory of an FTP site

To find an FTP client for our computer, we can consult Yahoo's directory of them at www.yahoo.com/Computers_and_Internet/ Software/Internet/FTP/

6. FTP in Unix Environment

Here we will discuss FTP client program that runs on Unix.

In order to use FTP to transfer a file, we need to know how to start an FTP session, specifying the FTP server we want to access; how to move through the directory structure on the FTP server to locate the document we seek; how to retrieve the document; and how to quit the FTP session. Let us see how to find useful information with FTP, such as subject-oriented compilations of reference information, and some online electronic books, journals or other materials.

First we need to know the address of the FTP site we want to access. "Frequently Asked Questions" FAQ is a compilation of those questions that are frequently asked on certain topics. The sci.space FAQ, for instance, is a huge compilation of useful answers to astronomical-and-space-flight-related questions. Uenet and FAQs wonderful resources.

6.1 Entering and Exiting

To connect to a FTP server, we have to type ftp <server address>, where <server address> is the Internet domain address of the FTP server we wish to access. Then we get connected to a UNIX host and at the system prompt, we can type address of ftp site pit-manager.mit.edu and press Enter. Our screen will display something like the following:

Connected to bloom-picayune.mit.edu

220 rtfm ftpd (wu-s.1c(17) with built-in ls); bugs to ftp-bugs@rtfrn.mit.edu

Name (pit-manager.mit.edu.jtiton):

If the FTP site is unavailable or not a known host, FTP will inform us of this and display the ftp> prompt. We can try the connection again using the open command. To access pit-manager.mit.edu from the ftp> prompt, we have to type open pit-manager.mit.edu of the ftp> prompt. Two ways are there to connect to an FTP site: full privilege and anonymous. We are using anonymous FTP when we use "anonymous" as the login name. Anonymous FTP is a standard convention on FTP servers. FTP was originally designed to provide access to only the legitimate users of the machine what is now called full-privilege FTP. When a need to come up with a scheme to make files available to the general public was felt, then anonymous FTP was devised. When we find a reference to information available via FTP, we can be sure that unless specifically told otherwise it's available using anonymous FTP. Type anonymous when asked for our name. We will see a response similar to the following:

```
487    Gust login ok, send your complete e-mail address as password.
Password:
```

We are asked to enter our e-mail address as our password in anonymous FTP. This way the server can keep track of the persons who access the system. We can enter our e-mail address (for example, ramannair_r@yahoo.com as our password. As we are entering a password, what we type will not be displayed. Then we will see a response similar to the following:

```
520 Guest login ok, access restrictions apply.
ftp>
```

7. Privileges in FTP

FTP has two access modes. The first is "anonymous" FTP. The second, which we will have is called "full-privilege" FTP. In this style of FTP, we will actually log in to a computer on which we have an account, much as we would log in to a Unix-based machine. If we have an account on a machine running an FTP server that is, if we have a user name and password that allow us to log on, it is likely that we can take advantage of full-privilege FTP.

We can try opening a connection to the machine on which we have an account. When asked for our username, we have to provide the one with which we normally login. When asked for a password, we have to provide our normal password. If our password is accepted, then we have full FTP privileges. This allows us to actually transfer files from and to our home directory. That means that we can retrieve the files that we have stored on that machine, and also store other files there. This kind of FTP access is most useful if we want to get files off that computer on to the computer we are currently using, which may be on some other part of the world. We can use full-privilege FTP just as we use anonymous FTP.

Now we are ready to start an FTP session. To quit the session, at the ftp> prompt we have to type quit and press Enter. Then the message 221 Goodbye is displayed and we return to our local computer.

8. Directory Organization

FTP servers organize files in a hierarchical structure. It is a tree-like structure. There is a root directory with a number of subdivisions, or subdirectories, each containing files and other subdirectories with a common subject matter. The following is a sample FTP directory. It is in upside-down tree structure. The top is the root of the directory. At the root level most are files like index-byname and directories like bin, dev, and pub. Most often, the pub directory contains files available to anonymous FTP users.

pit-manager.mit.edu

Index-byname	**Index-bytime**	**[bin]**	**[dev]**	**[etc]**
[ftp]	**[pub]**			
WorldMap	**chess.ps**	**[index]**	**[usenet-by-group]**	
[ac]	**[alt]**	**[aus]**	**[sci.space]**	**[zer]**
Space-FAQ				

In the pub directory, are some files like World Map and directories like Usenet-by-group. Moving right along, within the Usenet directory is a directory called sci.space, and under that, is a seen FAQ document on space science. Brackets denote a directory. By organizing files into directories, we can put related files into the same location. It's not like a filing cabinet, where we place reference materials for one class into one folder, reading materials for another class into a different folder, and all folders into one book. There are commands to move to the different levels in the structure, and there is a command to show the content at each level. The location of the file is listed by giving the directory levels separated by a forward slash. If we say pub/usenet/by-group/ sci.space/space-FAQ. It will specify the file space FAQ.

8.1 Changing Directories

We can also look around and find out what files and directories are there. We can then move from directory to directory, step by step. Two commands essential are dir and cd <directory name>. The dir command lists the contents of the current directory. The cd <directory name> moves us into the <directory name> directory. The command cdup moves back up one level. Let's explore the site pit-manager.mit.edu, and find the location of the FAQ archives. For this we have to reconnect to pit-manager as anonymous FTP. We have to type ftp pit-manager.mit.edu at the system prompt. We can give anonymous as our login name and our e-mail address as password. At the ftp> prompt we can type dir and press [Enter]. The screen display will look like the following.

```
200 PORT command successful
150 Opening ASCII mode data connection for/bin/ls.
total 3775
-rw-rw-r-      root  system        0 May 15  1997 .notar
-rw-rw-r-    1 root  system        149924 Mar 28 08:05 Index-byname
-rw-rw-r-    1 root  system        216223 Mar 28 08:05 Index-byname.gz
-rw-rw-r-    1 root  system        149924 Mar 28 08:05 Index-bytime
-rw-rw-r-    1 root  system        140777 Mar 28 08:05 Index-bytime.gz
-rw-rw-r-    1 root  system        249 Dec.11 17:46 Index-README
drwxr-x-x    3 root  system        12 Dec.11 17:17 bin
drwxr-x-x    2 root  system        12 May 15  1993 dev
drwxr-x-x    4 root  system        512 Dec.18 20:09 etc
lrwxrwxr-x   1 root  system        1 May 15  1993 ftp>
-rw-rw-r-    1 root  system        429800 Mar 28 08:09 ls-IR.Z
drwxrwxr-x   23 root  system1536 Feb.26 10:38 puv
226 Transfer complete.
795 bytes received in 0.71 seconds (1.1 Kbytes/s)
```

The information in the right-most column is the name of the files and directories in this directory level, and the information at the left-most column gives information about the content. The first character in each line tells whether the listing is a file we can retrieve or another directory we can explore. If the entry has a "d" or "l", as bin, dev, etc, ftp, and pub do in the preceding example, this is a directory. If the entry has a hyphen as Index-byname then it is a file. For moving from a directory to directory, we can use the cd command, which stands for "change directory". Type cd pub and press Enter to move into the pub directory. Then we will see the message: 250 CWD command successful. We can type dir and press Enter to get a list of contents. Then we will get a list of files and directories, but the list will scroll right through.

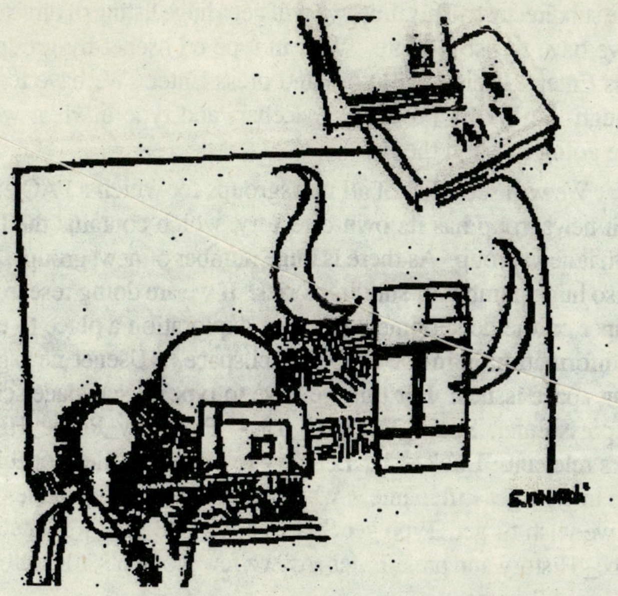

As an anonymous FTP user, the pub directory is where we are most likely to find files to which we have access. When we list the contents of a directory, if the directory contain more items than can be shown in one screen, it scroll and we could not read the listing. We can show one screen at a time by typing dir. [|]more. The "." stands for "the current directory", and "[|]more" is a flag that means "one page at a time." The [|] (pipes) key is the vertical bar symbol, often located above the backslash on the keyboard.

We can type dir.[|]more to get a listing of files, one screen at a time. We can hit Spacebar to get a new page. If we look at those list of files, we can see that it includes the following:

```
irwxrwxr-x  1 root system 15 May 18   1997  usenet—>usenet-by-group
drwxrwxr-x  8383009 3  24064 Feb 28   00:24  usenet-by-group
drwxrwxr-x  34 root 3   1024 Feb 27   01:00  usenet-by-hierarchy
```

As we are looking for Usenet FAQs, this is a very good place to start. Usenet is another link file, in this case, a link to Usenet-by-group. This tells that these two subdirectories are really the same subdirectory. This time, we will get a huge listing of directories, so we have to use [|]more. We can type cd usenet-by-group and press Enter. Then dir. [|]more and press Enter. We have to page through the list by pressing Spacebar; and type q when we are done going through the list.

We will see a list of all newsgroups for which a FAQ exists. Each newsgroup has its own directory, which contains the FAQs for that newsgroup. As there is huge number of newsgroups, there is also huge number of subdirectories. If we are doing research for a paper on the development of space exploration a place to check for information is in the FAQ for sci.space, a Usenet newsgroup about space issues. For this we have to type cd sci.space.science and press Enter. Space_FAQ_08_ 13_-_ Planetary_Probe_History looks relevant. Look at it. Let's try to retrieve a file. For this we have to type get <filename>, where <filename> is the name of the file we wish to get. Type get Space _FAQ_ 08_13_ -_Planetary _ Probe_ History and press Enter. After a few moments, the following display will come.

```
200 PORT command successful
150 Opening ASCII mode data connection for
Space_FAQ_08_13_-_Planetary_Probe_History (28606 bytes).
226 Transfer complete.
local: Space_FAQ_08_13_-_Planetary_Probe_History
remote: Space_FAQ_08_13_-_Planetary_Probe_History
32171 bytes received in 9.8 seconds (3 Kbytes/s)
```

Now we can type quit and press Enter. So we have transferred a file that was on another computer to our local computer. Unlike Gopher, we are not grabbing it and immediately displaying it. We have got this file and placed it on our local environment. If we are using Windows clients, it's actually on the computer in front of us. If we are logged onto a Unix-based machine, then it's on that machine. To view a document in Unix, we can type more <filename> where <filename> is the name of the document we want to view. So we have to type more, Space_FAQ_08_13_-_Planetary_Probe_History and press Enter. By pressing the spacebar we can view the next screen. We will be shown the document page by page. If we want to quit at any time, we can type q.

8.2. Viewing Documents

Let us try to get some information on current politics. Far getting information on various political, legal and economic affairs we can use Internet and FTP. White House is a government source online. The FTP server for the White House is ftp.whitehouse.gov. We can type ftp.whitehouse.gov and press Enter and Login as an anonymous user. Then when we type dir and press Enter, and then will come up a pub directory. Then we have to type cd pub and press Enter. Then dir and Enter, Here we will find that cd political-science is one of the sub directories. We can type cd political-science and dir and press Enter. Then there will be various sub directories on political science. We can go to the specific directory related to our subject of interest and type cd full-text and press Enter. Then we can type dir. [|]more and press Enter.

There will be many files in here. We have to took at the contents of these files without going through the process of retrieving a file and then later viewing it. It would be useful to be able to actually preview a document before transferring it to our own machine, to make sure we actually get what we require. If we type get chap-01.txt [|]more and press Enter the file is displayed, one page at a time. Again, think of the [|]more as a flag indicating that we wish to view this document one page at a time. There are the basic tools for getting in, taking a look around, moving to where the file is, and getting back out again to use FTP effectively. The following are some commands and functions that will be useful.

lcd	change our local directory (the directory on ourown machine that files will be placed in)
binary	set binary transfer mode (8 bit safe)
ascii	set ascii transfer mode (7 bit safe)
close	close your FTP session without quitting our client
open	open a new FTP session without restarting our client

9. Information Retrieval Tools

There are huge number of FTP sites available, and it's not always clear what piece of information is available where. But there is a guide named Archie. It was the first of the so-called "resource discovery tools" of the Internet. Archie's name is a shortening of the word archives. Gopher or Veronica provides a similar service.

What Archie provides is roughly analogous to the card catalogues of our libraries. Specifically, it provides something very similar to a catalogue of the titles of books in a library. We can then search this catalogue and find files on the Internet by their title like finding books in the catalogue. Archie does this work by keeping track of nearly all of the anonymous FTP sites. Periodically it searches these sites, compiling a list of all files. Then, once it has compiled its database, it sits content, waiting for queries from users. Archie is also based upon clients and servers. It is the server that searches FTP sites and maintains a huge database, and it is the client that asks the server to yield up this information to the user.

Let us take a possible situation in which we require information. Assume that we are doing a paper Herman Hesse's attitude to Indian thought on ultimate truth as depicted in Siddhartha and Glass Beadgame. Our user or we are also preparing the book in our computer at home or office, and we have to get a copy of Siddhartha for reference, which is not available at our library or personal collection. Here comes Internet, which has many electronic texts online. Let us check if Sidhartha is available. To check whether Siddhartha is available via FTP, we need to use Archie. We will use the Archie at archie.sura.net by telnet ting to the site. Although

Archie clients do exists for local systems, they are not as common as the FTP client. One may be installed on ours. At the system prompt, we have to type telnet archie.sura.net and press Enter and login as qarchie. Some introductory text will appear, followed by a prompt (>) indicating that Archie is ready to accept commands. The screen will be similar the following.

SunOS Unix(yog-sothoth.sura.net)

login: qarchie

Last login: Mon Dec. 3 03:01:53 from ux9000.weber.edu

SunOS Release 4.1.5 (NYARLATHOTEP) #3: Wed Jan.22. 15:26:21 EDT 1997

Welcome to the simple interactive archie query service at SURAnet.

This service only provides the ability to do queries. However, in general the queries should finish sooner than using the actual interactive client.

To enter a query, type prog <whatever>

To get more help, type help

To exit this program, type quit

We are now supporting a mail command, screen size setting, looking up i.p addresses, and optional screen clearing. The screen defaults to not clearing. To get the old behaviour, type set clear screen on. For more help on these commands type help and help set. Finally ctrl-d will log you out of the system

To get help we have to type help and press Enter. Then the following list of commands will appear.

>help

Commands available:

prog <filename>

Execute a search for filename using the current search type

mail address

mail the results of the last search to address

lookup host

Lookup the I.P. address of host

quit

Quit from the query program

set <variable> <value>

Help on variables which can be set

help [set]

Print this message, or the help message on settable variables

A command listed is prog <filename>. This execute a search for filename using the current search type. As <filename>, we can enter the search string that might be used to locate the file. This is a search based on the filename. The problem is that the titles of files of FTP sites are often less than descriptive. We can enter the word Siddhartha.

Archie permits several different types of searches. The one that it automatically uses is called "Case Insensitive Substring". What this means is that "Siddhartha" will match any title that contains the word "Siddhartha" and might have "S" of "Siddhartha" capitalized.

The case matters in searches. Uppercase and lowercase aren't always the same thing to computers, and "Siddhartha" might be considered to be different from "siddhartha".

We can also use another type of search, such as an "exact" search, if we knew more closely the name of the file we were trying to find. So, if we knew there was a file called "Siddhartha" , and wanted to find only it, we might do an exact search on "Siddhartha". Type prog Siddhartha" and press Enter. Archie will search for all file titles containing the word "Siddhartha". After a minute or two, a list will appear. We will be able to scroll through the list, a page at a time, using the spacebar at the colon (:) prompt. In the screen we can see the following.

Host sunsite.unc.edu

Location:/pub/docs/books/Hesse/novels

FIL-rw-r-r- 57278 Aug 26 1998 Siddhartha.Z

The host is sunsite.unc.edu.

We can figure out the location by now. The filename is Siddhartha.Z. The extension.Z mean compression format, but used by Unix computers. We will find many files on FTP as compressed files. The reason is very simple: a compressed file won't take as much storage and it is faster to transfer. We can scroll through the result from Archie to locate the listing from sunsite.unc.edu we have to note the listing, then quit by typing q. Archie will display a > and wait for a command. Once we have the > prompt, we can type quit and press Enter. Archie will quit, and we will be returned to the system prompt.

9.1 Uncompressing Files

It we are using a Unix host, we will get the file from sunsite.unc.edu. For this at the system prompt we have to type ftp sunsite.unc.edu and press Enter. We can login as anonymous. Then an introductory message will be displayed. Now, we can locate the document. For this first type cd pub and press Enter, then type cd docs and press Enter, then type cd books and press Enter, then type cd Hesse and press Enter, then type cd novel and press Enter. We will arrive in the proper directory to retrieve the file Siddhartha.Z. We can type dir and press Enter. We will see a list of files, as the following.

```
250-
250-
250 CWD command successful.
ftp> cd Hesse
250 CWD command successful.
ftp> cd Novels
250 CWD command successful.
ftp> dir
200 PORT command successful.
150 Opening ASCII mode data connection for /bin/ls.
total 615
-rw-r—r— 1 root daemon 82541 Jan 26 1998 Gertrude.Z
-rw-r—r— 1 root daemon 89563 Jan 26 1998 Glassbeadgame.Z
-rw-r—r— 1 root daemon 81625 Jan 26 1998 Klingsors last summer.Z
-rw-r—r— 1 root daemon 79315 Jan 26 1998 Knulp.Z
-rw-r—r— 1 root daemon 57733 Jan 26 1998 Narzis and gold mund.Z
-rw-r—r— 1 root daemon 77803 Jan 26 1998 Peter amenzind.Z
```

-rw-r—r— 1 root daemon 73999 Jan 26 1998 Rossalde.z

-rw-r—r— 1 root daemon 60853 Jan 26 1998 Siddhartha.Z

As we might have expected, this archive contains more than just Siddhartha. This can often play an important role in discovering Internet resources. We can get Siddhartha.Z and press Enter. We should not forget that Unix is case sensitive. The FTP client retrieves the file. Then we can quit the FTP session. Now the file is in our home directory for us to view. Since it is in a compressed format, we will need to convert it into something readable. A tool exists for this on most Unix machines, called uncompress.

At the system prompt, we have to type uncompress Siddhartha.Z and press Enter. Then we will see the system prompt again. We will see the text of the novel. We can type more Siddhartha and press Enter. We can page through using Spacebar or can type q to quit the display. Let us disconnect from the Unix host. These are the ways of using documents through Internet from libraries existing at locations at other end of the world.

9.2. Library Tool

FTP will continue as an important Internet tool for years to come at least in the libraries. It will be a little more difficult than the techniques of web browsing available now; but librarians and library users who are aware of the methods of organization of information for use will not find it difficult like the other Internet users. Many of the techniques used in Internet except the hardware and a few aspects of the software are highly related to library techniques or have got inspiration from library science. As FTP has been used highly by many libraries from the beginning of Internet; it will not be possible and feasible to get all such files transferred to the web. Hence FTP will continue to exist at least as a library tool.

9

WAIS and Catalogue Search

If we wish to find a definition for Advaita Vedanta in books on Indian Philosophy or locate a journal article on national movement of Kerala there are a number of methods we can use. We can scan the table of contents of all the books and journals for possible chapters or titles on these aspects. This is time consuming and we may not succeed in finding anything relevant even after turning pages and pages for hours. The effective strategy is to use an index of the work in question. Books and magazines are usually indexed. There are published indexes for magazines that often index the contents of several related magazines at once. We can look for the subject or author in the index and then chase down the indicated articles in the magazine stocks.

Now large amount of information can be stored in computers for later retrieval, such as magazines and articles. Wide Area Information System (WAIS) even though considered a primitive tool of Internet has some excellent library applications. It provides a method for indexing and accessing specific bodies of knowledge. It covers everything that we can obtain on the Internet like mail messages, text and electronic books, Usenet articles, computer code, image and graphics files, sound files, E-mail addresses, and raw-data databases. WAIS is powerful and flexible enough to index and store them for later retrieval. It was originally intended to create methods to allow speedy keyword access to information in some areas, which is to be constantly made available. Later WAIS has grown out of those limitations of subject boundaries to provide an index to the whole universe of knowledge.

The WAIS software architecture has four main components: the client, the server, the database, and the protocol. The WAIS client is a user interface program that sends requests for information to local or remote servers. Clients are available for most popular desktop environments. The WAIS server is a program that services client requests, and is available on a variety of Unix platforms. The server generally runs on a machine containing one or more information sources, or WAIS databases. The goal of the WAIS network publishing system is to create an open architecture of information clients and servers by using a standard computer-to-computer protocol that enables clients to communicate with servers. WAIS development began in October 1989 with the first Internet release occurring in April 1991.

As an aid to understanding the original WAIS implementation and its use, the historical design goals of WAIS are presented below with a brief description of the assumptions used to meet these design goals.

* Provide users access to bibliographic and non-bibliographic information, including full-text and images. Because it grew out of the bibliographic community, additional assumptions with the protocol were required to serve non- bibliographic information. They were also necessary to serve documents existing in multiple formats (e.g., rtf, postscript, gif, etc.).
* Keep the client/server interface simple and independent of changes in the functionality of the server. To achieve this, the text string entered by the user was transmitted to the server without parting the string into a Type-1 RPN (reverse-polish notation) query, as is common for bibliographic applications. Instead WAIS defined a new Type-3 query containing the text string. In this way, knowledge of the attributes supported by the server was no longer required by the client or the user, as is true of many existing implementations. In addition, the client software did not require modification to support the evolving functionality of the server.
* Provide relevance feedback capability. Relevance feedback is the ability to select a document, or portion of a document,

and find a set of documents similar to the selection. WAIS included documents used in relevance feedback as part of the Type-3 query.

* Permit the server to operate in a stateless manner. A WAIS server was designed to be "stateless", meaning that search result sets were not stored by the server. The server exercises its right to unilaterally delete a result set as soon as it sent the search response. For this reason, the Present Facility was not used, and retrievals were performed using the Search Facility.
* Provide the ability for a client to retrieve documents in pieces. Because retrieval of a portion of a document could be done several ways, specific assumptions were made to implement this functionality. Accessing a portion of a document was required for both retrieval and for relevance feedback.
* Run over TCP. It was designed to run in the application layer using the presentation services provided by the Open Systems Interconnection (OSI) Reference Model. Due to the popularity of TCP/IP and the Internet, WAIS was designed to run over TCP

1. Document Finding System

Wide Area Information Server (WAIS), are databases containing mostly text-based documents, (although WAIS documents may contain sound, pictures or video as well). WAIS databases are referred to as sources. The databases may be organized in different ways, using various database systems, but the user is not required to learn the query languages of the different databases. The WAIS client uses natural language queries to find relevant documents and the result of a query is a set of documents that contain the words of the query. WAIS databases are available on topics ranging from Agriculture to Zorastrianism. This network publishing system, Wide Area Information Servers (WAIS), is designed to help users find information over a computer network. The principles guiding WAIS development are the following

* wide-area network based information system for searching/

browsing/publishing.

* based on standards
* easy to use.
* flexible and growth oriented.

From this basis, a large group of developers, publishers, standards bodies, libraries, government agencies, schools, and users have been helping further development of the WAIS system.

1.1. Working of WAIS

The client/server model of computer communication was used in designing WAIS. The client-server model requires two programs to utilize WAIS. A WAIS server program running at several computers are repositories of WAIS indexes, and WAIS client software that enables access to these servers. The WAIS server program runs constantly on its host computer, waiting for requests from WAIS client programs. There are many different kinds of WAIS, client programs, ranging from desktop computer clients to Unix clients. They all have the ability to query and receive information from WAIS servers.

The institutions or groups run most of the WAIS servers, which owns huge stores of information on some related items. There are WAIS indexes for subjects from Aves to Zoology. Any one interested in past discussions on a specific subject can use that particular WAIS index to search for articles and items on their topics of interest.

WAIS indexes are arranged by keyword, which means that when a new index is created for a collection of data, WAIS looks through each item, recording which words are in which files. We cannot find index listing of all the occurrences of any specific word. But a WAIS index examines each and every word and decides whether to list it in the database. However, it is smart enough to discard words such as "a", "the", "and", "I" and the words that occurs frequently and in many contexts that where it is pointless to index them. When WAIS finishes examining everything, it creates the index and waits for requests.

WAISes are not alike. Early versions of the program allows

us to search for keywords, but do not allow searches based on multiple keywords using Boolean operators (AND, OR, and NOT). In older software, if we enter rats bats as keywords, WAIS would look documents with the words "rats and bats" occurring somewhere in the file. If we want to search for documents that contain "rats or bats", we could now search for "rats OR bats". Through WAIS client program, we can access any of the WAIS indexes that the client knows about or for which it has the computer address. The client program opens a connection with the server we select, sends it the words we specify, and receives the information that the server returns. The connections to other computers are rather brief, only long enough to convey requests and responses. The connection is then closed. The server waits for another request, and the client helps us to process the returns.

1.2. Nature of WAIS

For accessing WAIS servers we can use a WAIS client program directly or find WAIS servers on such network tools as Gopher and the World Wide Web (WWW). The Gopher and WWW access are, in a lot of ways, easier to access because searching and viewing results; mimic closely the Gopher and WWW environments. WAIS client programs often allow a great deal of flexibility, having more functions than the Gopher or WWW access. Although WAIS clients are available on a number of platforms here we will discuss client software on Unix available via Telnet. The concept applies to any platform, whether it is Unix or one utilizing a graphical user interface.

There are three versions of WAIS index software, each with different capabilities. We will not always know which WAIS we have. Let us see their common names and capabilities. If we see that the server we are using is of one of these types we can make use of its functions to the fullest.

"b5" WAIS', which is the common one is the original version, released by Thinking Machines, Inc. It does not allow Boolean operators. Searches are entered "rats, cats, bats" and the server interprets this as "rats or cats or bats". Indiana University version adds Boolean operators, but they must be in all capital letters for the server to recognize them. A search would be entered "rats

AND cats AND bats" not "rats and cats and bats", or the server will look for the work "and" as well. The version from CNIDR allows Boolean operators that are not in all capitals. In addition to Boolean operators, freeWAIS allows for truncation, which is the ability to type in the first part of a word and an asterisk at the end, and the WAIS server will return all files with words beginning in that manner. Entering "India" would return India, Indian, Indiana, and others when the server cannot be identified. We can test out the functions to see what we are dealing with.

2. Using WAIS

We must be on the international TCP/IP network (the Internet) in order to use a WAIS client on our computer to access WAIS sources. If we have e-mail access only, or if we are not on the Internet, we can still exploit some of the potential of WAIS. An interface, which gives e-mail access to WAIS databases, is available at the address: WAISmail@quake.think.com

There are many WAIS servers throughout the network. A directory of servers database is available at several sites, which can be queried to find out what databases are available on a particular subject. The directory of servers database is also available via anonymous FTP from ftp.wais.com in the directory /pub/directory of servers in the distribution wais-sources.tar.Z as file directory-of-servers.scr. If we do not have access to a WAIS client, at least two demonstration sites are available to allow us to get acquainted with WAIS. We can telnet to: quake.think.com (login: wais) or sunsite.unc.edu (login: swais)

The two demonstration sites above run swais (Screen WAIS), a simple WAIS client for Unix. There are many freely available WAIS client programs for various operating systems (Unix, VMS, MVS, MS-DOS, OS/2 and Macintosh) and for specific environments (e.g. X-Windows, Openlook, NeXT, and MS-Windows). The client interface differs slightly on different platforms, but the queries are performed in the same way whatever interface is in use.

* The user selects a set of databases to be searched.
* The user formulates a query consisting of keywords to be searched for.
* When the query is run, WAIS asks for information from each selected database.
* Headlines of documents satisfying the query are displayed. The selected documents contain the requested words and phrases. Selected documents are ranked according to the number of matches.
* To retrieve a document, the user simply selects it from the resulting list. The WAIS client retrieves the document and displays its contents on the screen.
* If not enough documents are found, the user can state the question differently or can select a set of documents.
* A further search will look for documents, which have a large number of words in common with the selected documents.

2.1 E-mail Access

We can query WAIS databases and retrieve documents by sending commands in the body part of an e-mail message to WAIS-mail@quake.think.com. The Subject: line is ignored. The important commands are given below (a vertical bar (|) indicates a choice of parameters):

* help: to get the help file
* maxres number: to set the maximum number of results (i.e. documents) to be returned.
* search source-name | "source-name1 source-name2 ..." keywords where: source-name : is a source name as found in the directory-of-servers (with or without the src ending). Use double-quotes (") to group several sources to be searched.
* Keywords: are the words we would normally type into a query. We may specify several search requests in a mail message. If we don't know what sources we can search, just we can try anything. If the source name is not recognized, we will be given a list of sources.
* retrieve docid: retrieves a document from a database
* Docid: is a Document Identifier as returned by a search. We may put more than one retrieval request in a mail message, but we must leave a blank line between requests. The docid must be written exactly as returned by a search request, including any spaces. We can retrieve non-text documents as well as text. If the document is of type TEXT or WSRC we will get the result directly. Other types will be UUENCODED before being transmitted.
* DocID: docid same as retrieve. This form is identical to the form, which is returned by a search request, which makes it easy to use the reply mail function to retrieve results.

2.2 Examples

When we log in to the demonstration site at quake.think.com, we have immediate access to the directory-of-servers database via the swais client software. To find recipes using papaya, we would select the recipes database and give papaya as the keyword. Here are the results of the search:

```
     # Score Source             Title                  Lines
001: 1000 (recipes) arielle@ta Re: Dawn's Muffins, Pt III   339
```

002: 1000 (recipes) arielle@ta Re: Muffins 3 632
003: 1000 (recipes) arielle@ta Re: Pineapple 678
004: 750 (recipes) arielle@ta Re: Pork and Papaya Salad 33
005: 750 (recipes) arielle@ta Re: Bread 681
006: 500 (recipes) roder@cco. Re: nonfat bakery collection 423
007: 500 (recipes) shiva@hoss Re: Juice Recipes 65
008: 250 (recipes) arielle@ta Re: Prawn Salad 49
009: 250 (recipes) arielle@ta Re: collection: Lots of Avoca 447
010: 250 (recipes) mecca@acsu Re: request: blender-made fru 29
011: 250 (recipes) Ann.Adamci Re: Re: request: blender-made 38
012: 250 (recipes) patth@Pani Re: Re: request: blender-made 49
013: 250 (recipes) arielle@ta Re: Avocados 459
014: 250 (recipes) red_trek@d Re: vegan: red beans and rice 78

We can then select any of the above documents for viewing. Here is the Pork and Papaya Salad recipe:

Newsgroups: rec.food.recipes
From: arielle@taronga.com (Stephanie da Silva)
Subject: Pork and Papaya Salad
Message-ID: <5BBP2SB@taronga.com>
Date: Mon, 29 Mar 1993 06:51:47 GMT
Lines: 23
1/4 cup dried currants
1/2 cup balsamic vinegar
1/4 cup walnut oil
1/4 cup chicken broth
1 tablespoon honey
1/4 teaspoon ground cinnamon
1 pound cooked boneless pork loin roast
1 head Belgian endive
Bibb lettuce leaves
2 papayas, seeded, peeled and sliced lengthwise
2 avocados, seeded, peeled and sliced lengthwise
1/4 cup broken walnut pieces
In a small bowl pour enough boiling water over currants to cover.
Let stand 5 minutes; drain. For dressing, in a screw-top jar combine vinegar, oil, chicken broth, honey, and cinnamon. Cover, shake well. Trim fat from

pork; slice thinly. Separate leaves of Belgian endive. Line 6 salad plates with lettuce leaves. Arrange pork, endive, papaya, and avocado on plates. Sprinkle with currants and walnuts. Drizzle dressing over salads. Stephanie da Silva arielle@taronga.com

If we give more than one keyword, then all documents containing any of the keywords will be listed.

3. Searching WAIS Databases

The full text of information on the Finance net server is indexed using the WAIS system. The indexing and searching is provided via software from WAIS, Inc. To perform a search, we enter what is termed a "search expression". A search expression can contain any combination of words, literal strings, Boolean operators, field name-value pairs, date or numeric ranges, and parentheses for grouping. The WAIS search engine also supports right truncation (wildcard searching) and relevance ranking. Each of these capabilities is explained below.

3.1 Documents Returned

After we enter our query, and click on "Search", we will see a list of the documents matching our query. In addition, at the end of the list of documents, we will receive a report by the server on how it interpreted our query. This can be very useful information, particularly if the results were not what we expected.

If our search did not result in any matching documents, we will receive, a query report. The query report will contain information explaining why no documents were returned.

4. Entering Search Expression

Search expressions consist of any of the following: words, literal strings, Boolean operators, field name-value pairs, date or numeric ranges, parentheses (for grouping) and wildcard words, all explained below.

Words: The simplest query is just one or more words separated by spaces. In this type of query, any documents containing ANY of the words (in any field) are returned. Words can be entered in either upper or lower case, and match words in any case. We do not enter quotation marks for a word search. Example: flexitime conflicts. This search will return all the documents that contain at least one of these words. The following points should be noted for simple word searches.

* Simple word searches aren't too useful in many databases unless the words are quite rare.
* We should understand the concept of "stopwords". Some words, such as "a", "the", "of", etc., appear in so many documents that they are useless in searching for specific documents. For this reason, they are not indexed at all, and are called "stop words". If we try to search on a stop word, the query report will explain that the word was a stop word, and was therefore ignored.
* In WAIS databases, numbers are words, so we can search on them. For example, we can search on ZIP codes. However, the search engine separates words on punctuation, so we cannot search for a number that is represented in the database with embedded commas, such as "1,000,000", unless it occurs in a numeric field.
* The documents returned are sorted, with the intent that the most relevant document is at the top. Relevance ranking may not be found totally intuitive for simple word searches. Suppose we enter the search: denver mitochondria . If our intent was to find documents that contain both of these words, we may be disappointed. Most likely, the top of the list will be documents that contains the word "denver" many, many times, and the word "mitochondria" not at all. So we have to use Boolean operators in this case: that is denver AND mitochondria

4.1 Literal Strings

We can search on phrases, such as "genetic engineering", by enclosing the phrase in quotation marks (this kind: "). In WAIS jargon, phrases in quotes are called "literal strings". A search on a phrase returns only documents containing the phrase. Literal string searches can be very useful, but they can sometimes produce unexpected results. We must be careful of stop words in literal strings. For example, if we issue a query on the phrase "conference on diversity", we will not get any matches, because of the stop word "on" comes between "conference" and "diversity". The query report will explain that "on" is a stop word, but the search will fail. In this case, re-issue the query with the phrase "conference diversity" which will work as we expect. We can also avoid this problem by using the Boolean ADJ operator explained below.

4.2 Boolean Operators

The Boolean operators, AND, OR, NOT, and ADJ are especially useful in narrowing down our search. Boolean operators MUST be entered in upper case as shown here and in the examples.

AND: The AND operator is helpful in restricting a search when a particular pair or larger group of terms is known. For instance, when searching for documents concerning mitochondria at institutions in Denver, a query such as "mitochondria AND Denver" will return only those documents that contain both the word "mitochondria" and the word "Denver". We can use more than one AND in a query, e.g. "mitochondria AND Denver AND Smith". Note that the C-like double ampersand (&&) may be used instead of spelling out the word AND. Example: mitochondria AND Denver AND Smith

OR: The OR operator is often used to join two different phrases of a Boolean search. A query such as "hurricane OR tornado" would search for all documents containing either the word "hurricane", or the word "tornado", or both. We can also use more than one OR in a query. The C-like expression "||" is equivalent to spelling out OR. Words separated by spaces are equivalent to using the OR operator. For example, the following queries are equivalent: Denver OR mitochondria, denver || mitochondria, denver mitochondria

NOT: NOT is a binary operator. That is, it has to come between two or more words or parenthesized clauses. NOT is used to reject any documents that contain certain words. For a generalize database, a query "basketball NOT college" would find all documents containing the word "basketball" that do not also contain the word "college". We should use care with this, since documents may contain words that we wouldn't expect. We have to be careful not to limit our search too much with the NOT operator, since we may miss documents that are relevant to our query.

ADJ: The adjacent operator, ADJ, is used to ensure that one word is followed by another in the returned documents, with no other words in between. For example, "cordless ADJ telephone" returns only documents containing "cordless telephone" and ignores documents that only contain one of the words or that contain both words, but not adjacent to one another. ADJ will work when stop words interrupt two words; for example, the preceding example will find occurrences of "cordless for telephone". Except for the way stop words are handled, the ADJ operator works just like a literal string query. The order of the words is significant. For example, "telephone ADJ cordless" does not work the same as "cordless ADJ telephone".

Right Truncation (Wildcards): We can specify right truncation by ending a word with the asterisk (*) wild card character. This tells the search engine to search on words whose first characters match the base characters before the *. For example, if we use "geo*" in a query, we will retrieve documents containing the words: geographer, geography, geologist, geometry, geometrical, etc. The query report will contain a list of all the words that the wildcard matched.

Grouping Search Terms: We can group search terms and phrases together using parentheses. For example, if we wish to search for information about snowstorms or tornadoes in New York City, we might search for the (snowstorms OR tornadoes) AND (New ADJ York ADJ City). We can nest parentheses.

Special Characters: The WAIS server uses any characters in a document that are not letters or numbers to separate words (which can consist only of letters and numbers). For this reason it is impossible to search on many strings that we might consider words. Here are some examples of things we cannot search on: "1,000,000" (except in a numeric field), "F.Y.I.", and "can't".

4.3 Relevance Ranking

An attempt is made to return matching documents with the most relevant at the top of the list. Here we will see how the scoring is performed. If we access this database through the WWW or Gopher, we probably cannot view the actual scores, although the list will reflect the correct order. Each document is scored based on its relevance to our query, where the most relevant document has the highest score, or rank — 1000 being the highest, 1 being the lowest. A document receives a higher score if the words in the query are in the title (the one-line description returned to us in the list of documents), if the words appear many times, or if phrases occur as they do in the query. A document's score is derived using techniques including word weighting, term weighting, proximity relationships, and word density. These scoring techniques are outlined below.

Word Weight: If a word in a document is found to match a word in our query, the word is assigned a weight, and this weight adds to the overall score of the document. The exact weight that a word receives depends on the emphasis given to the word by the document author, and on where in the document the word was found. For example, a word is weighted normally if it appears only in the text body with no capitalization, higher if the word has all capital letters or if the first letter of the word is capitalized, and highest if it appears in the headline.

Term Weight: Each word used in a document is assigned a numerical value, called the term weight, based on the frequency of occurrence of that word over all documents in the data set. Words that occur frequently are not weighted as highly as those that appear less frequently. Very common words are either ignored or diminished in the scoring. For example, since the term "animal" may occur frequently in many of the documents in a zoology data set, its term weight is small compared to a term such as "hippopotamus", which may occur only a few times.

Proximity Relationships: Proximity relationship scoring specifies that if the words in the query are located close together in a document, they are given a higher weight than those found further apart. The

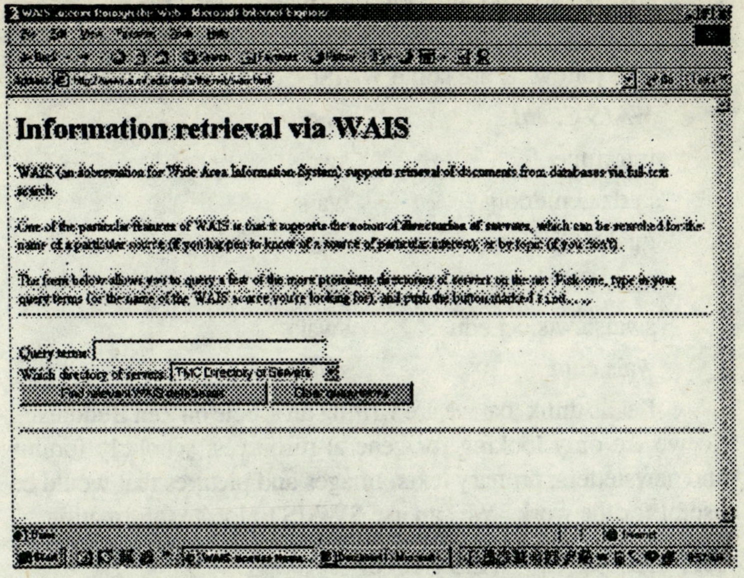

WAIS Search Mechanism

idea behind a proximity relationship is that if a document contains a phrase similar to one in our query, that document is more likely to be relevant.

Word Density: The ratio of the number of times a word appears in a document to the size of the document is called the word density. It is a measure of how important a word is to the overall content of the document. A higher word density results in a higher relevance ranking for that document with respect to that word.

The form of WAIS search seen in the picture of screen above can allow us to query a few of the more prominent directories of servers on the net. Pick one, type in our query terms (or the name of the WAIS source we are looking for), and push the button marked Find....

5. Unix Environment

The basic things we need to know in Unix environment are how to start the WAIS client software; how to specify which WAIS server we want to search; how to initiate the search by entering keywords; what to do with the information once we find it; and how to close the program when we have finished the search.

The following are some WAISes:

WAIS Client	*Login*
info.funet.fi	swais
kudzu.cnidr.org	wais
quake.think.com	wais
sunsite.unc.ed	swais
swais.cwis.uci.edu	swais
wais.com	swais

Let us think that we are writing an article on Zen Buddhism. So we are only looking for general resources: scholarly forums and newsletters, primary texts, images and pictures that would be useful for the work. We can use SWAIS to locate information.

5.1. Accessing WAIS Server

For this first we have to access a WAIS client. We will try the one at quake.think.com. At the system prompt we can type telnet quake.think.com and press enter. Then we will see a login screen, similar to the following.

```
Trying 192.31.181.1
SunDS Unix (quake.think.com)
login
```

We have to type wais and press Enter. Then a screen similar to the following will appears, asking for our identifier.

```
Last login: Sat Feb 12.04.27.28 from pt.olympus.net
SunOS Release 4.1.3 (SUN4C-standard)#9: Wed Oct.27   18:18;30 EDT
1993
Welcome to swais
Please type user identifier (optional, i.e., user@host):
```

We can type our username and press Enter. Then we will be asked about our terminal type. The default option is vt100 which can be accepted by pressing enter. Then an informational screen about the status of this WAIS client will appear. It will generally alert us to possible problems with the program. We can press spacebar to continue with the screen. Then we will be prompted to press q when we have read the message. When we press q the following main menu of the quake.think.com SWAIS client will appear.

```
SWAIS        Source Selection                  Sources: 1
#            Server                            Source          Cost
[quake.think.com]directory of servers                          Free
[
[
[
[
[
Keywords:
<space> selects, w for keywords, arrows move, <return> searches, q quits, or ?
```

5.2. Selecting Relevant Server

This is a WAIS index of WAIS indexes that can be searched by keyword to find WAIS servers that are relevant to our search. Doing a search for WAIS servers is not different from finding other resources. We can enter keywords for the topic we are interested in; in this case Zen Buddhism.

First we have to specify the WAIS server, we would like to search. Because we have just one option, this is irrelevant. By pressing spacebar we can select the directory-of-servers as the index we wish to search. An asterisk will appears in front of the "directory-or-servers" line. Then we have to enter the keywords for the topic, as per the instructions at the bottom of the screen. We can type w to enter keywords. The keywords: prompt appears highlighted near the bottom of the screen, followed by a cursor. Now we have to type words that are relevant. For Zen Buddhism suitable words may be "religion", "asia", "Buddhism" and "Zen". We have to type these words separated by blank spaces. We can type religion asia buddhism zen and press [enter]. After a brief pause, a menu similar to the following will come.

SWAIS	Search	Results		Items:17
#	Score	Source	Title	Lines
001	[684]	(directory-of-se)	ANU-Asian-Religions	93
002	[316]	(directory-of-se)	ANU-Dhammapada-Verses	91
003	[316]	(directory-of-se)	ANU-ZenBuddhism Calender	81
004	[316]	(directory-of-se)	ANU-ZenBuddhism	85
005	[316]	(directory-of-se)	OMNI-Cultural-Academic Res	31
006	[210]	(directory-of-se)	ANU-Pacific-Studies	88
007	[210]	(directory-of-se)	ANU-Tropical-Archaeology	86
008	[184]	(directory-of-se)	ANU-Pacific-Archaeology	81
009	[158]	(directory-of-se)	ANU-Aboriginal-Studies	73

<space> selects, arrows move, w for keywords, s for sources, ? for help

The matches are numbered down the left, then there are four columns: Score, Source, Title, and Lines. The sources are listed in the descending Score order. Score is a number that WAIS uses to rank returns. WAIS counts how many times it matches the keywords in the documents, and the one with the most get the highest score, 684, and appears at the top of the list. WAIS is guessing at which one will be of most value to us. Source and Title are self-explanatory: these returns come from the directory-of-servers WAIS and have these titles. Lines refer to the number of lines in the Introduction file for the index listed. Each WAIS index has an introduction file to describe its content.

6 Reaching Specific Subject

From titles, we can understand that many of our keywords are actually in these titles. We can also specify the WAIS index that will be used for our search. ANU-Zen Buddhism is a natural choice. We can use upward and downward arrow to move the highlight to the WAIS index titled ANU-Zen Buddhism and press Spacebar. After a pause, a screen with text describing this WAIS index will appear.

The displayed page will not make much sense, although the Description: sometimes will tell what version of WAIS is being used. There we can look at the introduction file. We can display the next screen by pressing any key. Eventually, we will return to the original menu. If we want to quit viewing introductory file at any point, we can press g. We can page through introduction file by pressing any key and then can return to earlier screen.

The selected service is relevant; so we have to highlight ANU-Zen Buddhism and type u for use. There should be a brief pause, during which the bottom of the screen will read "Adding Source: ANU-Zen Buddhism. Now we can tell SWAIS to include the selected index for search. For this we have type w for keywords. A screen similar to the following will come.

```
SWAIS         Search Selection                          Sources: 3
#Server       Source                                    Cost
001 [ coombs.anu.edu.au] ANU-ZenBuddhism-Calander       $0.00/minute
002[ coombs.anu:edu.au] ANU-ZenBuddhism-Cistsen         $0.00/minute
003:*[ quake.think.com ] directory-of-servers   Free
     Keywords: religion Asia Buddhism.Zen
     Enter keywords with spaces between them; <return> to search:
     ^C to cancel
```

WAISes that we have specified for use will be in screen. The same keywords we've entered appear at the bottom of the screen. We have to tell SWAIS that we want to use these additional WAIS servers. So we have to cancel the keywords entry. For this we have to press [Ctrl] and type C to cancel keywords entry. The keyword entry is canceled, and the first WAIS entry is highlighted. Then we can press Spacebar to select the first entry. An asterisk appears in front of it. We have to move the highlight to other entries we want to select and press Space bar to select. Asterisks will appear by each entry.

7. Keyword Search

We can make searches using keywords. If we want to get specific in our searching, we need to choose our keywords carefully.

A general term may return a huge volume of more than likely irrelevant files. An inappropriate or rare term may not return anything at all. When looking for information about a topic in a database, it is often appropriate to use keywords that are specific and narrow. For instance, the keyword Bible will certainly get us a lot of returns in indexes. But if we know more precisely what we are looking for we should use words related to it to narrow the search. For example, Vedanta will give whatever returns in the WAIS index containing these specific words. This will get us closer to the information that we want speedily.

If the information we are looking for is not available in the first instance, we have to try again with different related words. If, after a few attempts using different synonyms and related words, we don't succeed in getting any returns, this WAIS index or indeed any database we are searching may not contain information on our topic. This is a sign that it is time to move on to a different index or resource that more closely matches our topic of search.

8. Selecting Databases

To make a search we have to type w for keywords. Then we can backspace over the words we have already entered and then type Vedanta and press Enter. There should be a possibly long pause, during which the bottom of the screen will flash status messages about searching each database individually on a different computer. Then a menu of results, similar to the one shown below will came.

SWAIS Search Results Items:21

#	Score	Source	Title	Lines
001	[1000]	(ANU-Taoisn-List)	more chapter 47's	299
002	[1000]	(ANU-Asian-Relig)	Bibliographical reference..	11
003	[1000]	(ANU-Asian-Relig)	Bibliographical reference..	11
004	[1000]	(ANU-Asian-Relig)	Bibliographical reference..	12
008	[778]	(ANU-Asian-Relig)	Bibliographical reference..	12
009	[778]	(ANU-Asian-Relig)	Bibliographical reference..	11
010	[778]	(ANU-Asian-Relig)	Bibliographical reference..	11
011	[778]	(ANU-Asian-Relig)	Bibliographical reference..	12
012	[778]	(ANU-Asian-Relig)	Bibliographical reference..	11
013	[778]	(ANU-Asian-Relig)	Bibliographical reference.	11
017	[765]	(directory-of-se)	Hinduism	93

<space> selects, arrows move, w for keywords, s for sources, ? for help

All of these are not going to be relevant. We can narrow the search to only interesting Hinduism items now. We need to look for titles that look relevant and briefly look at the content. When we find one that may be of value, we have options to either mail it to our self or save it to a file on our local computer. Once we highlight a title, we can press Spacebar to view the document. Then we can type m to mail the document to a valid e-mail address or we can type S (uppercase) to save the file on our local computer. We will be prompted for a filename, which is to be given by us. To exist the WAIS server, we can type q for quit. Then the message Connection closed by foreign host is displayed, and we return to the local Unix computer.

9. Using through Gopher

We can go to WAIS index through Gopher. It is a bit different from the SWAIS client, but the basic idea is same. If we have a Gopher client on our computer, we can access the Gopher gopher-gw.micro.umn.edu, port 70. For this at the Unix prompt, we have to type gopher gopher-gw.micro.umn.edu 70. Then the Gopher menu is displayed with just one option, WAISes. We can Select WAISes/.

Regardless of the route we took, a screen similar to the one as below will come up.

Internet Gopher Information Client

WAISes

1. **READ THIS!**
2. **List of all WAIS Sources/**
3. **WAIS Databases sorted by Letter/**
4. **WAIS databases sorted by Subject (Experimental), UB2, Lund, Sweden/**

Press? for help, q to Quit, u to go up a menu

The list of all WAIS Sources option will give us a list of all the WAIS sources available at this site. Just as with the SWAIS client, we don't particularly want to page through hundreds of entries looking for likely WAISes. Instead, we will open WAIS Databases sorted by Letter/, because it contains as an option Director of WAIS servers <?>. As in the SWAIS session, we can use this directory of WAIS servers to find indexes that relate to our topic. We can select WAIS Databases sorted by Letter/, and then Directory of WAIS servers <?>. Then we will be prompted for keywords. Let us type the words we used earlier with WAIS, Zen Buddhism and press Enter. After a pause, we should see a new menu with some familiar titles.

These returns will be similar to those we got in the SWAIS session. The drawback of using Gopher, as a WAIS client is that: we must here individually search each WAIS index that looks relevant. But in SWAIS we could simply mark each one as desirable and type in keywords. But here we have to go through each one in turn. There is the advantage of the relatively easy-to-use Gopher interface. This is all about gopher and WAIS.

9.1 Further Support

A bibliography of documents, services and sources for WAIS is maintained by Barbara Lincoln Brooks of WAIS Inc. The bibliography is available from ftp.wais.com in the directory /pub/wais-inc-doc along with many other WAIS documents. WAIS Inc. provides commercial WAIS software and services. The Clearinghouse assumes the support for the freely available version, called freeWAIS, for Network Information Discovery and Retrieval (CNIDR). We can check these sites to become aware of the current developments related to WAIS.

10

Scientific Communication

Internet can be used for voice and video conferencing that may help scientific and academic communication. Both the Netscape Communicator and Internet Explorer suites include a program for live, real time conferencing through the Internet. In Communicator, it is called Conference, and in Internet Explorer, it is called NetMeeting. But the two programs are similar, and still more such programs are available from the web. With one of these programs, we can have a live conversation, much like a telephone call with anyone else on the Internet who uses the same program that we use. Presently Internet telephony is not permitted in our country. Depending on availability of such service from our Internet Service Providers (ISP) and what we pay for Internet service and how far away our caller is, conducting such "Internet telephone" calls may be substantially cheaper than making a long distance telephone call, because the call costs us nothing beyond what we already pay for our Internet account. We can, in effect, make a one our call to France without any charges if our French friend has an Internet account and the same conferencing software we have. These programs do more than just carry a conversation. We can have a text based chat like a chat client, draw and type messages on a collaborative whiteboard, and even add video to the conversation.

1. Conferencing

Conferencing is a different process from the Internet activities we have discussed up to now. Most Internet activities are standardized; that is, they are based on already agreed rules that enable all different programs and systems to interact. For example, because of standards, we can send a message with one email program, and our recipient can read it in another. The difference in programs does not matter, because all Internet email programs follow the same standards. Conferencing has yet to be standardized although standardization efforts are underway. For that reason, those with whom we share a conference must use the same conferencing program we do. Using NetMeeting, we can conference only with other NetMeeting users.

The latest version of Netscape's Conference supports an emerging standard, called H.323, which enables different programs to join in a conference as long as both programs support H.323. Few other programs support this standard today. But among the supporting programs, compatibility is not reliable. For now, in general, we must conference only with others using the same program we use. This is a severe limitation. We cannot simply dial up any friend on the Internet and conduct a conference. Rather, we must first contact our conferencing partners by phone or email, and agree upon what conferencing software we will use when we call one another. In effect, we must establish our own standard for our community of conferencing partners. If our partners use a variety of programs, nothing prevents us from installing different conferencing programs and using different programs to talk to different folks. Microsoft NetMeeting and Netscape Conference are included in their respective suites. We can also download them. Some programs and sites are listed below.

NetMeeting	www.microsoft.comnetmeeting/
Conference	home.netscape.com/ comprod/products/ communicator/conference.html.
Internet Phone	www.vocaltec.com,
PowWow	www.tribal.com/powWow.

We can find other conferencing programs in Yahoo!'s Internet Telephone programs directory at www.yahoo.com/ Business_and_Economy/Companies/Computers/Software/Internet/ Internet_ Phone/ Titles/

2. Hardware Requirement

The most popular form of conferencing through these products is voice conferencing, speaking and listening just as we would in a telephone call. In addition to voice conferencing, some programs also support video conferencing, in which we can see the person with whom we are speaking and they can see us also; and text conferencing, which are conversations carried out through typed messages. To have a voice conference, we must have the following equipment installed and configured in our computer:

* sound card
* microphone either attached to our sound card or built into our computer. In a voice conference, we speak into the mike.
* speakers or headphones attached to our sound card or built into our PC. We will hear our partner's words through the speakers or headphones.

The sound quality of voice conferences is highly variable. An Internet voice conference never sounds as clear as a phone call, even on the best equipment. Still, it is important to know that the better our equipment, the more clearly the call will sound. More expensive, 32-bit sound cards enable a much clearer conversation than cheaper, 16-bit or 8-bit cards although those work. An external microphone connected to our sound card is usually preferable to any built in mike. Built in mikes tend to be low quality, and pick up too much background noise from the computer. Most sound cards made recently support full duplex communications; that is, when having a voice conference through them, we can talk and listen at the same time, just as we would in a phone call. Older, cheaper cards support only half duplex sound. When conferencing through a half duplex sound card, our partner and we must take turns speaking and listening, as if we were using a speakerphone or walkie-talkies. The speed of our Internet connection also plays a role. The faster our connection, the clearer the conversation will be. Connections of 56.8Kbps or faster provide acceptable sound. We will hear heavy static and occasional interruptions.

3. Conference Set Up

Before we can use a conferencing program, we must supply it with a little information. The first time we start Conference or NetMeeting, it launches a Setup Wizard to collect this information from us. We have to work our way through the steps to configure our conferencing program. We will now see how we can set up Microsoft NetMeeting. Note that setting up Conference is nearly identical. To set up NetMeeting, we can follow the steps listed below.

* First we have to open NetMeeting. We can open NetMeeting from within Internet Explorer by choosing Go > Internet Call. The wizard opens.
* Read the introductory message, and then click the Next button to get started.

The required dialog box will now appear. The first thing we need to decide is whether we want to log on to a NetMeeting directory server when we start the application, and if so, which one. In most cases this is a good idea because the directory server is where we will probably find the people we want to talk to. The server can also list our name in the directory so that other people on the Internet know we are online and can call us. It is better to leave the Log On to a Directory Server When NetMeeting Starts; check box checked, and leave the What Directory Server we would like to use? List set to ills. Mcrosoft.com for now. We can change both options later if we need to.

* Now we have to choose our server options and then click Next. A dialog box will appear. NetMeeting wants to know some things about us. This information will show up on the directory server that we chose in the preceding dialog box whenever we are logged on.
* We have to type the information we want to have listed, and click the Next button to continue. Before the Setup Wizard will let us continue to next step, we have to enter at least our first and last name and our email address in the dialog box.

  As with Chat it pays to be discreet and cautious when using

personal information in NetMeeting. Directory servers, like some chat servers, are cruised by some people to whom we may not want to reveal too much about us. In the, dialog that is open before us here, we can consider using a phony name and email address, just to preserve our privacy. :

* On the next screen we decide which category in the directory list us in: Personal Use, Business Use, or Adults Only Use. Choose the option that is appropriate for how we intend to use NetMeeting, and then click the No button to continue. A dialog box informing us that we are about to configure our sound card for NetMeeting opens.
* Click Next. A dialog box opens, listing our sound card that NetMeeting will use for recording that is sending our voice to others and playback that is playing others' voices to us.
* If the device listed is our sound card, we have to click Next. Otherwise, we can use the drop-down lists to select the correct devices, and then click Next. Another dialog box opens. Here we can tell NetMeeting what type of connection to the Internet we have.

4. NetMeeting

NetMeeting has a simple interface that is easy to figure out. In the main screen, the biggest section is the list of people logged on to the directory server that we chose. To its left are tabs that enable us to change what we see in the main view. Above the directory listing are the Category and Server drop down lists. Above those lists is the audio level adjustment toolbar. Finally, the tool bar and menus are at the top of the window, as with most Windows applications. We will have a glance through each of these areas, one at a time.

4.1 Directory Listing

When we first start NetMeeting, we see a list of people. These are the people in the category we selected and on the server we selected when we ran the NetMeeting Setup Wizard. Because we chose ils.microsoft.com as our server and put us in the For Personal Use category, we can see the list of everyone who made the same choices. In this list, we see eight columns:

* Email: The person's email address.
* Audio: A small yellow speaker in this column means that this person can talk to us.
* Video: A small gray video camera in this column means that this person can send live video over the Internet.
* First Name: The person's first name.
* Last Name: The person's last name.
* The city and the State: Exact location.
* Country: The country that this person is in.
* Comments: Comments, if any, that this person entered in the comments field.

We have to keep in mind that the person using NetMeeting enters all this information, other than that in the Audio and Video columns. Some people choose not to reveal their true identities or locations. We should not accept the information listed here as 100 percent accurate. By default, the listing is sorted by email address, but we can sort it by any information we like. To sort the entries by a different column, click the column header. For example, if we want the entries sorted by country, we can click the Country heading above the listings.

4.2 Category and Server Lists

Above the directory listing are the Category and Server drop down lists. These lists control who shows up in the directory listing. When we start NetMeeting, by default it logs us on to the server we chose in the NetMeeting Setup Wizard and displays the category we chose for our entry. If we want to see the entries on a different server, we have to just click the down arrow to the right of the Server drop down list and choose the server that we want to use. Similarly, to see the list of people in a different category than our self, we have to just choose the category we want to see from the Category drop down list. Setting the Category field to, say, Business, will let us see the list of people who have designated that their information is For Business Use.

4.3 Tabbed Call Windows

To the left of the directory listing is four tabs:

* Directory
* Speed Dial
* Current Call
* History

The Directory tab contains the Category and Server fields and the directory listing. The first time we start NetMeeting, the Directory tab is the one we see. Clicking the other tabs enables us to see different information pertaining to calls we can make, the current call, or calls we have received.

Current call is how NetMeeting describes the conference in which we are currently engaged. We can use the Speed Dial tab the same way we would use a Speed Dial button on our telephone. This tab keeps a short list of people we call regularly so we do not have to search for their names in the main directory listing. We can also have people who frequent different servers on the same Speed Dial list so we do not have to keep changing servers to find the person we want to call. After we have added someone to our Speedballs, NetMeeting starts on this screen instead of the Directory screen, because we are more likely to want to call the person whose number we have saved than someone we have not talked to before. The Current Call tab shows a list of the people in the current call. We will always find at least two names in this list if we are in a call, or none if we are not. Also, if we or another person is sending video, we will see it in the video boxes on the right side of the screen on this tab.

Finally, the History tab holds a list of all the calls we have received from other people. The caller's name, the date and time of the call, and whether we accepted, rejected, or ignored the call are all listed on this tab.

4.4. Audio Level Controls

Using the audio level controls, we can change the level of our voice and the voice of the person on the call. The audio level controls enable us to adjust the volume of our voice and the voice of the person we are talking to. We have to just drag the slider for either the microphone for our voice or the speaker the other person's voice to the left to lower the level or to the right to increase the volume. In most cases, we will not need to adjust the microphone level because the NetMeeting Setup Wizard should have set that automatically. We can change the speaker volume to suit our taste for each individual call, however. We can also use the check boxes on the audio level controls to temporarily mute our self or our conversation partner.

5. Answering Calls

To talk to someone on the Internet with NetMeeting, we have to call someone or someone has to call us. We will understand here how we can answer a call. When someone calls us, the first thing that happens is we hear the phone ring. It is not really the phone ringing. The sound is coming out of the speakers of our computer. Next, we will notice at the bottom right side of our screen a NetMeeting dialog box that says who is calling. It also has two buttons, Accept and Ignore. If we do not want to talk to the caller, we can click the Ignore button. To answer this call, click the Accept button. After we accept a call, the NetMeeting window switches automatically to the Current Call tab. Here we will see the name of the caller and our name, along with some information. To the right of each name are several columns as follows :

* Audio: A little yellow speaker in this column means that this person can talk over the Internet.
* Video: A small gray video camera in this column means that we should also see live video in the Remote Video frame on the right.
* Chat: A small white and blue rectangle in this column means that the chat window is open.

It will take a few seconds for NetMeeting to complete the connection between our computer and the caller's computer. After it has finished we can put our conference underway. When we finish talking to the caller, one side has to hang up. In NetMeeting, this means clicking the Hang Up button on the tool bar. We can hang up at any time, just like we can on the telephone.

6. Placing Call

Calling someone with NetMeeting is actually easier than using the white pages and a telephone. We do not need to remember or dial anyone's phone number. We just have to double click a name in the directory list. After we have connected with someone, we can have NetMeeting automatically save the listing for us. Let us now make a call. For that we have to complete the following steps:

* We have to prearrange the conference, via email or other means.
* In Net Meeting, we have to log on to the directory server where our partner is listed.
* Find our partner's name in the listing.
* Double click the name to make the call.

When our partner answers, NetMeeting switches over to the Current Call tab, and we may proceed with our conversation.

7. Advanced Techniques

Most people use their conferencing software for voice calls and nothing else. However, we may want to know about the three other forms of conferencing and collaboration enabled Internet conferencing software, videoconferencing, text chatting, and whiteboard drawing.

7.1 Videoconferencing

Few conferencing programs today support videoconferencing, and for good reason they does not work very well. Making live video looking good requires moving and processing tons of data quickly, and even the fastest modems and computers are not up to the task. The video image we will see of our conference partner and the one they will see of us will be small, fuzz and jerky, like watching a bad station on a TV in a thunderstorm. Besides not always looking good, videoconferencing often degrades the audio quality in the call. Our partner and we may find it preferable to shut off the video so that we can hear each other more clearly.

A program that supports setting up and using video in Net meeting is a breeze. All we really need to do is install a computer video camera on our computer. These cameras are usually designed to sit on our desk or mount on top of our monitor and they come in color and black and white models, and can cost less than Rs. 2500. After a video camera has been installed and configured in Windows, NetMeeting automatically senses and takes advantage of it. If our partner has a video camera installed, the image from that camera automatically appears in a small square on the right side of the Current Call tab; this is called the Remote Video Frame. If we have a camera installed, our partner also sees us.

7.2 Chatting

Chatting is using our conferencing software to conduct a conversation through a series of typed messages, just like using Chat. It is important to remember that a text conference is not the same thing as IRC Chat, which we will discuss elsewhere. A text chat in a conference program is private, between users of a conferencing program, while bona fide IRC sessions take place on a public chat server among users of any IRC program, There are several reasons for preferring a text chat over a voice chat. They are the following.

* One or more of the participants is speech or hearing impaired.
* One or more of the participants has insufficient hardware, or too slow a connection, to support a voice conference.
* Text conferences require no sound card, and work fine over slow connections.
* The conference requires the input of more than two participants. Voice and videoconferences are limited to parties of two; however, a text chat can include three, four, or more participants.

To hold a text chat in Conference or NetMeeting, we have to establish the call just as we do that for a voice conference. All participants then switch to text chat mode by clicking the Chat button. Everyone types whatever they have to say, and all statements typed by all participants appear in a scrolling display in the conference program. Each statement is labeled with the name of the speaker, so everybody knows who said what.

7.3 Whiteboard

We would have seen many meetings where the speaker feels he needs to present his idea visually, so he jump up and starts drawing on a blackboard, or the more modern office whiteboard. In NetMeeting and Conference, we can do the same thing. Click the Whiteboard button while in a call, and a separate window opens' the whiteboard; a space in which we can draw and jot notes. Whatever anyone in the call draws on the whiteboard appear to all participants, so partners can even add to one another's drawings. Using a whiteboard is just like using any drawing program. We select a drawing tool from a panel of buttons, and then use our mouse to draw lines or shapes in the drawing area. We also click a colored square to choose the color the tool produces, and even click a text that is the 'A' button among the drawing tools to type notes on the whiteboard.

Using a conferencing program through the Internet is unimaginably useful, as long as those with whom we like to converse or collaborate use the same program we do. This capability of the Internet has yet to grow up, but when it does, we all will be using it in one way or another.

8. Chatting Live

Chat puts us online in a live conversation with other Internet users, anywhere in the world. Lots of chat clients are available, but the Microsoft Chat, which we get free from Microsoft, does everything most chat clients do. Microsoft Chat also displays the chat in a cool way. So our discussion on Internet chatting will be mainly on Microsoft Chat, which is available either as part of the full installation of the Internet Explorer suite or separately. Netscape Communicator does not include a chat client. If we are using Communicator, we can download and use Microsoft Chat or any other chat client right alongside Communicator.

We have to be very cautious about one factor. Most of the

chat traffic on the Internet is dedicated to sex chats of various persuasions. Many sex chat rooms exist, and sex chat oriented chatters often wander into non-sex oriented rooms looking for new friends. If we have an aversion to such stuff, we have to tread very carefully in Chat. If we have a severe aversion to it, it is best to totally stay out of Chat. Regardless of our own interests, it is strongly advised against permitting children to use Chat, especially unsupervised.

When we are in an Internet chat, everything we type appears on the screens of everybody else participating in that particular chat. Thousands of different chats are underway at once, each in its own chat room. When we join a chat, we enter a room, and from then on we see only the conversation that is taking place in that room. A chat room is a space where a single conversation is taking place. In Internet chat parlance, a chat room is sometimes known as a channel. But now the word channel has a new and completely different meaning on the Internet, so it is best to stick with the term chat room.

We can see that in most chat rooms, the conversation is focused around a given subject area. In a historical chat room, participant's chat about history and that is the only topic participating historians will like to talk about. In a geology chat room, people generally talk about rocks and earthquakes.

When we are in a chat room, everything anyone else in the same room types appears on our screen. Each participant's statements are labeled with a nickname to identify who is talking. Those participating in a chat known as members choose their own nicknames and rarely share their real names. In a chat, we can be who ever we want us to be, and so can everyone else. Our nickname, which we choose, is how others know us in a chat. Our nickname appears on every statement we make, so everyone knows who is talking.

Other than IRC type chatting, there is another type: web chatting. A web chat takes place within a web page, and is generally hosted as a discussion related to the web page's topic. To join a web chat with our browser, we need the right plug in for the type of web chat underway. Several types of plug-ins exist, but most web chat is supported by the ichat plug-in. We will usually find a link for downloading ichat on any web page where a chat takes place. We can also get ichat directly from the source at www.ichat.com

8.1 Microsoft Chat

If we have to chat, we must have a program called a chat client. Internet Explorer's own chat client, included in the full installation is called Microsoft Chat, and it is an excellent program. If we do not have Microsoft Chat, but want it, we can download it from www.microsoft.com/ie/chat

To learn about or download other chat clients, we can apply the file searching techniques we have understood earlier for finding programs and files, or check out www.yahoo.com/ Computers_ and_Internet/Internet/Chat/IRC/Software/Clients_ and_Servers/

Here wherever we mention the word Chat; it means Microsoft Chat. Like any chat client, it lets us communicate with chat servers. We can view the list of chat rooms, join a chat room, read what everyone says in the chat room, and make our own contributions to the discussion. What is different about Chat is the way it displays the conversation. A chat takes place on a chat server; more properly called an IRC server. IRC stands for Internet Relay Chat, the full formal name for Chat. Just as we need a web browser to communicate with a web server, we need a program called a chat client to communicate with a chat server.

Like the chat client seen earlier which is really just Chat in its text mode, which we will discuss in detail later, most chat clients show the text of the conversation, a line at a time, and label each line with the speaker's nickname. Chat, however, displays the conversation like a comic strip, using little cartoon characters to represent members and showing the members words in cartoon word balloons. Microsoft think seems to think that this approach makes chatting feel more human, more fun. In its first versions, Chat was actually named Microsoft Comic Chat. The balloon is the little bubble we see in comics in which the words and thoughts of characters appear.

We should understand that chat servers support any IRC client, so most of us will end up chatting with out using Microsoft Chat.

Many use ordinary text IRC clients. So they see our statements labeled with our nickname but do not see our comic character. On our display, Chat converts all statements in a chat even those made by users of text only clients into comics. Other Chat users in the room with us appear as their chosen cartoon character. For users of other chat clients, Chat automatically assigns and shows an unused character.

8.2 Joining Chat

Now that we understand what chatting is all about, it is time to access a server and see how it functions. We will also perform some automatic configuration that Chat needs to open properly. Before opening Chat, we can be online or offline. If we are offline when we begin, Chat connects to the Internet automatically. Also, our browser need not be open for us to use Chat, although it will not hurt anything if it is open. We can start Chat and display the Chat Rooms List if we follow the steps listed below.

* First we have to open Chat. In Windows 98, we do so by choosing Programs > Microsoft Chat. The Connect dialog box opens.
* Then we have to select the Show All Available Chat Rooms option, and then click OK. After we go online, a list of all chat rooms available on the server appears. We are now connected to a chat server and ready to chat except that, as a new user, we have not yet selected a nickname and a comic character, as described below.

8.3 Choosing Identity

Before we can join in a chat, we must create a nickname. Because of Chat's unique presentation style, we must choose a comic character, too. In addition, we can select a background that appears behind the characters in each panel of the comic, as we see it on our screen. After we choose a nickname, character, and background, Chat remembers them for future sessions. We do not need to choose them again, unless we want to change them.

We can follow the steps listed below to choose our Chat character and get a nickname.

* First we have to choose View > Options. The Options dialog box appears.
* Choose the Personal Info tab if it is not already open.
* Click in the Nickname box and type a nickname for us. Our nickname should be one word, using no spaces or punctuation, and it should also be unusual to reduce the chances that another member has chosen the same nickname. If we attempt to select a name that some one has already taken, Chat prompts us to change our nickname before entering.

On the Personal Info tab, we can enter other information besides our nickname, such as our real name and email address. We have to think carefully before doing so. Whatever information we supply here can be seen by other members whose clients like Chat can display Member Profiles. If we want to keep our anonymity, we should enter only our nickname and nothing else.

* Click the Character tab. This is where we select our character.
* Select the character we want to play by clicking a name in the Character column

Note that someone else in the chat may use the same character as we use. Chatters can share characters, but not nicknames. The Preview column shows what the selected character looks like; what we will look like to other Chat users if we stick with that character. When choosing a character in the Character tab, we can click the faces in the emotion wheel beneath the character preview to see what the character will look like when we apply to it a given emotion when making a statement. We will learn about choosing emotions also.

* Click the background tab. This tab enables us to select from several cartoon backgrounds to use one for us.
* Choose a background. When we select an entry in the Background column, the background appears in the Preview column.
* Click OK.

8.4. Entering Chat Room

If we want to enter a chat room, we should select a room from the chat room list. Each server has its own list and the lists change often. The chat room list reappears after we finish selecting our identity. We can open the chat room list any time we are connected to the server by clicking the Chat Room list button on Chat's toolbar. In the list, the name of each room begins with a pound sign {#). The name of the room followed by the number of members currently in the room, and sometimes also by description of the conversation that usually takes places there. On most servers, there is a chat room specifically set up to practice chatting, called Newbies. We can give it a try.

We can follow the steps listed here to enter a Chat Room. We have to scroll down the chat room list which is found organized alphabetically until we see the #Newbies. Then we have to double click #Newbies. The Chat window opens, and we are in the chat. We can see that the Chat window is broken up into five sections, or panes covered clockwise from upper left. The biggest pane is the viewing pane, where we see the chat session as it progresses. The small pane in the upper right is the member list pane, which lists all members in the current chat room. The pane showing our character is the self-view pane, which reminds us of who we are. The ring of faces is the emotion wheel, from which we can select our character's facial expression. The small text box at the bottom of the window is the compose pane, where we type our statements. Instead of double-clicking the chat room name, we can click it once to select it, and then click the Go To button in the chat room list.

When we first arrive in a room, we may not see any comic panels right away. The server shows us only what is been said since we entered the room. After we enter, statements begin appearing, one by one, as members make them. We can switch Chat into a text mode so that it skips the comic characters and displays the conversation as scrolling series of text messages, like any other IRC client. If the room is crowded with five or more members, we may prefer chatting in text mod. If we want to switch to text mode, choose View > Plain Text. To switch back from text mode to comics, choose View > Comic Strip. We can switch back and forth at any time, even in the middle of a conversation.

8.5. Contributing to Chat

Now that we are in a room, we can just listen to the conversation, or we can contribute to it by sending our statements for all others to see. Note that we are not obligated to add anything to the conversation. In fact, just lurking in a chat room is a great way to learn more about chats before jumping into it.

When we contribute, we can choose the style of the comic word balloon in which our words will appear to us and to other Chat users. We choose the style of the word balloon by clicking a button next to the compose pane, the text box at the bottom of the Chat window in which we type all our statements. For example, for a particular statement, we can choose a think balloon so the words appear in the balloon style generally used in comics to represent what the character is thinking. We have to keep in mind that while we are typing and editing our statements, no one sees them but we only could see them. A statement is sent to the chat only when we press Enter. That gives us a chance to choose our words carefully and correct typing errors before committing our statement to the chat. When we want to add statements to a chat, we can do that by following the steps given below.

* First we will enter a chat room that interests us and follow the conversation until we understand what is being talked about.
* When we are ready to contribute, we can begin typing. Anything we type while in a chat room appears automatically in the compose pane, the text box at the bottom of the Chat window. As we type, we can use the Backspace, Delete, Insert, and arrow keys to edit our statement and correct mistakes. When wording on a statement, we have to keep in mind that Chat automatically gives our character certain gestures based on words in the statement. Also, always we have to observe the rules of netiquette when contributing; that is no flames, no sarcasm, and so on. We have to be prepared, however,

because a chat room is the place we will see others breach netiquette the most.

* When our statement is worded the way we want, we have to press Enter. After a few moments, our statement appears as part of the scrolling conversation displayed in the chat window. It appears at the same spot in the list in the display of everyone else in the room. Those in the room using regular chat clients see our statement labeled with our nickname, so they know we said it. Those in the room using Microsoft Chat see our chosen comic character speaking the words in a say balloon, the type that surrounds words that comic characters say aloud. The say balloon is the default balloon style the one Chat uses automatically when we do not select a different balloon style.
* We can type a statement that is more a thought than a statement and opinion perhaps. Before pressing Enter to submit the statement, we have to click the Think button which is second from the left in the compose pane. Then press Enter. Chat users see our character thinking the words in a thought balloon, the type that surrounds the thoughts of comic characters.
* Think of a statement our character might whisper, rather than say aloud. Type the statement, click the Whisper button, which is third one from the left, and then press Enter. Chat users see our character whispering the words in the type of balloon that surrounds the whispers of comic characters.

8.7 Showing Emotions

The emotion wheel in the lower left corner of the Chat window lets us change the expression of our character's face when making a statement. Because some members in the room may not be using Chat and therefore cannot see expressions, we have to remember that our words alone carry our meaning. When we want to change our character's expression, we can do that by using this method. First we will get into a chat. Then we can type a statement, but we should be careful not to press Enter. Then we have to select a face from the emotion wheel. The character in the self-view pane changes to show how our character will appear if we commit to using the selected expression. As long as we do not press Enter, we can choose a different expression until we find one we like. To choose our character's normal, neutral expression, we can click the + at the center of the emotion wheel. When the self-view pane appears the way we want it to, we have to press Enter to submit our statement.

8.8 Gesturing

If we watch a chat for a while, we will notice that the characters are not static. They change body position and gestures, panel to panel. The gesturing is selected automatically by Chat based on words we use in our statements. For example, if a statement contains the wo sounding expression, when speaking that statement our character will appear to point to him or her. We can use other members' nicknames to control to whom the gesture is made. For example if we say "Hi," our character appears to wave to the group. If we say "Hi, Nair," our character appears to wave at the member using the nickname Nair. Some gestures are based on words used to begin a statement and others are based on words within the statement. When a statement begins with a gesture word, Chat applies the gesture for the beginning word. Gestures used automatically by Chat characters are the following.

Statement Begins With	*Character's Action*
I	Points to itself
You	Points to another member
Hello or Hi	Waves
Bye	Waves
Welcome	Waves
Howdy	Waves
are you	Points to another member
will you	Points to another member
did you	Points to another member
aren't you	Points to another member
don't you	Points to another member
I am	Points to itself
I will	Points to itself

6.9 Switching Rooms

Sometimes we may find that not much is going on in a chat room we enter, or that the conversation has taken a turn we do not care to follow. At such times, all we have to do is leave the room we are in and enter a different one. When we leave the room, a message appears in the chat to inform everybody that we are gone. We cannot "sneak out" without anybody knowing, as we can in life when a conversation turns beyond one, which we can tolerate.

We can switch to another room. That can be done by this method. While in a room, we have to click the Leave Room button on Chat's toolbar. Click the Enter Room button on the toolbar to open a dialog box that prompts for a password. Some chat rooms are set up for private conversations; to enter, we must type a password. Most chats are public, however, so we generally ignore the password box. Then we have to type the name of the room. Be sure to include the pound sign (#) at the beginning of the room name, as in #Newbies. After that we have to Click OK. If we do not know the name of the room we want to go to, click the Chat Room List button on Chat's toolbar to open the chat room list, and then choose a room from the list.

For any one Chat is informative and entertaining, as long as we stay among those whose reasons for chatting are the same as ours. But chat is an entertaining place to be enjoyed with caution. If we are careful, we can have safe, interactive fun and information there and if we are not results are unpleasant to think of.

9. Making the Web Deliver Pages

Earlier if we want to get information from the Internet we go online, reach the concerned site and get it. Each time we want to catch up with the latest information, we have to follow the same procedure. To make this procedure easy and unrepetitive, channels, also known as Net Casting, has come into existence. When we want to stay abreast of a particular kind of information, the information should be delivered to us, automatically, whenever there is news. If we use Navigator or Internet Explorer we can use the techniques explained here to set up channels to bring the web to us. Depending on how we use a channel, all of a channel's new content can automatically be downloaded to our computer so that we can, read it offline, any time when it is convenient to us. Unlike whatever we discussed earlier what we are going to experiment here will require either Microsoft's Internet Explorer or Netscape's Navigator (Communicator) for all practical purposes, only these two browsers support channel technology. If we want to use other browsers, service called PointCast Network is to be used to supply to them the effect of channels.

9.1 Channels in Internet Explorer

If channels catch on, we will not need to go looking for them. We will come across them. For example, when we first visit a web page about a topic that interests us, we may discover the buttons that enable us to subscribe to that page as a channel. Because channels are new, Microsoft is trying to help us find and use them in two ways. Microsoft has created the Active Channel Guide, a channel for finding other channels. The Active Channel Guide contains links for subscribing to many of the channels currently available online.

If we choose to install the web-integrated desktop or Active Desktop, when installing Internet Explorer, a button bar called the Channel bar appears on our desktop. As we begin subscribing to channels, it will show those we have signed up for. We have to note that the initial group of buttons on the Channel bar contains shortcuts to web pages where we can subscribe to channels. As we subscribe to these and other channels, new buttons will appear on the bar. We can delete Microsoft's shortcuts or any other button from the bar by right clicking the button and choosing Delete from the pop up menu that appears.

In the Channel bar, there is a button labeled Active Channel Guide. We can click it, and the Active channel Guide will open, offering links to channels and general information about channels. We can also open the Active Channel Guide from within Internet Explorer by clicking the Channels button on the toolbar, which opens a list of channels in the Explorer panel on the left side of the window. At the top of the list is a link to the Channel Guide.

Internet Explorer looks a little different when we view the channel Guide. The toolbars look smaller and simpler, and the menu bar is gone. This is Explorer's full screen view, which kicks in automatically when we open most cannels. We can switch back and forth between full screen and regular view by clicking the full screen button on the toolbar. Besides finding channels in the Channel Guide, we can also visit the Active Desktop Gallery find new active desktop items. To open the Active Desktop Gallery, we have to go to www.microsoft.com/ie/ie40/gallery

An active desktop item is a special kind of channel that displays not in the browser, but in its own little box or window right on our desktop. Desktop items are used most often to display a little box showing regularly updated weather reports, sports scores, financial news etc.

Figure 17.3

9.2 Subscribing to Channels

We can subscribe to a channel by first navigating to a channel or a web page that contains a link for subscribing to the channel, such as Microsoft's Channel Guide. Wherever we have the option to subscribe to a channel, we will see a buttons labeled; Add Active Channel: for a regular, full screen channel and Add to Active Desktop: for a desktop item. Some pages offer both buttons; so that we can choose the way we want the channel content to be displayed on our computer. Click the button, and the Add Channel dialog box opens; just we have to follow its prompts to complete the subscription. We will see below how to use that dialog box to subscribe to the National Geographic Connection. Different channels may allow different subscription options, so the following dialog boxes and steps may not apply exactly for every channel we wish to subscribe to. However the general idea is always the same.

For subscribing to a channel in Internet Explorer, we can follow the steps listed here. On the Channel bar or in the Channel list in the Explorer bar, click the button labeled Lifestyle & Travel. IE opens in full screen view, and a list of Lifestyle & Travel channels appears. We can click National Geographic Connection to go to the channel. Wait for the page to finish downloading, which takes a while due to the multimedia content, animation and music. We should keep our speakers on. After the page has fully arrived, we can click the button labeled Add Active Channel. The Modify Channel Usage dialog box opens. The dialog box asks "Do you want to subscribe to this channel?" and offers three subscription options listed below.

* *No, Just Keep It in My Channel Bar*: A button for this channel is added to or kept in our Channel bar so that we can easily visit the channel online at any time. We are not subscribed to it, however.
* *Yes, but Only Tell Me When Updates Occur*: When we update channels we will be notified when this channel has new content, but the new content will not be downloaded automatically. We will visit the channel online to see the new content.

* *Yes, Notify Me of Updates and Download the Channel for online Viewing*: When we update channels, we will be notified when this channel has new content and that content will automatically be downloaded to our computer so that we can view it anytime, even offline.

From the above we have to choose a subscription option, and click OK to finish subscribing. Alternatively, we can customize the subscription by clicking the Customize button. The Customize button opens the Subscription Wizard, which leads us through a few simple dialog boxes on which we can choose when new content should be downloaded and whether we should be notified by email when new content is available. After we subscribe to a channel, a button for it appears in the Channel bar, and an item for it appears in the Channels folder of our Favorites menu. We can use it to navigate to that channel at any time we want to.

9.3 Subscribing to Web Pages

Besides subscribing to a channel, we can subscribe to any web page. Channel and web page are entirely different even if they seem similar. A channel is smart. It has been specially designed to deliver to us only the new information, and only under certain conditions. It knows what we need to know, and when to tell us. A web page is not smart, so when we subscribe to a web page, the whole page is downloaded to our computer every time there is news, even if only a small part of the page has changed, or that change does not really amount to "news." Still, the overall effect is a lot like a channel.

To subscribe to a web page, we go to the page and choose Favorites Add to Favorites just as we would to add the page to our Favorites list. The Add Favorite dialog box offers three of the following options much like those for a channel.

* No, Just Add the Page to My Favorites: This option creates a regular Favorite.
* Yes, but Only Tell Me When Updates Occur: When we update channels, we will be notified when this web page has new content.

* Yes, Notify Me of Updates and Download the Page for Offline Viewing: When we update channels, if this page has any new content, the page will be downloaded so that we can read it offline at any time convenient to us.

After we choose an option from those listed above, the page is added to our Favorites list. If we choose the second or third options, the page is updated along with our channels when we update channels.

9.4 Updating Channel Content

When and how channel content is updated depends on the choice we make for the Schedule option when subscribing. By default, most channels are updated automatically, according to a schedule set by the channel's publisher. We can use the Subscription Wizard to choose a different schedule. On the final dialog box of the Subscription Wizard we will see a drop down list from which we can choose one of several predefined scheduling options. Alternatively, we can select the Manual option at the bottom of the dialog box to prevent all automatic updates; and update only when we choose to do that.

After subscribing, we can change the schedule and other options for a subscription from the Subscriptions list. We have to open the list from within Internet Explorer by choosing Favorites > Manage Subscriptions. Point to the channel whose subscription options we want to change, and wait until the icon is selected. Then click the Properties button to open a dialog box on which we can change any of the options for that subscription.

If we choose the Manual option, we can update channels manually in a variety of ways. From the Internet Explorer menu bar, we can update all channels at once by choosing Favorites > Update All Subscriptions. Or from the Windows Start menu, we can update all channels at once by choosing Settings > Active Desktop > Update Now. After a channel has been updated regardless of how or when it was updated we may disconnect from the Internet and read the channel content at our leisure, offline that is without connecting to the Internet.

9.5 Removing Channels and Subscriptions

After adding a lot of channels, items, and subscribed web pages we will be forced to decide on separating them for convenience and removing some of them. We can delete channel and web page subscriptions from the subscriptions list. But desktop items do not show up on the subscriptions list, so we cannot remove them from there. Instead, we can delete them from the Web tab of the Display Properties dialog box. If we ever delete a channel, a web page subscription, or a desktop item, and decide later that we want it back, we have to subscribe it again as we did the first time.

If we want to unsubscribe to a channel or web page subscription, we have to use the Subscriptions list. In Internet Explorer, we have to choose Favorites > Manage Subscriptions. The Subscriptions list appears. To delete a subscription, we have to click it once in the list to highlight it, and then press the Delete key. A warning appears, cautioning us that we are about to delete the channel or web page subscription permanently. It is a normal warning given by the windows. We can always re subscribe later. Click Yes to delete the subscription. We do not have to actually delete a desktop item to get it off our desktop. We can simply disable it, which clears it from our desktop and prevents its further updates. If we want to restore it later, we can re enable it and save the difficulties for re subscribing to it.

We can remove a desktop item by doing this. We have to Right click the desktop and choose Properties from the content menu. The Windows Display Properties dialog box opens. In that choose the Web tab. The Web tab lists all items on our desktop. In it click the item to select it. To disable the item, we can click its check box to remove the check mark. If and when we want to restore the item, simply return to the Web tab and check the check box. To delete it, click the Delete button. Clicking the Web tab's New button opens the Active Desktop Gallery so that we can find and subscribe to a new desktop item.

9.6 Navigator Net Caster

The channels capabilities in Navigator's Net Caster are similar in many ways to Internet Explorer's channels, as are the basic steps for using them. However a few important differences exist. They are the following

* Net Caster is an optional component of Navigator. Today, it is included in most copies, but if we have an early release of Navigator or Communicator, we may not have Net Caster. To learn how to download and install it, we have to click the Net Caster button on the toolbar, or choose Help > Software Updates in Navigator.
* Net Caster's desktop items are called WebTop. Subscribing to a WebTop channel or one that displays in the browser window is identical. The channel generally decides itself whether it belongs on the desktop.
* Net Caster has its own family of channels; it is not compatible with channels designed for Internet Explorer. However, we can use Net Caster to schedule downloads of ordinary web pages, just as we can with Internet Explorer. We may use that capability to subscribe to web pages that contain Internet Explorer channels, even though Net Caster as dumb web pages, not smart channels will handle them.

When Net Caster is installed, a tab labeled Net Caster appears on the right side of the Navigator window. We have to click it and Net Caster opens, showing its Channel Finder, which is a directory of available channels and a toolbar for subscribing. We simply scroll through the list, pick a channel we want, and then click the Add button on the toolbar to subscribe. A channel properties window opens, on which we can choose options for the channel, such as an update schedule:

To view content for channels we have subscribed to, we can click the Net Caster tab and choose My Channels, then choose one of our channels from the list. To manually update a channel, we have to right click it in the My Channels list, then choose Smart Update. To unsubscribe from a channel, we have to right click it in the My Channels list, then choose Delete.

11

Listserv for Information Dissemination

Discussion facilities provided by the Internet attracts a lot of people to the net. They are of two types and both are known as discussion groups. They differ only in the medium on which the discussion takes place. In the type of discussion group we deal in this chapter, which is called listserv, we read the discussion in email messages we receive, and contribute to the discussion by sending email. The listserv are also known by other names like mailing lists, list processors, and mail reflectors. Listserv and mailing lists are the popular terms and here also both mean the same. In the type of discussion group called the newsgroups discussed elsewhere in this book, we read messages on, and send messages to, a news server. Regardless of the discussion method we use, discussion groups are a great way to keep up with news about any imaginable topic, and to engage in conversation and debate with others online who share their experiences, knowledge and information. We already know most of what we need to know to use them. We know how to send and receive email. All that is required to learn is where and how to find the mailing lists that is of interest, how to sign up, and how to quit a mailing list if we lose interest in it. Here we will discuss those aspects in Windows and Unix environment.

1. Working of Listserv

For a listserv or mailing list to work, someone has to handle its management and administration. Mostly that work is signing up new members and removing members who have asked to be removed. In a few listservs, a real person handles the administration task. Most listservs, however, are managed not by a person, but by a listserv program. Sometimes, the mailing lists managed by people are called manual mailing lists, to distinguish them from the lists automated by listservs. A listserv is a program that automatically manages a mailing list. Actually, several programs are available that manage mailing lists, including Listserv, List proc, and Majordomo. But the term listserv is used generically to refer to all such programs, and often to the lists they manage, as well.

The listserv functions like this. There will be one address to which we can send mail. This mail will in turn be distributed to every one whose address appears on the mailing list. If we want to get our address included in a specific list we can send a message to the listserv, which manages that list. It makes us a subscriber to that list. Then our messages will be mailed to all those who subscribe to that list.

Thousands of listservs are there on the Internet. Topics discussed on a list can be anything about which a group of people might want to talk. For example, there are listservs on Albert Einstein's writings, information on film actors, novelists, villages, tourist resorts various types of music, ecology and the biosphere, World War II, and medicinal and aromatic plants, and the like. Some lists are designed for very practical discussions, others are more scholarly, and some are just plain and simple.

2. Uses of Listserv

We can use listserv for discussion. It can also be used as a resource for getting answers to our questions. We can post a message asking for a particular piece of information, and within a few hours, other subscribers will provide answers. Some lists are used to distribute electronic journals. An electronic journal is much like a print journal. But is not in print format. It will come to our e-mail address in electronic format. We can subscribe to receive an electronic journal in the same way in which we subscribe to a listserv.

Listservs are powerful communication tools. They can put us in contact with others who have interests similar to that of us even if they are thousands of miles away. As librarians we would like to find listservs pertaining to libraries or the subjects on which library users work. Using listservs we can help our users find required sources of information and people specialising on that top.

3. Finding Listserv of Interest

Many listserv addresses are on BITNET, as listservs originated on the BITNET, which is a network, founded in 1981 to link universities and other academic institutions that didn't at that time have ARPA, NFSNET or other network access. By 1988 there were over 1,500 nodes in the network, up from 65 in 1983. BITNET uses a different network and transmission protocol and relies heavily on e-mail to move information back and forth whereas TCP/IP networks can support non-mail applications such as FTP and Gopher. The listserv software was originally written for BITNET sites and still supports a large user base. BINET addresses do not end in standard Internet geographical or administrative domain names, such as in, aus, edu, gov, com, and net. Usually we need to send mail to a BITNET address from the Internet by adding.bitnet at the end of the BITNET address. For example, if the address is epp-l@buacca, then we address it to epp-l@bucca.bitnet. If our host computer does not understand the use of .bitnet, we must use the format listserv%host.bitnet@<an.interbit. gateway>. The same applies to the mailing addresses of the lists themselves.

Like all other Internet resources, there are different categories of listservs to satisfy various interest groups. The first step in using listserv is finding one that interests us. When visiting web pages devoted to our favorite topics, we will often see mention of related mailing lists, along with the email address required for signing up which is the subscription address. We may also visit any of several web pages that help us find mailing lists related to a particular subject. A good first stop is Find Mail (www.findmail. com), a search tool dedicated to helping people find and use mailing lists. We can browse through FindMail's categories to find a list, or use its search engine to find lists related to a search term we enter. Besides FindMail, other good places to find mailing lists and instructions for using them include the list of Publicly Accessible

Listservs at www.neosoft.com/internet/pam/, Liszt, a searchable database of lists and instructions at www.liszt.com and Yahoo!s directory at www.yahoo.com/ Computers_and_Internet /Internet/ Mailing_Lists/

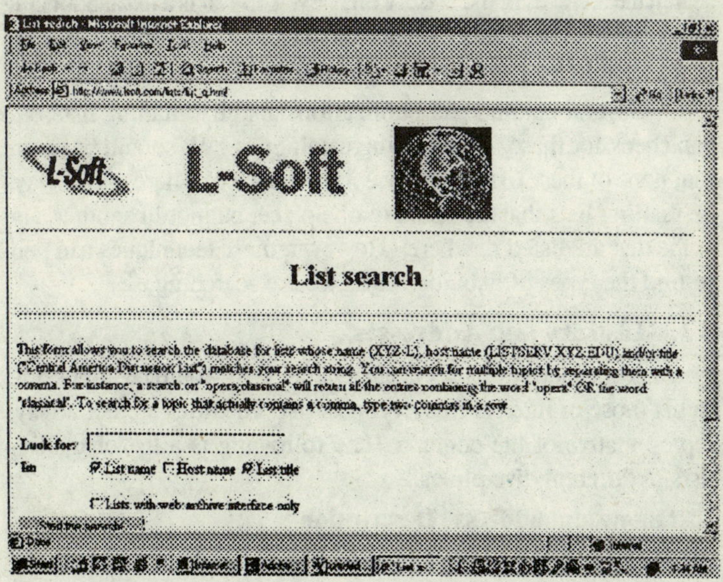

Search Mechanism for lists

4. List of Lists

If we need a list of all lists, we can obtain the global list from a listserv, using its electronic search and retrieval capability. To get a complete list, we can send the message; list global. The file we receive in return will be quite large. We will probably prefer to search the global list for discussion groups on a particular subject by adding the option /<topic> where <topic> is one or more words describing the subject in which we are interested. Let's say that we are interested in finding listservs that deal with library science. Then we can send an email to a listserv address. Leave the subject line blank, with the body of the message as : list global/ library science

Each line in the global list will contain a list's name, the BITNET address of the list, and a brief description of the topics discussed in that list. Usually those lists will be very long. An easier way is to search the list; using Gopher, which will be discussed afterwards. Another approach that can yield useful results is to search the archives of the listserv on NEW-LIST. It is a list announcing the creation of new lists. We may also want to subscribe to this list if we want to keep abreast of lists as they become available.

Several commercial publications also list mailing lists. We can check for these in publishing catalogues. We should be aware that none of these lists are truly comprehensive. There may always be mailing lists that are listed in one place, but not in another, and some that are listed nowhere. However, these techniques can help to find the types of lists for which we are searching.

4.1. Listserv and Addresses

Thousands of listservs are available. It would be impossible to list those of interest to everyone. Also, the titles are not always representative of the content. The following is a list of mailing lists in different disciplines.

List name and address	Description
epp-l@buacca	Albert Einstein
anthro-l@ubvm	Anthropology Research Technique
arch-l@dgogwdgi	Archaeology-Archaeology Software
caah@pucc	Art History-Architectural History
chemic-l@taunivm	Chemistry Research
china@pucc	China-Chinese Culture
cinema-l@auvm	Cinema-Film Criticism
econed-l@utdallas	Economics-Business
burg-cen@hearn	Fluid Mechanics
folklore@tamvmi	Folklore-Cross Cultural Studies
history@uwavm	History
hound@beloit.edu	Holmes, Sherlock Literature
chug-l@brownvm	Humanities and Computers

jpinfo-l@jpnsutoo	Japan-Japanese Culture
mclr-l@msu	Latin American Studies
ilas-net@technion	Linear Algebra
classm-l@brownvm	Music-Classical Music-Research
enord-l@ubvm	Philosophy
photo-l@buacca	Photography
photosyn@net.bio.net	Photosynthesis
physics@miamiu	Physics
play-1@hg.uleth.ca	Play-Games-Sport
politics@ucfivm	Politics
pmc-list@ncsuvm	Post modern Culture-Post modern Literature
cchd-l@uncvmi	Psychology-Human Development
religion@harvarda	Religious Studies
finino@utoronto	Renaissance Studies - Reformation Studies
russia@arizvmi	Russia-Russian Culture
superguy@ucfivm	Superheroes-Science Fiction Literature

4.2 Listserv and List

We have to make the distinction between; when we send a message to the listserv which is the program managing things like subscription requests and the list which will distribute the message to the subscribers. The listserv address is where we can send commands to subscribe and unsubscribe. The list address is where we send messages that we wish to distribute to everyone on the list.

One major listserv mistake about which we are to be care full is mixing up the list address with the management address, and vice versa. If we accidentally send our list contributions to the management address, the others on the list will not see them. If we send management commands to the list address, those commands will not be carried out. Worse, the message containing those commands shows up in the mailing list of everyone in the list, which will not win us any friends. We should never forget that contributions to the discussion go to the list address, commands for managing our subscription go to that other address; subscription, management or whatever it is called, which is usually the same one we used to subscribe.

5. Subscribing to a List

To use any listserv, we need to know two different email addresses; the address of the person, or listserv program, that manages the list which might be called the management or subscription address; and the list address, an email address to which we send all our contributions to the list and the Comments or questions we want all others in the list to see.

5.1 Composing the Subscription Message

When we are ready to sign up, we should send a simple email message containing the command required to subscribe to the subscription address. But the command differs from list to list. Most references to mailing lists including those we will turn up in the directories described earlier include subscription instructions. Those instructions typically tell us the command we must send, and also where in the email message in the Subject line or the message body we must type that command. Command instructions use a syntax diagram to tell us what to type. Even manually managed lists generally require a particular command syntax, although they are more forgiving of command mistakes than listservs are. A syntax diagram shows what we must type to properly phrase a command to control a computer program, such as a listserv. In a syntax diagram, the exact words we must type are shown in normal type, and any parts of the command we must add are surrounded by brackets or shown in italics. For example, to phrase the command indicated by the syntax diagram subscribe last name first name or subscribe [last name] [first name]

We have to type

subscribe Raman Nair

Notice that we have to replace any portions in italics or brackets with the information indicated, and that we do not have to type the brackets. To subscribe to a list, we have to read the instructions to find the syntax diagram for subscribing, the part of the message in which to type the command either the Subject line or body and the subscription address. As an excersize we can compose an email message containing only the command indicated by the instructions, and send it to the subscription address.

When composing our message, we should not type anything the instructions do not ask for. If the instructions tell us to put the command in the Subject line, leave the message body blank. If the command belongs in the message body, leave the Subject line blank, and put nothing but the command in the body. Many lists do not care whether we follow this rule, but because we cannot predict which lists do care; it is best to always follow the rule. Because many listservs manage more than one list, the subscription command syntax often includes the name of the list, so the listserv knows which list we are subscribing to; for example: subscribe list name first name last name

5.2 Welcome Message

Immediately after we send our subscription message, we will receive a reply message from the list. A listserv may reply within a minute or two. After sending a subscription message to a listserv we can stay online and be there. Some listservs and manual lists may take a day or more to reply, so we have to be patient, and we should not resend the subscription message if we do not get an immediate reply. If we did not phrase our subscription message properly, the reply reiterates the subscription command syntax and usually includes instructions. We must compose and send another subscription message, carefully following any instructions in the reply. After we subscribe successfully, we will receive a welcome message.

We should read and save the welcome message because it contains the instructions for unsubscribe to, or quitting, the mailing lists if we choose to do so later. The welcome message also contains a lot of valuable information, particularly a syntax diagram for phrasing the command to unsubscribe. If and when we decide that we no longer want to receive messages from the list, we will need to send this command to the subscription address. It also contains the list address to which we must send all our contributions and the management address, which is usually the same as the subscription address, but not always. Then it will give the syntax for other commands we may use to manage the way messages come to us. For example, many lists let us send a command to temporarily stop sending us messages if we go on vacation or want messages paused for any other reason. The message is also a document to refer any other rules or policies all members of the list are required to observe. These typically include the basic rules of netiquette.

Sometimes the Welcome message includes instructions to send a reply to the Welcome, to confirm our subscription. In such cases, we are not officially subscribed until we send a reply as instructed. Always we have to read and save the Welcome message, so that we can refer to it when we need to know a command or policy or want to unsubscribe. If our email program lets us organize our messages in folders, create a special folder for Welcome messages, so that they are easy to find and we do not accidentally delete them when cleaning up our Inbox. We may also want to print the Welcome message and file it.

Shortly after we receive the Welcome message and reply to it, if so instructed, we will begin receiving email messages from the list. How many and how often depends on the list, but it is not unusual to receive a dozen or more messages per day. Read anything that looks interesting; ignore or delete the rest. Some listservs are purely informational. Listservs are designed not as a discussion forum, but to keep us abreast of news and developments in a particular field or organization. Usually, such lists do not have list addresses to which we can contribute. It's a one way of conversation. We just subscribe, and then read whatever they send us.

5.3 Sample Subscription

For understanding the method let us subscribe to a list. The following steps will enable us to subscribe to the Ballroom list, which is devoted to ballroom and swing dancing. But if we have already found the address of another list we are interested to subscribe that list can be used.

* At first in our email program, we have to start a new message.
* In the To line, put the Ballroom list subscription address: listserv@mitvma.mit.edu
* The instructions for the Ballroom list say that the command must be typed in the message body. So leave the Subject line blank, and skip to the body.
* The syntax of the subscription command for this list is 'subscribe ballroom your name'. We have to enter the command in the message body, replacing the words your name with our actual name. The command does not say whether the name should be last name first or vice versa. So it doesn't matter which we use.
* Then we can Send the message. After a few minutes, we can check our email. We will probably have received a welcome message, prompting us to reply if we really want to subscribe.
* To start receiving messages about ballroom dancing reply to the message as instructed. To avoid subscribing, do not reply. The welcome message expires in a period specified in that message. Unless we respond to it before that we will not be included in the mailing list.

6. Contributing to Listserv

We are not required to contribute to a listserv. Many people simply read and enjoy the messages they receive, and never add their own comments or questions. If we do feel inspired to contribute, we can send a message to the list address. If the contribution is related to a previous message, we can use our email program's Reply feature to reply to the group, and include in the reply a quote of any portion of the original message that is relevant to our comment or question. When using Reply to send a message to a listserv, we have to always double check the To line in our message to be sure that it shows the correct list address.

7. Expressions with Smileys and Shorthand

Over the years, a system of symbols and shorthand has developed to enable folks to be more expressive in their messages.

They are smileys and shorthand. We will see both used online often, in discussion groups and in email. Although we will see here smileys and shorthand next, that is mainly to help us understand them in messages we receive; except for the occasional, simple smiley face, using these in our contributions to discussion groups is not advisable. There are many newcomers online today who do not know smiley or shorthand. So if we use these, many of our readers will not understand us. We have to try to put all our meaning in our words, so that everybody gets the message.

7.1 Smileys

Smileys are used to communicate the tone of a message, to add an emotional inflection. In fact, smileys are sometimes called emotions or emotional icons. They are little pictures, usually of faces, that are built out of text characters. To see the picture, we tilt our head to the left. For example, tilt our head to the left or tilt this book to the right while looking at the following smiley, which is made up of three characters: a colon, a dash, and a close parenthesis:

:.)Looks like a little smiling face. Folks follow a statement with this smiley to indicate that the statement is a joke, or is made facetiously; for example: Just for that, I'm leaving you everything in my will. :-). Many different smileys exist, some so obscure that only the real net jocks use or understand them. We are likely only to see the basics, including the basic smile shown earlier, and also these:

:-(	Frown
;-)	Wink
:-0	Surprise
8-)	Smile with glasses or bug eyed
:-D	Laughing

People also nose from their smileys. For example: :) ;) ;0

7.2 Shorthand

Shorthand abbreviations are used to carry a common phrase efficiently, to save space and typing. Some of these are commonly used offline, everyday, such as ASAP (As Soon As Possible). Another shorthand expression used commonly online is IMO (In My Opinion) and its cousin, IMHO (In My Humble Opinion). For example: The Godfather is the greatest film of the '70s, IMHO. Other popular shorthand expressions include

BTW	By The Way
B4	Before
FWIW	For What It's worth
IBTD	I Beg To Differ
IOW	In Other Words
LOL	Laughing Out Loud (generally used to declare that a statement is laughable)
OTOH	On The Other Hand
ROTFL	Rolling On The Floor Laughing generally used to declare that a statement is extremely laughable

8. Listserv Through Unix

As in Windows environment we need to know the name of the list; the address of the listserv that manages the list; instructions on how to subscribe as well as how to unsubscribe to a list or stop subscription.

To subscribe to a list, we have to send a mail message to the listserv address with the message: subscribe<listname> <our name> where <listname> is the name of the list and <our name> is really our name. That is, if our name is Gayathri Devi type Gayathri Devi. There is no need to enter the subject line.

Let us subscribe to the list on Sherlok Holmes Literature. Its address is hound@beloit.edu. For example, if our name is Gayathri we should send the following e-mail.

```
to:     hound@beloit.edu
cc:
subject:
subscribe:  hound Gayathri
```

We will receive a message back from the listserv confirming that we are subscribed and giving us additional information about the list. This includes information about how to unsubscribe to the list. From this point on, we will receive any mail that anyone sends to hound@beloit.edu. If we send this message to the list address, hound@beloit.edu everyone subscribed to the list will receive a copy of the message. Sometimes a list will not send a copy of the message to the person who posted it. A list will only be sending us a copy of messages that we posted if our mail is set to "ACK" nowledge. Like this if we want to subscribe to TOURBUS which is a free Internet Magazine giving road maps and information on places of interest we can send to listserv @ listserv.aql.com the message subscribe tourbus. aql. Some lists are very busy, with many messages being posted in a short period of time. It is easy for our mailbox to become full, very fast! If we do not or cannot check our mail on a regular basis, we should not subscribe to a list. If our mailbox becomes overstuffed, our local system administrator will go into problem. To unsubscribe from a list, we can send an e-mail message to the listserv address with the message: unsubscribe <listname> where <listname> is the name of the list from which we wish to unsubscribe to. To unsubscribe from a list we have to send the message to the listserv, not to the list address.

8.1. Listserv Commands

The following is a list of some commands that most listservs will accept. These commands must be sent to the listserv @ address!

subscribe<listname> <our name>	subscribes us to the list
unsubscribe <listname>	unsubscribes us from the list
review <listname>	sends us a list of all the people who are subscribed to the list
index <listname>	sends back the names of any files that are archieved on the list.
info <listname>	an information file about the listserve will be sent to us which can be useful in determining what commands and mail options are valid.

get <listname>	gets a file that is archived on the listserv and e-mails it to us.
set <listname> nomail	temporarily stops mail from the list or set <listname> mail postpones stops mail
set <listname> mail	restarts mail after temporarily stopping mail or set <listname> mail ack restores mail.
set <listname> repro	has the listserv send us a copy of whatever we post to the list.

After we have subscribed to a list we can begin posting messages to it. Some lists allow anyone to post, others will accept postings only from subscribers, and still others are moderated, meaning that there is a moderator who reads all incoming postings to make sure they are appropriate for the list. He or she decides which messages are to be send to all.

8.2 Archival Search

Unless we happened to be reading the list when a topic was brought up, we may miss it. Sometimes it will be referred to a previous discussion on the list when we ask a question. We may be wondering how to get hold of past postings to the list. Many BITNET listservs and UNIX listprocs maintain archivs of all list correspondence, which can be searched using e-mail. If we are dealing with a BITNET-sytle listserv we can use the following commands. Send a message to the LISTSERV address (not the LIST address).

```
//database search dd-rules
//rules dd
search KEYWORD(S) IN LIST
index
```

In this command KEYWORDS(S) are the words that we are searching for, and LIST is the name of the list in which we want to search. For example, to search with KEYWORD=conference in a list called. HISTORY we have to enter

```
//database search dd-rules
//rules dd
search conference in history
index
```

After sending this message, we will receive a message from the listserv containing an access number and the subject line of all messages that contained our keyword or words. To retrieve the messages we wish to read. We have to send the following command in an e-mail message to the listserv, with the same keywords and list name, and the numbers (number1, number2,...) of the messages that we wish to retrieve.

```
//database search dd=rules
//rules dd
search KEYWORD(S) in LIST
print all of <number1> <number2>
```

For example, to receive messages 005541 and 005542 from

the previous example, we have to type.

//database search dd-rules

//rules dd

search conference in history

print all of 005541, 005542

If this does not work for the list we are searching we have to send the command "info" to the listserv for any search on information unique to that listserv. To search a Unix listproc, we have to send the command Search LIST KEYWORD to the listproc address. LIST is the name of the list, and KEYWORD is the word on which we are searching. We should get a reply from the listproc listing all the files in that list's archive, with each line in that file in which the key word appears. Listprocs do not always store messages individually, but sometimes a week or month's worth of messages is dumped together in one file. We can read through, looking for lines of text that seem to relate to the subject we seek. When we have a file or two picked out that we would like to retrieve, we have to send the command get LIST FILENAME to the listproc.

We have to enter the filename exactly as it appears in text, because generally the listproc is not quite "smart" enough to figure out which file we mean. The file will be returned to us by the listproc. If the list in question is high volume, we may receive quite a bit of text in our mailbox. If these commands don't get any results, we have sent the command "info" to the listproc for information on methods meant specially for that particular list proc.

9. Code of Online Conduct

Mailing list can get distributed to literally thousands of people. Hence it is wise to think about the types of messages we post. In email everything is between our friends and us. But after we begin contributing to discussion groups, mailing lists and newsgroups we are participating in a public forum, and have an obligation to follow a code of conduct that keeps the conversation pleasant and productive for all. Netiquette; the unofficial code of online conduct can be boiled down to the Golden Rule; Do unto others as you would have them do unto you. As we gain experience, we will begin to notice things. Quoting too much or writing sloppily is not good. Such and many other things against netiquette we must remember not to do our self. The basics of being a good cyber citizen, particularly in discussion groups, are given in the following list. Note that none of this stuff is law. If we skip a rule, the cyber police will not show up at our door. Like all forms of courtesy, netiquette is not required, but highly recommended.

***Using Uppercase*:** Some people like to type all messages only in capital letters, and some others overuse capital letters for emphasis. Capitalize like a person, and use your word choices and phrasing for emphasis, saving the all caps trick for rare, extreme emphasis.

***Stay on topic*:** Each list has different personality and, often, its own rules of etiquette and protocol. It's good to find out these things before we subscribe. The name or the description of the list can be quite misleading. Nothing's more aggravating than subscribing to a list and then receiving all sorts of messages that has no relation to the list. If our message does not pertain directly to the discussion group's stated topic, we should not send it.

***Keep current*:** Newcomers to a list or group, or folks who only drop in occasionally, tend to ask questions that have already been asked and answered a dozen times, which annoys the regulars. We have to keep up with the conversation, so we know what is going on. We have to read the FAQ if one is available.

***Frequently Asked Questions (FAQ)*:** it is a file that contains a general list of common questions and answers pertaining to a particular list, newsgroup, web page, or other topic. By reading FAQs we can quickly get up to speed on the background information shared by others in the group. When an F AQ is available for a mailing list, we will find instructions for obtaining the F AQ in the Welcome message.

***We should not use sarcasm*:** It is difficult to communicate sarcasm effectively in a written message. Often, exaggerated messages intended as sarcasm are taken literally by those who read them, and confusion or arguments ensue.

***We have to keep personal discussions personal*:** Before sending any message, we should ask our self; would this message interest the whole list, or is it really a personal message to just one member? If the message is really for one person, we can find that person's email address in the header information quoted in all list and newsgroup messages, and send our comment or question directly, in private. We have to avoid small, conversational contributions that add little information: For example, if someone posts a message with a great idea in it, we should not send a reply to the group just to say Great ideal. No one wants to go to the trouble of receiving and opening a message with so little to say.

***We should not over quote*:** When replying, we should cut quotes down to all that is necessary to show what we are replying to. When a series of replies builds up and nobody cuts the quotes, each message can be pages long even if it contains only one new sentence. We should try to leave enough information so a newcomer to the conversation can tell what is being discussed, but cut everything else.

***We should write and spell well*:** In the name of speed and efficiency, some boil their messages down to a grip of abbreviations and shorthand, or write too quickly. We should do our readers the courtesy of writing whole words and complete sentences, and fix mistakes before we send.

***Neither flame nor counter flame should be there in a message* :** a flame is an angry attack in a message, the kind that flares when a debate grows into a spat. No matter how hot the argument gets, we should try to keep cool. When flamed personally, we should not rise to the bait. Some flame others for breaches of netiquette, but that is hypocritical. Take responsibility for our own online behavior, and let others worry about theirs.

***Fit in* :** Usually every mailing list and newsgroup has its own, insular culture. After reading messages for awhile, we will pick up a sense of the general technical level of the group, whether they are experts or novices or both on the topic at hand, the overall tone, catch phrases, vocabulary, and so on.

***We have to be our self* :** Any group needs fresh ideas, new personalities. So we should try to be our self within the style and culture of the group, to ensure that all can understand us.

9.1. Information Dissemination

Listservs are not very difficult. After we understand the difference between the list address and the management address and understand the way in which a subscription command is to be phrased things become smooth. Listservs are not for everyone, however. We must manage so much work related email traffic that the steady flow from a mailing list gets in our way. We can also participate in the same kind of discussion in another way in newsgroups. Posting to lists can be a great way to exchange ideas, ask and answer questions, and get to know others on the Internet who share our interests. When dealt with some care, they can be an astoundingly rich resource. As we have seen listservs offer an important feature. It is the electronic ability to search and retrieve files that are archived under listserv.

12

World Wide Web Through Unix

The powers and possibilities of the World Wide Web (WWW) are unique and it is the most popular part of the Internet. It is the result of a project initiated by CERN High Energy Physics Lab in Switzerland in 1990 to develop a system that can take advantage of computer networking, to allow researchers to share information with each other. There was already a huge amount of data in the lab, but navigating through the data was very difficult. We might, for instance, be reading a report that refers to a different set of data somewhere else. In order to go and look at that data, we would probably have to jump through several hoops with some other program, first finding, and then retrieving the desired information. Once we had finally found the information, it was often not simple to keep track of it for later use.

CERN High Energy Physics Lab project had much in common with the Gopher project of the University of Minnesota. Both intended to provide a single interface to many different kinds of information with the capability to link them together. The approach of CERN proposal - the World Wide Web proposal - did not call for Gopher-style menus, but instead involved a concept called hypertext.

1. Hypertext

The article in The Atlantic by Vannevar Bush in "As We May Think" has given birth to the idea of hypertext. Bush described a machine, which he calls a memex, which has turned out to be an accurate prediction for the computers of today. The article predicts that the challenge facing us is no longer to make new discoveries, but instead to make sense of the huge amount of knowledge we already have. A "memex" would be like a secretary, storing information, and more importantly storing connections between information. By making connections among related ideas and information, the memex could help us to find the specific information we are looking for. We would simply start with a related concept; and follow the "most promising scent" until we come to what we require.

But the word hypertext was not coined until the late sixties. In 1960 Ted Nelson was fascinated by the machine described by Bush, and wrote a pair of books, Computer Lib and Dream Machines, which laid out in great detail how he saw the future of computers and the hypertext. Nelson's vision of hypertext has yet to be realized. He continues to work on Xanadu, which he first proposed in Dream Machines. But the World Wide Web comes awfully close to his dream. By late 1991, the software developed by CERN project was available to the Internet community and the Web was born. In 1993 the Web began to really take off, with the development of two really slick browsers; Mosaic, a graphical multimedia browser; and Lynx, a good text-based browser for the rest of us.

2. Mosaic

Mosaic is a very popular World Wide Web client. It is a program developed by the National Centre for Supercomputing Applications at the University of Illinois. Mosaic has provided much of the forward push that has brought the Web to the forefront of Internet tools. Mosaic introduced multimedia to the WWW. With Mosaic, it became possible to have not only hypertext "documents," but also pictures, sounds, and movies. This extension, combined with an easy-to-use point-and-click interface, has made Mosaic a very attractive program for exploring the Web and, therefore, most of the Internet.

The methods in WWW can be easily used on Mosaic also. The ways in which we perform certain actions such as scrolling, searching, and following links will be different, but Mosaic has a very friendly interface and we will have no problems in using Mosaic.

Mosaic is available for the Macintosh, Microsoft Windows, and for some other platforms.

3. Nature of WWW

In Internet, World Wide Web (WWW) brings every thing together. Gopher ties together text documents, Telnet sessions bind sound, graphics, file transfers, and more in an easy-to-use menu-driven format. But the WWW takes Gopher one-step further by using hypertext. Hypertext document is a document that not only contains information, but also contains references, or links, to other documents that contain information related to the topic at hand. Like footnotes and bibliographies contain references to other books and articles that deal with whatever we may be reading about, hypertext links are also references to other documents. But there are some differences. When we find a reference in a book, we have to go elsewhere to find the reference, if we can find it at all. On a hypertext document, we simply click on the link, and then not just the name of the author and the title, but the document itself is displayed.

Gopher and WWW have many similarities. Both organise previously unrelated information and provide ways to navigate across the network easily, and make it possible to access many different types of information such as text, pictures, sounds, and movies. The important difference is that a Gopher document is only inert text. In Gopher, after viewing a document we can only go back to the Gopher menu to start on another search path through the menu system. In hypertext documents, upon viewing a document, we can select different links pointing to relevant documents and information.

4. Working of WWW

WWW is based on a client/server model. When we use the Web, we are using two programs, namely the client and the server. The client program is the program that is running on our local terminal, whether it is a PC, Macintosh, or a UNIX station. It displays information on our screen, takes our keystrokes and our mouse clicks, and retrieves the information we request. It retrieves the information from the server. The server program runs on a computer system that provides the Web information. It waits for an information request. Upon such a request, it then handily provides the information to the client when requested.

The client program is the program we will be using, and everything that has to do with servers should be transparent to us. In the course of using the Web, we will probably be handed off among dozens of different servers on the Internet. The only reason for us to understand what is going on in the background is that when some documents we request are mysteriously unavailable, we should know that this most likely means that the servers we attempted to access was not working at the time when we requested.

WWW deals with a wide variety of information. The most common documents on the WWW are written in a form called Hypertext Mark-up Language (HTML). Documents are marked up in this format, meaning that codes for formatting and linking are inserted into the text. Each client program interprets the codes differently, depending on the limitations of the platform it is serving. A fancy graphics workstation has more graphics and formatting capabilities than a text-based, dumb terminal. With the appropriate client software, we can take full advantage of the display capability of the platform. In any platform, the same text and links will be present. In addition to the hypertext document, we utilize almost all Internet tools through the Web. It can deal with FTP, Gopher, WAIS, Newsgroups, and Telnet sessions. This is a comforting thought. The skills we have acquired elsewhere can now serve us in WWW also. But WWW has its own set of skills, which we should learn to become able to use the program.

5. Clients for WWW

Clients are available for the WWW, for most of the popular platforms. The following is a selection.

Macintosh: Mosaic for the Macintosh is one. Mosaic is a popular World Wide Web browser developed by the National Centre for Super computing Applications. It is available via FTP at ftp.ncsa.uiuc.edu, In/Mac/Mosaic.

Mosaic for Windows: Mosaic for Windows, Available via FTP at ftp.ncsa.uiuc.edu, in/PC/Mosaic is one Client. Cello is another one: Thomas Bruce of the Legal Information Institute of Cornell Law School develops Cello. It is available via FTP at ftp.law.cornell.edu, in/pub/LII/Cello.

Unix: Lynx as a text-based browser developed by the University of Kansas is a popular client. It is available via anonymous FTP at ftp2.cc.ukans.edu, in/pub/lynx.

A list of browsers is available, online at http:// info.cern.ch/ hypertext/ WWW/ TheProject.html.

6. Entering and Exiting WWW

To use the Web, we should know how to start WWW client program; recognize and select links; follow the link; go back to previous screens; specify a Universal Resource Locator (URL) and open; and quit WWW. The WWW client program we are discussing here is Lynx, a text-based programme of Unix systems. Although it cannot display graphics or play sound, it can show the concept behind WWW. The concept is transferable to all WWW clients.

WWW represents the integration of different kinds of Internet resources. Let us take history - an area that is a little bit political science, a little bit sociology and a little bit philosophy, for sample search. To make it more specific we will search for Electronic Journals. First, we have to find out if the client software is available on the Unix computer we are using. If not, there are other ways. Let us connect to our Unix host. For this at the system prompt, we have to type in lower case lynx and press enter. If lynx is available, the home page, opening screen for a Web server is displayed.

<Name of> University World Wide Web Home Page ()

Welcome

Welcome to University's World Wide Web Home Page. Any material found herein is provided AS-IS from indivdiual members of the university community, and does not necessarily reflect the views of the University.

X-Terminal Users - Click here for the latest

exciting news: (9/29/98)

Local Resources

- * HTML authors
- ** What's New *in the University *Infostructure *(9/29/98)
- ** All the documents in our Web (automatically) generated Monday and *Wednesday evenings)
- ** University Gopher
- *** Ph Loopup Gateway *or *Ph Lookup Form (needs Mosaic 2.0) Press space for more; use arrow keys to move, for help, to quit
- * Arrow Keys: Up and Down to move, Right to follow a link: Left to go b H)elp O)ptions P)rint G)o M)ain screen Q)uit /=search [delete] = history list

If the message lynx command not found appears, then Lynx is not available on our host computer. We need to telnet to the computer at the University of Kansas that will allow us to run Lynx. For this we have to type telnet kufacts.cc.ukans. edu to use a public access Lynx client. The instructions on the screen that come, tell us to enter a username. At the login prompt, we can type kufacts and press Enter. It then asks for terminal type. We have to press Enter to accept VT 100. The home page, similar to the one shown below will come up.

The University Online Information

How to use this system

Everything you always wanted to know about the University.

About the University of <name>

Information about the campus, policies, and admissions, Events, activities and announcements.

Happenings at and around KU and Lawrence.

Courses:

Timetable of classes and catalogue of course description.

Departmental information

Info about people, classes, events, and services by department.

Campus organizations

Groups of students, faculty, and staff recognized by <>

Reference shelf

Reference materials, phone books, and worldwide resources.

Index

Commands: Use arrow keys to move, '?' for help, "q" to quit, '<-" to go back

*Arrow Keys: Up and Down to move, Right to follow a link: Left to go b H)elp O)ptions P)rint G)o M)ain screen Q)uit

/=search [delete] = history list

Links are text in bold characters. The first link is currently highlighted and selected. It is the links that allow us to navigate. By following a link, we will be taken to another document, or to another part of the document. If we want to quit at any time we can press q for quit, and we will return to the local system. To select a link, we can use upward and downward arrows. Each time we press downward arrow, the next item is selected, and each time we press upward arrow the previous link is selected.

To follow a link, that is, to display the linked document or menu, highlight link and then press forward arrow. If we press backward arrow, the previous screen is displayed. We will be back-tracking the link. We can highlight a link and press -> (forword arrow) to follow it. Then we can press <- (backword arrow) to return to where we were. We have to keep doing this until we feel comfortable with both seeing and following links.

7. Universal Resource Locator

National Centre for Supercomputing Application's (NCSA) the developer of a Web clint called Mosaic, maintains a rich collection of links to the rest of the Web and will serve us well in our Internet search. We can open a document directly without following through a series of links. We can do this by providing the document's address on the Internet by providing its Universal Resource Locator name. Right now, we canl go to the Universal Resource Locator: http://www.ncsa.uiuc.edu/SDG/Software/Mosaic/ MetaIndex.html. This is a very long name, and the entry is case-sensitive. We must be very careful in typing this address.

We can type g. and then Lynx will prompt us for a URL to open. Then we can type http;//www.ncsa.uiuc.edu/SDG/Software/Mosaic/MetaIndex.html and press Enter. the meta/Index similar to the one shown below will come up.

Internet Resources Meta-Index (p1 of 7)

This document is intended to be a loosely categorized meta-index of the various resource directories and indices available on the Internet. Please send suggestions for new entries on this list (any index or directory of resources) to mosaic@ncsa.uiuc.edu.

World Wide Web

* **Searchable indices:**
* W3Catalog. a searchable catalogue of WWW resources at CUI, Geneva, Switzerland, updated automatically every day from a variety of sources.
* WWWW - the World Wide Web Worm
* Meta-Library index at the Global Network Academy
* **Subject indices:**
* Whole Internet Catalogue from O'Reilly and Associates, a part of the Global Network Navigator
* WWW Virtual Library, a subject listing from CERN. Press space for next page
* Arrow Keys: Up and Down to move, Right to follow a link: Left to go b H) elp O) ptions P) rint G) o M) ain screen Q) uit, /=search [delete] = history list

This is only the first section of this document. There is more text "below" that which we can currently see. In Lynx, we can scroll through the text by pressing Spacebar. Each time we press Space bar, the next screen is displayed. We can press [-] to scroll up one screen.

The client we are using need to know only what format and protocol we expect of the desired information, and it retrieves it by that protocol. The Web author specifies this by using an appropriate Universal Resource Locator (URL). URLs are a relatively new standard for specifying any kind of information on the Internet, and though they may at first seem cryptic, they are really very simple.

URL usually specifies three things: <method>://<host computer>/< host name>. In this <method> is the general kind of protocol or method to use to retrieve a document: "Gopher" for Gopher documents and directories; "ftp"for FTP; "http" for HTMAL

documents on the Web; "news" for Usenet news groups; and "telnet" for Telnet sessions. The <host computer> refers to the specific computer at which the information is located; for example, Gopher, FTP, and HTML documents have a server on a specific host computer. Telnet sessions have a specific destination computer. Newsgroups are the only exception, instead of a hostname, we provide a newsgroup like "news;new.answers". The <pathname> refers to where such as Gopher or FTP or HTML this information is to be found. We can scroll through the screen we have just described to find the following text.

Gopher

* Searchable indices

\+ Veronica (alternate interface at Library of Congress)

\+ Jughead at Washington & Lee University, see also WLU's

Finding Gopher Resources

Scrolling through the screens can take some time if the

document is lengthy. Another method is to find specific words using the Find command. We can invoke this by pressing the forward slash key. We will use this to find the word "telnet". The search is not case-sensitive, meaning that we can use both upper and lowercase when entering the text for which to search. We can press [/] and then Lynx will prompt us to enter a search string. Here we can type telnet and press Enter. After some time the following text will appear.

Telnet

* HyTelnet listing of online library services and other interactive services (served from the University of Kansas)
* Yanoff Internet Services List at UWM (also Indiana University version)

All information in this Meta-Index is not World Wide Web specific. We can access information from Gopher, WAIS, Telnet, and FTP as well. On the Web, these distinctions between different tools are invisible.

8. Subject Catalogues

The best place to start looking for information is to take advantage of the work that other people have already done. Just as Gopher had subject trees, the World Wide Web has "virtual libraries" and subject oriented collections of pointers to information available on the Web. Fortunately, the Meta-Index lists some of the virtual libraries. In the Meta-Index screen we have seen earlier we can find the text "WWW Virtual Library, a subject listing from CERN". From this we can follow WWW Virtual Library by highlighting it and pressing [->]. Our screen will clear, and we will be presented with a list of resources organized by topic area, similar to the one shown below.

The World-Wide Web Virtual Library: Subject Catalogue (pl of 249

The WWW Virtual Library

This is a distributed subject catalogue. See also arrangement by service type, and other subject catalogues of network information.

Mail to maintainers of the specified subject or WWW-request@info.cern.ch to add pointers to this list, or if you would like to contribute to administration of a subject area.

See also how to put your data on the web

Aeronautics; Mailing list archive index. See also MASA LaRC

Agriculture: See Agricultural infl. Almanac mail servers; the Agricultural Genome (National Agricultural Library, part of the U.S. Department of Agriculture): North Carolina Cooperative

Press space for next page

This is the virtual library maintained by CERN. Unlike a real library, this virtual library contains no books. Instead, it contains a series of links to information in other places on the Web. Topics in the virtual library range from archaeology to economics and religion. We can find the text with the word History and by highlighting it and pressing [->] we will be taken to the history resource screen, as shown below.

The World-Wide Web Virtual Library: History (p 1 of 2)

History Resources

Information categorised by subject. See also other subjects. Please mail Ihnelson @ ukanum. cc. ukans. edu if you would like to register your WWW server or know of online information not in these lists.

History Indexes

* Alphabetical list of history resources
* Regional tree of resources,
* Subject tree of resources (not yet implemented, suggestions?)

Historical News Groups and Discussion Lists

Press space for next page

We can browse this document to find the information we require. If we select Alphabetical list, we will be provided with the full index of available references as follows:

Full index (p1 of 37)

Full Index of Available Resources.

This is a full index of all resources to which this server currently provides direct connections. The listing is alphabetical according to the acronym or name of the resource, but the entire list may be searched by pressing the /-key and entering the word for which you are looking. If you find any of these connections not operating, please press the C-key and tell us which resource you could not reach. If you know of resources that should be on this list but are not, please let us know of that also.

* ABSEES: American Bibliography of Slavic and East European Studies [login = absees pw = slavibib] (US)
* Academe This Week: News from the Chronicle of Higher Education (US)
* ACLU Reading Room (US)
* ADFA: Australian Defence Force Academy (AU)
* African Art Graphics Files (US)
* ALIS (DK)

Press space for next page

There will be a lot of items listed here. We can read through this list, seeing what seemed appropriate and select that. While going down the screen we will find the text. We can follow that and then we will be connected to an FTP site, as indicated by a screen similar to the following one.

Index of <Name> FTP site (p1 of 48)

FTP Site Categories.

Introduction to <site name>

Catalogue <name>

The catalogue listing of all files in the Malin ftp site

Asia files

Europe files

Electronic history journals

This FTP site archives several electronic journals as a service to the historical profession

KU History

KUHIST serves KUHIST-L@UKANUM, the University of Kansas, Department of History's list for members, alumni, and friends. It contains a graduate student's guide to the City of Lawrence.

Press space for next page

We have to notice some points here. The first is that this is actually FTP site, whatever that means. But on the Web, it really does not matter. Second is that this FTP site looks like everything else on the Web. In fact, they seem to be no difference between one kind of service and another. We can find and follow electronic history journals to have an extensive list of such journals published worldwide. Like this we can follow the list to the specific journal and article we are looking for.

While pages of one required journal, article open before us, we will notice that the menu at the bottom of the screen tells us that we can press P to print this document. Type P. Then the screen displays some information about the document and gives us further choices. We can have this document mailed to our self or we can transfer it to our local computer using the program Kermit. During the search if we need to go back to the previous screen we can press [<-]. Each time we press it, we backtrack one link.

9. Keyword Indices

The familiar way to find information on a specific subject is through an index. In a book, an index helps us to find specific information quickly without messing around with the table of contents to try to figure out in which chapter the information might be. Similarly, indexes on the Web allow us to use specific keywords to find information that matches what we are looking for without trying to figure out what links might lead to it. We can do this from a searchable index called the W3Catalog. Let us return to the Meta-Index by returning to the URL http://www. csa.uiuc.edu/ SDG/ Software /Mosaic/MetaIndex.html. We can do this using the g command or back tracking using [<-]. We will come to the screen described earlier and find the following text in it.

* Searchable indices;
  - W3Catalog, s searchable catalogue of WWW resources at CUI, Geneva, Switzerland, updated automatically every day from a variety of sources.

We can follow W3Catalog and then its main page will appear as shown below:

CUI W3 Catalogue (p1 of 28)

Provide a Perl regular expression as a search pattern. Submit

NB: Searches are case-insensitive,

Welcome to CUI's W3 Catalogue, a searchable catalogue of W3 resources. There are currently 7335 entries. You may also consult the list of recent changes.

For information about the contents of this catalogue, see the W3 Catalogue overview.

NB: For clients without support for forms, an alternative interface is

(Normal link) Use right-arrow or (return) to activate

As indicated on the screen, this is a searchable index. The W3 Catalogue indexes several collections of information about what is on the Internet. One source we will notice is the W3 Virtual Library - where we just came from. The W3 Catalogue allows us to search the contents of all of these indexes by allowing us to provide keywords and returning a list of all items that match. This is different from the search we did earlier, where we looked for text within a document. This time we will be searching a database, and will get back a completely new document based on the keywords we supply. The "————" that appears after the word "submit" in the screen described above. It is the search text entry field.

In WWW usually we can highlight any word from the text that appears on the screen and go to information on that topic. From there to the next link and so on till we reach relevant and specific information we were looking for is accessed.

13

Libraries in Cyberspace

Libraries accessible through Internet are digital libraries. The words like "digital library," "electronic library," "virtual library," and "library without walls," refer to the library of the future. Additionally, these terms have different meanings among the different interested parties involved.

To some it suggests computerization of traditional libraries. To others, it calls for carrying out of the functions of libraries in a new way, encompassing new types of information resources; new approaches to acquisition, cataloguing, interaction, etc. To computer professionals it is a distributed text-based or multimedia information system. Some see it as linked multimedia objects that encompass humanity's store of information. Some see digital libraries as the space in which people communicate, share, and produce new knowledge and knowledge products.

1. Digital Libraries

This statement reflects two different but complimentary ways of thinking about the concept. One is to think in terms of digital products in traditional libraries. That is, the definition of a digital library is a more or less traditional library that uses CD ROMs, online searching, online public access catalogues, e-mail, and other electronic products and tools to serve its clientele. Indeed, libraries are increasingly using digital products, tools, and resources to serve very traditional functions. Part of the ever-growing body of literature is concerned with the issues revolving around this side of the concept

Based on all these aspects Digital library can be defined as electronic information collection containing large and diverse repositories of digital objects, which can be accessed by a large number of geographically distributed users. Digital objects include text, images, maps, sounds, videos, catalogues and indices, and scientific, business and government data sets as well as, hyper textual multimedia composition of such elements.

2. Virtual Libraries

Another approach is to think more in terms of virtual libraries. This approach focuses not on traditional libraries in library buildings, but rather on online information resources used by people in all kinds of settings. Virtual libraries sometimes "look" like traditional libraries. An example is the Internet Public Library developed by the University of Michigan School of Information and Library Science (URL: http:/ /ipl.umich.edu). More typically, virtual libraries are personal, ad hoc creations, developed to meet the informational and recreational needs of one individual or a small group. They might be related to a specific project or developed and maintained throughout a lifetime of research and interest by an individual. Or, virtual libraries might be developed for public use in much the same way public libraries have been developed. There are, however, commonalties among the variety of projects and the multiple definitions being offered for the "digital" or "virtual" library which are:

* geographically distributed users
* large and diverse collections
* information represented by a variety of electronic objects
* seamless access.

The virtual library would allow users to seamlessly connect and interact with information with no regard to geographic location or time. No buildings, no containers, no staff. Librarians of the digital library of the future should assume the role of information manager, both in creating and facilitating access to a variety of information objects across multiple platforms. Libraries as places will continue to serve useful informational and communal functions.

Also, containers of information will be around for a long time, and they will continue to be selected, acquired, catalogued, indexed, and referred to. In fact, among the definitions and descriptions of digital libraries, Nunberg describes the electronic library as 'an aggregation of catalogues, lists, and indexes of documents of every imaginable type, organized according to myriad schemes of classification, and linked and cross-indexed for searching, so that they come to behave as a single database in which the lines between individual collection and catalogues are blurred.

3. Advantages of Digital Libraries

The key feature of digital libraries is that they are network-based distributed systems with individual servers responsible for maintaining local collections of digital documents ranging from sets of electronic texts to video-on-demand services. A digital library would provide a coherent, consistent view of many repositories of information allowing users to seamless connectivity and interaction with information with no regard to geographic location or time. The term 'seamless' in the context of digital libraries means that the user need not be aware of the computer and communication related heterogeneous environment that could exist between him and the information sought. The key components of digital libraries can be listed as follows:

* geographically distributed digital information collection and users
* information represented by a variety of digital objects
* large and diverse collections
* seamless' access

The advantages of digital libraries are many. In the area of search for information, fast online search is replacing printed abstract journals. Ubiquity, in the sense a single electronic copy can be accessed from many locations by many simultaneous users, is another advantage. The other advantages are in the area of preservation. Since the digital information can be copied by many without error and preserved without deterioration, making up-to-date current literature available to users and access to new kinds of multimedia materials have no equivalent in any traditional format.

4. Major Digital Library Projects

In a number of establishments and academic institutions, 'Digital Library has been established to deal with the information in digitized as well as in electronic form. The present status and an intelligent guess on the future shape that the field of information is likely to take are two vital inputs to resolve both the long- term and short-term investment issues. An experiment involving many of the parameters like generation and publication of information in computer accessible form, its communication to the users, hardware and software issues involved, user preferences etc. that influence the shape of things to come were conducted in the United States during 1991 to 1995. The code name of the experiment was TULIP (The University of Licensing Program). The focus of the experiment was to test one key aspect, namely, networked delivery of journals to user's desktop and the extent of their usage. The results and conclusions of the experiment are helpful in providing pointers to the resolution of not only to journals issue but also the future of information in electronic form. Another study with similar objectives though specific to the field of chemistry is the CORE (Chemical Online Retrieval Experiment) project also in US, based at the Cornell University. It is a large experimental electronic library project involving realistic laboratory environment.

The TULIP study by a consortium of one of the leading technical literature publishers (Elsevier Science) and nine renowned universities (Carnegie Mellon, Cornell, Georgia Institute of Technology, MIT, California, Michigan, Tennessee, Washington and Virginia) is to jointly test the systems for networked delivery and use of journals at the user's desktop. The technical conclusions of the study are the following:

* The first technical conclusion was on the web. The web is a set of protocols that give Internet users interactive access to a huge variety of content on the Internet. In many people's view, the web is the content itself and not the underlying protocols. Though the web does not provide some real-time

functionality features like image zooming available in the windows applications, users favored and shifted to the web.

* The bandwidth restriction and other limitations of the prevailing transmission schemes do not permit large-scale Internet FTP (File Transfer Protocol) transfer.
* The electronic collection building of institutions is likely to be layered, composed of local servers for primary relevant material and remote servers for material of secondary importance.

The TULIP study has brought out that the end users have certain requirements regarding functionality, ease of use and critical mass of electronic information services. With respect 'to ease of use, the services should be as intuitive as possible and should be preferably from a familiar interface. The access to all information should be from one source. The search capabilities should be very effective with high processing speed. The information should be timely and there should be linking of information. The quality of image text should be good. The number of journals covered should be sufficient and their time coverage should be adequate. While there is enthusiasm about the desktop access to electronic information, the end of print media is far away still, if at all it happens. The reason is that there are practical benefits of paper products besides 'emotional' ties with paper for many users.

The CORE project is primarily concerned with the conversion of large text and graphics collections to an electronic format and use the same to serve the document delivery needs of scholars in a distributed networking environment. The technological problems of full-text retrieval and delivery are investigated in this project. The five objectives of the CORE project are to

* Define a suitable architecture for delivery of full-text information in a distributed networking environment with heterogeneous workstations;
* Convert and mount a critical mass of chemistry journal data in a database format suitable for effective retrieval and display;
* Study the elements of full-text interface functionality necessary

to serve the needs of scholars in a network document delivery environment;

* Advance the understanding of suitable document mark up for electronic full-text databases, and Investigate information retrieval questions genuine to the coming era of full-text delivery.

5. Libraries With Collections Online

In most of the advanced countries libraries are digitizing their collections during the last decade and have succeeded in putting on their site most of the important documents sought for reference. Many conservation projects also are under way which are transforming rare and antique materials from libraries. In universities and other organizations Information Infrastructures are priority item now and as information store has to act as the central hub of those infrastructures the first thing such developments concentrate on is automating libraries and transforming highly used library materials to digital form. So most of the libraries in advanced countries have now established their web presence.

If we search Internet for libraries we will find libraries that have made valuable collections and services available in Internet from most of the countries in the world including China, Pakistan, many African and Gulf Countries and even Sri Lanka. But we will fail to find Indian Libraries except a few which have established their presence recently. Check for our National Library, or the National Agricultural Library of India coming under the ARIS program or any university library. Libraries of some NGOs and a few institutions have stayed for some time on the net due to voluntary effort of individual and have gone away due to the lack of institutional or government support. We are spending more than any similar country for Information infrastructures but we failed to recognize that it is for information. So we lost the libraries as well as failed to put information in concerned infrastructures. But among this confusion and turmoil a notable developments have occurred in Indian Institute of Science, Kerala Agricultural University, Indian Institutes of Management etc of which a few are listed below.

Here we will have an overview of some selected libraries online and discuss in detail the Internet Public Library, Library of congress and Indian Institute of Science Library.

5.1 InfoCentre

Hertfordshire Libraries, Arts and Information (HLAI), UK, has officially launched Public Information Network, 'InfoCentre' which is the first UK public library catalogue on the Internet in 1996. InfoCentre is the most extensive UK public library information database available on the Internet. Computers housed in fifty-three libraries across the county are freely available to the public to find out thousands of facts and figures. Public terminals, which are installed, have touch screens or keyboards and feature attractive GUIs (graphical user interfaces). Infocentre has details of more than 11,000 organizations, clubs, services and societies. Along with the basic information other key facts such as dates of meeting are also available. Searching the system is simple and user friendly-exploring different sections of the database at random using hypertext links. As the system grows, it is probable that information and databases accessible in InfoCentre will be expanded. Full multimedia (text, still pictures, sound and video clips) is also available from the site subject to copyright.

5.2 British Library

Other libraries have embarked on similar projects. The British Library began an "Initiatives for Access" project in 1993 to investigate hardware and software platforms for the digitization and subsequent networking of a range of library materials. It includes a patent information system, "Electronic Beowulf" digital manuscript, photographic collections, and an OPAC.

In 1994, the National Science Foundation (NSF), the Department of Defense's Advanced Research Projects Agency (ARPA), and the National Aeronautics and Space Administration (NASA), through a joint initiative, announced the funding of several digital library development projects, mostly among academic institutions. The focus of the digital library initiative is to dramatically advance the means to collect, store, and organize information in digital forms, and make it available for searching, retrieval, and processing via communication networks. Each project is described briefly below. More information may be found at the World Wide Web addresses (URL's) shown. The differences in how the grantees define "digital library" are especially instructive.

5.3. University of Michigan

The University of Michigan project defines digital libraries as "electronic libraries in which large numbers of geographically distributed users can access the contents of large and diverse repositories of electronic objects. Electronic objects include networked text, images, maps, sounds, videos, catalogues of merchandise, and scientific, business, and government datasets. It will concentrate on earth and space sciences. URL http:/ /http2. sils.umich.edu/UMDL/HomePage.html.

5.4. Stanford University

Stanford University is developing the enabling technologies for a single, integrated, virtual library, allowing users to access information through interfaces that hide the unimportant details of diversity of materials and provide ways to navigate and manage the information space in a consistent and unified way. Stanford's project will include a mix of virtual and traditional libraries URL: http:/ /www.diglib.stanford.edu/diglib

5.5. University of California

The University of California at Berkeley is producing a prototype digital library with a focus on environmental information. Its goal is to develop a system in which large numbers of geographically distributed users can conveniently access the entire contents of very large and diverse repositories of electronic objects. These repositories will exist in locations physically near or remote from the users, and will contain objects comprising text, images, maps, sounds, full-motion videos, merchandise catalogues, scientific and business data sets, as well as hyper textual compositions of such elements. URL: http:llelib.cs.berkely.edu.

5.6. University of Illinois

The University of Illinois believes that the international network will evolve from distributed computer nodes to distributed information sources supporting object interaction. Users will browse the Net by searching digital libraries and navigating relationship links, as well as share new information within the Net by composing and publishing new objects and links. The Net will thus appear as interconnected spaces of information objects. URL:http:// Iwww.grainger.uiuc.edu/dli.

5.7. Carnegie Mellon University

Carnegie Mellon University is developing an online digital video library, allowing users to access, explore and retrieve science and mathematics materials from video libraries. This project is more concerned with connecting to an existing storehouse and accessing the information in television videos URL:http:llfuzine.mt.cs.cmu.edu/im/iformedia.html.

5.8. University of California

The University of California at Santa Barbara is working on a project called Project Alexandria, which is primarily concerned with maps and geographical images and geographical information systems. UR. http:llalexandria.sdc.ucsb. edu.

6. FUNCTIONING OF SELECTED LIBRARIES

Now most of the libraries of national importance in all countries have digitized their important collections; that is collections of rare materials, highly sought documents in different media and or programs needed continuously in campuses or buildings or offices located in different regions of the country where their activities extend to. The libraries and information is also presented in the most attractive way than we could have dreamed off yesterday using computer stimulation techniques and multimedia applications. Most countries including Pakistan and Sri Lanka have developed such information sources, which are to function as hearts that pump blood into those country's information systems and networks. Today also while finalizing this manuscript I have surfed through the net to see if at least our national library is having a page even if it is not having a site. To our shame I failed. I could retrieve the beautiful websites of National Library of China, Sri Lanka and also many underdeveloped countries. And going into them we can find the importance they have shown and devoted work they have put in to develop content, transfer the content of their libraries into digital form. But we can see many web sites and home pages of libraries like that of the College for Women, Trivandrum and KAU Library which are voluntary efforts of individuals who have suffered much to establish a web presence while institutional effort has not become fruitful due to unknown reasons for the last half decade or more during which every one is getting sufficient fund for Information Technology development.

6.1. Internet Public Library

As per its statement of principles, the Internet Public Library Project (IPL) seeks to challenge and redefine the roles and significance of libraries in an increasingly distributed and digital world. Libraries have always been places of learning and excitement, opening new

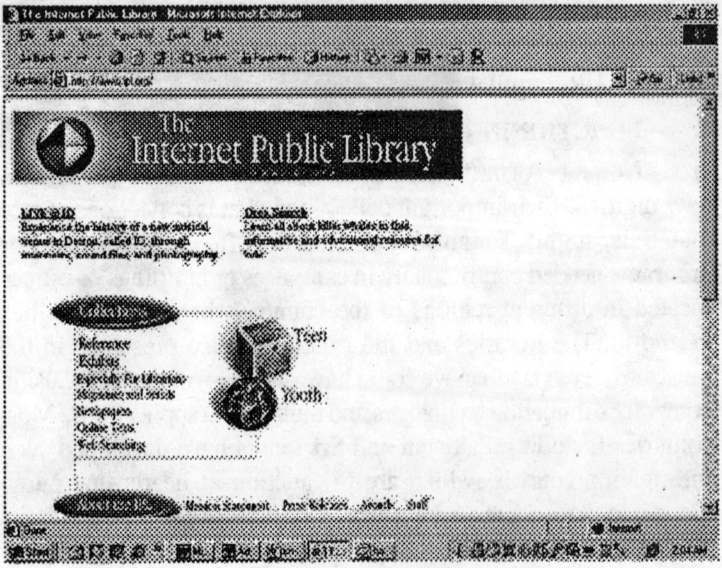

Figure 21.1

worlds of information, enlightenment and entertainment to all who enter. Libraries and the people who work in them are committed to democracy and equality of access, the dignity of their patrons, and the freedom to express and investigate all points of view.

This is a noble and honorable professional mission. Technologies have always permitted libraries to accomplish their aims more effectively. The rise of libraries as we know them today is due in large part to the explosion in volume and diversity of printed and recorded matter. Simultaneously, however, each new medium brings with it difficulties and change. The technologies of global internetworking now present yet another set of challenges and opportunities to the library community.

Internet Public Library Project has a twofold educational mission:

* First, and foremost, the planning, development, design, and thinking about the Library serves as an opportunity for its members to learn—about users, about technologies, about management—in short, about all the issues motivated by the translation of the library perspective into a networked environment. Further, we hope that by conveying our experiences, we can help others to share in our lessons.
* Second, the Library itself exists to; provide services and information which enhance the value of the Internet to its ever-expanding and varied community of users, work to broaden, diversify, and educate that community, communicate its creators' vision of the unique roles of library culture and traditions on the Internet. The members of the Library affirm that they will.
* work to provide service of the highest quality possible to our community of users.
* uphold the highest standards of professionalism, including commitments to equality of access, and intellectual freedom. In particular, we endorse the principles of the Library Bill of Rights.
* strive for creativity and originality in all our work, within appropriate constraints.

* endeavor to extend the scope of our work on a global scale: to incorporate the participation of people around the world in the development and work of the Library, and also to acknowledge and access collections of interest everywhere.

The School of Information & Library Studies of the University of Michigan hosts the Library. The Internet Public Library group through their website seek the participation and collaboration of individuals and organizations around the world. They will maintain the nucleus of the Library here. Now we will visit the Internet Public Library before further discussing on it.

To connect to the web site of the Internet Public Library we can follow the steps given below.

* Connect to the Internet and open the web browser.
* Find the address box, and click in it once.
* Type the URL: http://www.ipl.org. That URL will work in any browser, but if we use latest versions of Internet Explorer or Navigator we can optionally omit the http:// prefix.
* Press Enter. The Internet Public Library web site appears.

The Internet Public Library Project is inspired by the American Library Association Bill of Rights, which affirms that all libraries are forums for information and ideas. The following have been stated as the basic policies that should guide library services.

* Books and other library resources should be provided for the interest, information, and enlightenment of all people of the community the library serves. Materials should not be excluded because of the origin, background, or views of those contributing to their creation.
* Libraries should provide materials and information presenting all points of view on current and historical issues. Materials should not be proscribed or removed because of partisan or doctrinal disapproval.
* Libraries should challenge censorship in the fulfillment of their responsibility to provide information and enlightenment.
* Libraries should cooperate with all persons and groups

concerned with resisting abridgment of free expression and free access to ideas.

* A person's right to use a library should not be denied or abridged because of origin, age, background, or views.
* Libraries, which make exhibit spaces and meeting rooms available to the public they serve, should make such facilities available on an equitable basis, regardless of the beliefs or affiliations of individuals or groups requesting their use.

The Internet Public Library Mission Statement which follows the same lines adopted in 12th April 200 is as follows.

The Internet Public Library (IPL) is a public service organization and learning/teaching environment at the University of Michigan School of Information. It will engage in activities in the following areas:

* SERVE: Provide library services to Internet users. Activities include: finding, evaluating, selecting, organizing, describing, and creating information resources, and direct assistance to individuals.
* TEACH: Use a learn-by-doing approach to train information professionals and students to work in an increasingly digital environment.
* BUILD: Develop technology and best practices for providing library services via the Internet, including digital reference service and collection management.
* LEARN: Conduct research aimed at improving our services and increasing the body of knowledge about digital libraries and librarianship.
* SHARE: Promote our services. Share what we've learned with the professional community. Participate in efforts to create and promote relevant standards. Disseminate technology and practices to others. Develop relationships with organizations pursuing similar goals. Provide leadership in these activities.
* GROW: Develop a model and plan for long-term sustainability and growth for our organization and services.

* We approach the above activities via the values and principles of the profession of librarianship.

From the beginning, the Internet Public Library project, based at the University of Michigan School of Information (SI), has been driven by its mission to educate library school students about the practice of librarianship in the digital age. An integral part of that education has been providing students at SI and other library schools with the opportunity to get hands-on experience in being a "virtual librarian" by answering questions for the Internet Public Library's Ask A Question service. The "Ask a Question" service is one of the most popular e-mail based reference services on the Internet. Patrons from all over the world submit questions, which are then answered by the library school students, library paraprofessionals, and professional librarians who staff the virtual reference desk. With their help, the IPL has answered over 30,000 reference questions to date.

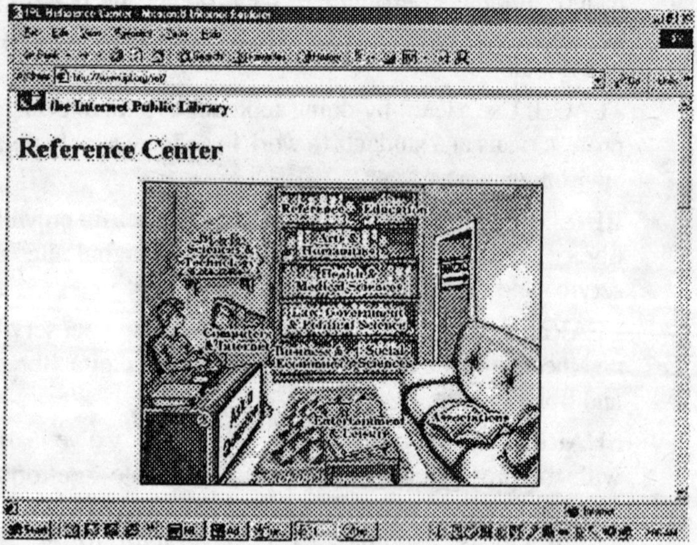

Figure 21.2

More than this, though, the "Ask a Question" service is a learning laboratory for students and librarians who want to learn more about the benefits and drawbacks of offering electronic reference services to library patrons, the challenges and rewards of using the Internet to answer reference questions, and the impact of the Internet on the practice of librarianship. Internet Public Library staff members supervise the service; providing training, feedback, and guidance to students & volunteers as they tackle the diverse questions that the service receives. Collaboration tools also enable the students and volunteers of this project to help each other out with difficult questions, adding to the learning experience.

In the statement published in their website Internet Public Library group has expressed that they are currently interested in recruiting library school faculty members who would be interested in working with the IPL to offer their students the opportunity to answer questions for the "Ask a Question" service. There are several successful models for such a partnership. Most notably, IPL has worked with a faculty member at Kent State University for 3 years in a row. Students in the faculty member's introduction to reference course are assigned an IPL "practicum" in which they each commit to spending 40 hours over the course of the semester answering questions for the IPL's "Ask a Question" service. They have also made similar arrangements with faculty at the University of Washington, University of Illinois, and the University of Alabama, in which, as part of their coursework for a reference class, the students were each assigned to answer a set number of questions over a several week time period, for the service.

Internet Public Library Group is open to other ideas for how they might involve classes and/or individual students in our project. Their goal is to do as much as they can to enable students to participate in what we believe is an exciting project that helps enhance students' skills and experience!

Internet Public Library staff members' time spent training and supervising students who participate is free of charge. Faculty who wish to arrange for a staff member to visit their school in person to offer a training seminar to get the students started, though, would have to cover travel, room and board costs. Staff members are also available for "virtual visits" to the faculty's class through videoconferencing technologies.

Supervision and monitoring of the students' work is usually mostly be handled by IPL staff. They have staff coverage of the service for most of the 24x7 hours a week that the service operates and an interest in seeing that their patrons receive high quality service but we also work closely with the faculty member to be sure that they are kept in the loop about their students' progress.

Students who participate will need to have Internet access and their own email account. There are no special software requirements to access the IPL's web-based system for viewing and answering reference questions, besides access to a web browser. Question queues allow students to choose from a list of questions that are available to be worked on. Once a student chooses a question, they are responsible for seeing that the patron receives an answer by their deadline, or within one week from when the IPL accepted the question, whichever is sooner. All questions and their answers are archived, and are available for students and faculty to review at any later date. Faculty who are interested in collaborating with the IPL can contact them.

6.2. Library of Congress

The Library of Congress has long maintained many information resources on the Internet. The Library of Congress (LC) has been a key leader in the use of automation to promote inter-library collaboration and in developing standards such as MARC and Z39.50. The LC is conducting a five-year Digital Library program to assemble a core digital collection of American historical and cultural primary source material. These collections, collectively referred to as American Memoir', derive from heterogeneous resources and are intended to serve a range of users including scholarly researchers and school children. Most of the books and papers have been encoded in SGML with embedded links to the images of original pages. However these are also converted to HTML to support a wider user group. The LC has recognized a number of special challenges. For example digitizing historical collections poses special requirements since it is necessary to minimize the handling of fragile or deteriorating originals. Similarly significant staff time and technical expertise are required to create workflow plans and process materials through to successful digitalization. Other conclusions made include recognition of the need for a naming scheme and the impracticality of expecting uniformity in description. The American memory collections are also linked to the INQUERY search systems to offer both browsing and full text searches. The digital archive expected to be 50 TB by the year 2000 requires management and preservation. Other related LC projects are THOMAS to provide public access to legislative information and CORDS to accept materials in digital form for copyright registration and deposit. LC is also a participant in the National Digital Libraries Federation (NDLF) established in 1995 a consortium of the country's fifteen largest research libraries and archives. In addition LC participates in the G-7 program on the Global Information Society. This program emphasizes international cooperation in projects such as the Electronic Libraries Project, which aims to build a prototype global library. We will discuss this library in detail at the end of this chapter.

The Library's mission is to make its resources available and useful to the Congress and the American people and to sustain and preserve a universal collection of knowledge and creativity for future generations. As per its mission statement its priorities are the following.

The first priority of the Library of Congress is to make knowledge and creativity available to the United States Congress. The Congress is the lawmaking body of the United States. As the repository of a universal collection of human knowledge and the creative work of the American people, the Library has the primary mission to make this material available and to identify, analyze and synthesize the information it contains to make it useful to the lawmakers who are the elected representatives of the American people.

The second priority of the Library of Congress is to acquire, organize, preserve, secure and sustain for the present and future use of the Congress and the nation:

* a comprehensive record of American history and creativity;

has to be maintained in order to fulfill the mandates which are twofold: to protect intellectual property rights (a constitutional mandate statutorily exercised by the Copyright Office) and to preserve the record of the past for the sake of present and future creativity (the constitutional mandate "to promote the Progress of Science and useful Arts")

* a universal collection of human knowledge: A universal collection is essential to meet the present and potential needs of the Congress (the statutory work of the Congressional Research Service) and of the government more broadly (Law Library, Federal Research Division, general reference services).

All other services and activities of the Library of Congress support the core mission of maintaining and continuing to build on the world's greatest treasury of recorded human knowledge. The collections must continue to be comprehensive in order to keep pace with the rapid proliferation of information. The Library of Congress is the only library in the world that collects universally. If this time-honored tradition is diminished then the Federal government and the American free enterprise system will be the poorer for it. Except for technical agriculture and clinical medicine, which do the National Agricultural Library and the National Library of Medicine cover respectively?

The third priority of the Library of Congress is to make its collections maximally accessible to (in order of priority) that is a) the Congress, b) the U. S. government more broadly, and c) the public. It is unprecedented in human history — and a uniquely American offer — to open public access to an institution that is in many respects the working library of a government and a de facto national library.

The unifying purpose of providing the public with essential library services, such as cataloging and reference help, is to afford as much access to useful information as possible to each of these three constituencies. In addition to on-site service, the National Digital Library will provide remote electronic access to the most interesting and important documents of American history and culture for local schools, libraries, businesses, and homes across America.

The unique and ambitious mandate that the Congress has given its Library during the past two centuries is a stunningly original expression of a broader American democratic ideal. For a democracy to be dynamic and self-correcting, its governing institutions must be not only continuously accountable to the people but also solidly based on a body of knowledge that is both constantly expanding and available equally to those who legislate and to those who elect the legislators.

Equal access to knowledge for both governors and governed, rich and poor, represents an essential minimal form of empowerment in a pluralistic democracy - and has found expression in our system of public libraries and public schools. The Congress has given to the Library a series of centralized national functions to perform that are essential to the health of these local institutions: setting bibliographic standards, providing subsidized cataloging, storing the records and artifacts of the copyrighted creativity of America, and creating and delivering nationwide reading materials for blind and physically handicapped persons.

The Congress has now recognized that, in an age in which information is increasingly communicated and stored in electronic form, the Library should provide remote access electronically to key materials. For the general public, the Congress has endorsed the creation of a National Digital Library Program through a private-public partnership that will create high-quality content in electronic form and thereby provide remote access to the most interesting and educationally valuable core of the Library's Americana collections. Schools, libraries, businesses, and homes will have access to important historical material in their own localities together with the same freedom readers have always had within public reading rooms to interpret, rearrange, and use the material for their own individual needs.

The fourth priority is to add interpretive and educational value to the basic resources of the Library in order to enhance the quality of the creative work and intellectual activity derived from these resources, and to highlight the importance of the Library's contributions to the nation's well being and future progress. Implicit in the broad and international inclusiveness of the Library's clientele (both here and elsewhere) is another ideal of American democracy: the desire to promote the free exchange of ideas. There are three essential aspects to this priority that are uniquely available through the Library of Congress:

* greater use by the Congress, government officials, and the private sector of the vast special (i.e., non-book) and foreign language collections that are unique to the Library and that have generally been underused resources.
* greater use of the Library's Capitol Hill facilities by scholars for the kind of interdisciplinary, cross-cultural, multimedia, multilingual, and synthetic writing that is important to Congressional deliberation and national policy-making, but inadequately encouraged both by special interest groups and by advocacy-oriented think tanks; and
* greater use by the general public through programs that stimulate interest, increase knowledge, and encourage more citizens to use the collections on-site and electronically.

The library staff will increase its role as knowledge navigators by helping more people find appropriate materials in a swelling sea of unsorted information and pointing them to services and resources unique to the Library of Congress. This requires not merely more development and retraining of staff than the library has previously been able to do, but also facilitating in new ways more extensive and systematic use by researchers of the distinctive materials that only the Library of Congress has. Programs for the general public, such as exhibits or publications, must demonstrate the value and usefulness of the collections.

To accomplish its mission and support the library's four priorities, the library has built up an efficient and effective infrastructure with five key components:

* the mobilization and motivation of human resources in all parts and at all levels of the library. There are four important elements within this category which are recruiting, assessing, rewarding and holding accountable employees on the basis of objective evaluations of knowledge, skills and performance;

training, developing and, where needed, retooling the work force to perform new functions in new ways; promoting fairness, equal opportunity, and respect for diversity at all levels and in all parts of the library; and fostering communication by using early and frequent consultation to promote innovation and increase participation in decision-making and in implementing change.

* The provision and delivery of electronic services in order to serve the departments of the library in the execution of the library's mission and priorities with speed, quality, and economy.
* The allocation and use of space and equipment in order: to preserve and make accessible the artifactual collections; and to maximize the efficiency, productivity and well being of the staff.
* The operation of modern financial and information systems to facilitate decision-making and ensure accountability.

The operation of effective security systems that ensure adequate access and at the same time provide maximum protection for the staff and patrons, facilities, data, and collections.

Collections: The Library of Congress; the oldest federal cultural institution in America founded in 1800 is the largest library in the world, with more than 120 million items on approximately 530 miles of bookshelves. The collections include more than 18 million books, 2.5 million recordings, 12 million photographs, 4.5 million maps, and 54 million manuscripts. The library receives some 22,000 items each working day and adds approximately 10,000 items to the collections daily. The majority of the collections are received through the Copyright registration process, as the library is home to the U.S. Copyright Office. Materials are also acquired through gift, purchase, other government agencies (state, local and federal), Cataloging in Publication (a pre-publication arrangement with publishers) and exchange with libraries in the United States and abroad. Items not selected for the collections or other internal purposes are used in the library's national and international exchange programs. Through these exchanges the library acquires material that would not be available otherwise. The remaining items are made available to other federal agencies and are then available for donation to educational institutions, public bodies and nonprofit tax-exempt organizations in the United States. Approximately half of the library's book and serial collections are in languages other than English. Some 460 languages are represented in the collections.

The Law Library of Congress is the world's largest law library, with some 2.4 million items, including one of the world's best rare law book collections and the most complete collection of foreign legal gazettes in the United States. The Law Library contains United States congressional publications dating back to the nation's founding. The library's African and Middle Eastern Division hold some 600,000 volumes in the non-Roman script languages of the region. The library's Asian Division collection of some 2 million items represents the largest assemblage of Chinese, Japanese and Korean materials outside of Asia, and one of the largest Tibetan collections in the world. The library holds the largest collection of Russian-language materials in the United States and the largest outside of Russia (more than 750,000 items). The library's Iberian, Latin American and Caribbean collections, comprising more than 10 million items (books, journals, newspapers, maps, manuscripts, photographs, posters, recordings, sheet music and other materials) are the largest and most complete in the world. The library holds the largest rare book collection in North America (more than 700,000 volumes), including the largest collection of 15th century books in the Western Hemisphere. The collection also includes the first extant book printed in North America — The Bay Psalm Book. The library possesses approximately 100 extremely rare children's books, including The Children's New Play-Thing (Philadelphia, 1763) and The Children's Bible (Philadelphia, 1763). The smallest book in the library of Congress is Old King Cole. It is 1/25" x 1/25", or about the size of the period at the end of this sentence. The pages can only be turned with the use of a needle. The largest book in the library of Congress is John James Audubon's Birds of America, containing many life-size illustrations of birds. The book is 39.37" (1 meter) high. The oldest example of printing in the world - passages from a Buddhist sutra, or discourse, printed in 770 A.D, is housed in the library's

Asian Division. The oldest written material in the library is a cuneiform tablet dating from 2040 B.C. Foremost among the Manuscript Division's holdings are the papers of 23 presidents, ranging from George Washington to Calvin Coolidge. The Gutenberg Bible, one of the treasures of the Library of Congress, was purchased in 1930. It is one of three perfect copies on vellum in the world.

The Prints and Photographs Division of the Library of Congress contains some 13.6 million visual images (such as the one at right, Billie Holliday by William Gottlieb), including the most comprehensive international collection of posters in the world, the most comprehensive visual record of the Civil War and pioneering documentation of America's historic architecture. The largest and most comprehensive collection of American and foreign-produced films and television broadcasts in the world is housed in the library's Motion Picture, Broadcasting and Recorded Sound Division. The library has been collecting films and documentation relating to the production of motion pictures since the 1890s, including "The Edison Kinetoscopic Record of a Sneeze," the oldest extant copyrighted

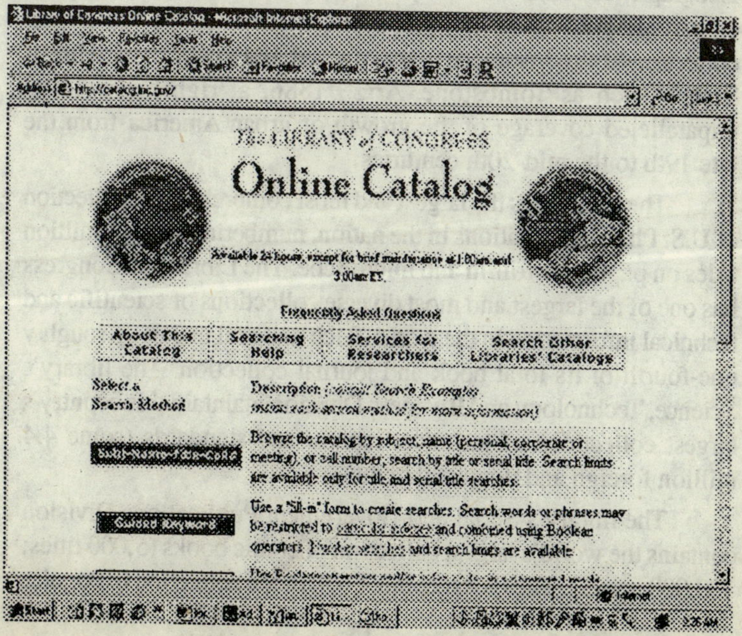

motion picture (copyrighted in 1893 by Thomas Edison). The library holds the most comprehensive collection of American music in the world, including an extensive assemblage of original manuscripts by composers of the American musical theater and the largest collection of any one kind of musical instrument (flute) in the world. The library sponsors a long-running broadcast concert series of chamber music. The Library of Congress holds the nation's largest public collection of sound recordings (music and spoken word) and radio broadcasts, with some 2.5 million recordings. Recordings represent more than 100 years of sound recording history in nearly every sound recording format and cover a wide range of subjects and genres in considerable depth and breadth. With more than 1.5 million items, the Archive of Folk Culture in the American Folk life Center is the largest repository of traditional cultural documentation in the United States and one of the largest in the world. It contains the largest collection of American Indian music and spoken word, including the earliest ethnographic field recordings made anywhere in the world. Other fascinating facts the library's Geography and Map Division holds is the world's largest collection of cartographic materials, 4.5 million items. It has the largest collection of fire insurance maps of cities and towns in the United States (such as Tombstone, Ariz., 1886, at right), providing unparalleled coverage of the growth of urban America from the late 19th to the mid-20th centuries.

The library has the largest and most comprehensive collection of U.S. Ph.D. dissertations in the nation, numbering about 1 million titles on paper, microfilm and microfiche. The Library of Congress has one of the largest and most diverse collections of scientific and technical information in the world. Such material makes up roughly one-fourth of its total book and journal collection. The library's Science, Technology and Business Division maintain this country's largest collections of technical reports and standards (some 4.4 million foreign and domestic items).

The library's Serial and Government Publications Division contains the world's largest collection of comic books (5,000 titles; 100,000 issues). The oldest comic book in the collection is Popular

Comics, February 1936. The division also holds the world's most extensive newspaper collection. The oldest original newspaper in the collection is Mercurius Publicas Comprising the Sum of Foreign Intelligence, December 29, 1659.

Scientific and Technical Information **:** Let us have a tour through the Library of Congress before further discussions on it. To connect to the web site of the Library of Congress we can follow the steps given below.

* Connect to the Internet and open the web browser.
* Find the address box, and click in it once.
* Type the URL: http://www.loc.gov. Press Enter. Library of Congress Web site appears.
* We can see the interior of the dome of the building and various sections listed around it on the page.
* By clicking the Exhibitions and further links we can view an exhibition made of documents of different media that preset before us the past in an unimaginably effective way.
* By clicking the Library Today we can view current news and announcements from the library.
* In the options listed at the top we can select the search the catalogue that will open the site for Library of Congress Online catalogue. All the access methods we use in any of the library cataloguing schemes can be used here with a thousand more possibilities and unimaginably seedy engine will reveal within seconds what is available and its details from an ocean of world documents produced up to the present.

Online Catalog**:** The Library of Congress Online Catalog is a database of records representing the vast collection of materials held by the Library. In addition to these records, the Online Catalog provides cross-references, notes, and circulation status, as well as information about library materials still in the acquisitions stage. The Library of Congress Online Catalog contains approximately 12 million records representing books, serials, computer files, manuscripts, cartographic materials, music, sound recordings, and visual materials. The Catalog also displays searching aids for users, such as cross-references and scope notes. The catalog records reside in a single integrated database; they are not separated according to type of material, language of material, date of cataloging, or processing/ circulation status.

As an integrated database, the Online Catalog includes 3.2 million catalog records from an earlier database. These catalog records, primarily for books and serials cataloged between 1898 and 1980, are being edited to comply with current cataloging standards and to reflect contemporary language and usage. The legend [from old catalog] indicates that the headings may deviate from current Library of Congress cataloging policy. For a complete search of books and serials cataloged prior to 1980, researchers onsite at the library should also use the Main Card Catalog.

Many items from the library's special collections are accessible to users but are not represented in this catalog. In addition, some individual items within collections (microforms, manuscripts, photographs, etc.) are not listed separately in the Catalog, but are represented by collection-level catalog records.

The Catalog includes romanized records for Chinese, Japanese and Korean language material cataloged since 1984, Hebrew and Yiddish cataloged since 1988, and Arabic and Persian cataloged since 1991. These catalog records appear in the Library of Congress Online Catalog in the Roman alphabet and with English language subject headings. In the future, the Online Catalog may display catalog records in the scripts used by these languages.

Each catalog record indicates where onsite users should request library materials. Other users should consult the interlibrary loan policy for the Library of Congress. Records in the Online Catalog will generally indicate that the library holds one copy of a work, even though additional copies may actually be available in the library's collections. Library staff will begin entering information about additional copies in the near future. The library will also be incorporating more detailed information about serials holdings, indicating which issues are available and where they should be requested.

In addition to holdings and location information, the catalog record supplies information on the circulation status of library materials. Initially, some circulation information may not be complete, since many materials in the library (including many special collections materials) are not handled by the circulation system at this time. Catalog users should consult reference staff if they have questions about holdings or the circulation status of any materials.

In addition to the Library of Congress Online Catalog, users have access to recent issues of the Handbook of Latin American Studies (HLAS). HLAS is accessible by selecting the [Databases] button from the top button bar on most Catalog screens. Other electronic research tools, some of which provide supplementary access to the library's collections, can be found on the Library of Congress Web Site.

***Factors of Interest to Librarians*:** There are several notable features and changes important to librarians using the Library of Congress Online Catalog:

* Name and Subject Authority records cannot be directly searched or retrieved in the new Online Catalog. However, the Catalog provides information from authority records by means of cross references (marked with the icon) or scope notes (marked with the icon) which can be accessed from the Headings List produced by using the Subj-Name-Title-Call # search method.
* MARC 21 is the Online Catalog's content designation standard, including a number of locally defined fields.
* Searching by Library of Congress Control Number (LCCN) is only available using special index codes in Guided Keyword or Command Keyword search methods.
* It is not possible to store search results sets for further manipulation; however, searches may be refined and combined using the Guided Keyword and Command Keyword search methods.
* An online guide to Command Keyword Index Codes is available.
* CONSER (Cooperative Serials Cataloging Program) records

of other institutions cannot be searched or retrieved in the new Online Catalog; only those serials the library has acquired and continues to acquire are available.

***New Catalog*:** In addition to being "year-2000" compliant, the new Library of Congress Online Catalog replaces many of the library's older, separate automated systems — some of which date back to the late 1960s and early 1970s — with a single, client/server system that supports all standard library operations, including acquisitions, cataloging, inventory and serials control, circulation, and the online public catalog. The library expects to improve control over its collections, increase the efficiency of its operations and provide better service for its many researchers. In addition, two large card files — the 12-million-card manual shelf list and the 900,000 title serials check-in file will be converted from paper to electronic format.

In 1998, following a competitive procurement process, the Library of Congress awarded a contract to Endeavor Information Systems of Des Plaines, IL, for its Voyager Integrated Library System (ILS) software. The library began using the Voyager software for its ILS on August, 1999 for its cataloging operations and has added additional modules since.

Approximately 11.7 million bibliographic and 4.9 million authority records were migrated to the new system from various files in the old catalog like the following:

* Over 4.7 million records from the former BOOKS file (15,000 records for CIP materials never published or never received from publishers were not migrated).
* Over 4.7 million records from the former PREMARC file.
* 256,000 records from the former APIF file (76,000 records for older "in process" records for materials never received by the Library were not migrated).
* Over 223,000 visual materials records from the VM file (86,000 records from the "AV Datasheet" program that did not represent LC holdings were not migrated).
* Ten and a half thousand manuscript records from the Mixed Materials (MX) file.

* 187,000 records for cartographic materials from the MAPS file.
* 223,000 records for scores and sound recordings from the MUSIC file.
* 375,000 records from the JACKPHY file (records containing vernacular scripts for Japanese, Arabic, Chinese, Korean, Persian, Hebrew, and Yiddish works cataloged in the RLIN system).
* 375,000 serial bibliographic records from the SERIALS file representing the subset of CONSER records of titles held by the library (over 530,000 non-LC CONSER records were not migrated to the new system).
* Approximately 600,000 records from the SERLOC file of serial holdings, including several hundred thousand records for titles not kept by the library — records in this latter category are "suppressed" from view in the Online Catalog.
* Around 19,000 brief bibliographic records from the ACQUIRE system (the former acquisitions management system).
* 250,000 subject authority records from the former SUBJECTS file.
* 4.6 million name authority records from the former NAMES file.

***Access to the New Online Catalog*:** The Library of Congress Online Catalog is available using the World Wide Web at http://catalog.loc.gov/. The Library of Congress Online Catalog is available 24 hours a day, 7 days a week. Maintenance and updates are done during the late evening and early morning hours—U.S. Eastern Time—and during those short periods of time some features may not be available. Users anywhere in the world beyond the walls of the Library of Congress can access the Online Catalog using the World Wide Web at http://catalog.loc.gov/. Users inside the Library of Congress utilize the Windows-based version of the Online Catalog. While there are some differences in the two versions, the catalog data is the same—only the interface is different.

6.3 Indian institute of Science Library

The Indian Institute of Science (1ISc), Bangalore has set up a digital library, the first of its kind in the country. The new cyber library uses the IBM's Digital Library software running on fast computers. This software has already been installed at the Vatican and in many large universities in other countries. With good communication links, the IISc's digital library will be accessible from anywhere in the country and the world.

This digital library is much appreciated a national resource. Universities and colleges suffered because they were unable to afford books and journals. If they had good communication links, these educational institutions would be able to access the information in the Institute's digital library. The IISc produces about 1,000 papers a year and around 200 doctoral theses. These will be available from the digital library as also the scientific journals published by the Institute. Some scientific journals have started appearing in electronic form on the Internet, and within a short while they too will be provided through this library. Many journals and other publications are available on CD-ROM. In addition, the Institute's computer networks already hold high-quality course material. The digital library can provide access not just to textual material, but also to multimedia. To demonstrate what can be done, the video of some recent functions, such as the reception given to Dr Abdul Kalam, have been digitized and put in the library. This multimedia capability can be used to generate visually rich material, with sound also, such as lectures, talks and presentations. These new digital libraries will be accessible over the Internet through the Institute's Web site www.iisc.ernet.in. Such access is at present likely to be slow and time consuming. But an initiative by the Department of Science and technology to establish high-performance computing facilities with good communication inks at many educational and research institutions throughout the country could provide better access to the IISc network and its digital library.

Let us connect to the web site of the Indian Institute of Science for which we can follow the steps given below.

* Connect to the Internet and open the web browser.
* Find the address box, and click in it once.
* Type the URL: http://www.library.iisc.ernet.in/
* Press Enter and then the JRD Tata Memorial Library of Indian Institute of Science opens before us.
* Now we can explore the hundreds of possibilities offered by IISc library by our self.

6.4 Indian Digital Library in Agriculture

Under the initiative of Dr. A.M. Michael the Vice Chancellor Kerala Agricultural University has obtained support from various national and international agencies and developed during 1995-98. Kerala Agricultural University Library and Information System named KAULIS, which can pool and share traditional and digitized agricultural information resources available at various centers under the university as well as permit access to it from anywhere. KAULIS consist of the University Central Library with Digital Library, IT Training Facilities and a Building LAN connected to the main campus network as well as automated libraries in distant campuses of the university connected to concerned campus networks.

The University Library and its Digital Library and Networks completed in 1997 were formally commissioned in 1998. It faces a serene and beautiful landscape and provides comfortable and peaceful environment for the seekers of knowledge.

KAULIS has designed and developed an Electronic Library. Various national and international institutions have provided support toward this. The Library has customized some search engines according to requirement, which will enable automatic pooling of resources in a subject group and retrieving information from that at a single stroke of the key. The electronic library storage systems that can manage storage in a cost effective way and disseminate information efficiently consist of three types of hard wares; meant for highly used information, middle level usage information and less or rarely used information. In this Electronic Library the storage systems and the Alpha Server 1000 A; stores very costly specialized software and databases and agricultural research information worth about approximately Rs. 2.87 crore received and downloaded under various MOUs and licenses. The PhD dissertations of KAU are available in this electronic library. The Electronic Library has a storage capacity of approximately 6.5 crore printed pages and it already has full text libraries copied under various MOUs and books and other documents acquired in electronic medium consisting of 5.5 crore pages and about hundred and twenty hours video/ audio files in its storage systems. The Electronic library was experimentally put on Internet using a temporary connection the library got in December 1998 and was found successful. The library has also temporarily experimented the teleconferencing and conference digitizing facilities during IASLIC 1998 conference held in the campus. The video and sound files of the conference was recorded in the library's storage systems during December 1998. Immediately after the library gets a Vsat or leased line connection, which is a part of the project, the library will become accessible through Internet. Then the digitized books, interactive multimedia programmes, video films on agriculture related aspects and other information stored here would become accessible from any distant campuses or Krishi Bhavans of the State. The electronic library systems installed here has the capacity to maintain a web portal on agriculture for the

State. This can provide online information to farmers on cropping agricultural practices, technical aspects of agriculture, and government schemes. Farmers can also get customized information from agricultural scientists of the university through this system. Extension activists can take access equipments to remote areas and there the whole multimedia information resource kept at this library will be accessible for their presentation and demonstration through the portable access systems. The electronic library has all the facilities for hosting a virtual university on agriculture.

The content of the Electronic Library comprises specialized information on; genetic engineering, animal cell culture and virology, plant tissue culture, photosynthesis, and plant molecular biology, oncogenes, reproduction physiology, cell transformation, nucleic acid and protein sequences, immunology, enzyme engineering, immobilised biocatalysts, microbial fermentation and bioprocess engineering received from DBT and other agencies which can be accessed online by KAU scientists and students.

The electronic library contains all the publications originally brought out by 19 international agricultural research centers including ICRISAT of India. It contains in full results of 24 years agricultural research recorded in documents including key books, serials, conference proceedings, reports, maps, graphs and photographs produced by research centers worldwide on practical problem solving research in key areas like productivity, management of natural resources, improving policy environment, institution building, germless conservation and building linkages in agricultural system. All this collections are available for use through KAULIS Network.

The full database of International Development Research Center, (IDRC) Ottawa containing information on development research going on all over the world supported by World Bank, FAO and other international organizations is also available on this electronic library and is continuously updated under a resource sharing programme which is accessible through KAU Library System.

The databases developed by Center for Agriculture and Biosciences International an intergovernmental organization covering subjects like agricultural engineering, animal breeding, animal diseases, arid lands, diary sciences, forestry, forest products, horticulture, nutrition, veterinary science, entomology, plant breeding, plant pathology, soils and fertilizers, weeds and world agricultural economics is also available in the electronic library. This database contains information including abstracts of papers published in 8500 journal on agricultural topics in 37 different languages, and also books, reports, thesis, conference proceedings, patents, annual reports and guides. The coverage is from 1970. Over 1,60 000 items are included in the database every year and is added to KAU electronic Library also. This database on agriculture and allied subjects covering the period from 1970 to present consisting of 3, 000, 000 records is an asset to the state's agricultural research and development programmes.

To connect to the web site of the KAULIS we can follow the steps given below.

* Connect to the Internet and open the web browser.
* Find the address box, and click in it once.
* Type the URL kaulis.org. That URL will work in any browser, but if we use latest versions of Internet Explorer or Navigator we can optionally omit the http:// prefix.
* Press Enter KAULIS web site appears.
* We can explore the site from this page.

7. Bibliographic Sources on the Net

Bibliographic services give information about locating information sources and information itself. This is the most important service provided by libraries. Though it is not an easy task, it is a necessary for libraries and information centers to provide this service. Presently this task has become much easier with Internet. Internet has a tremendous number of resources available and hosts many bibliographic information sources which are of more importance to libraries. It is required that library professionals are familiar with these resources and their features, to harness them from the Net and use it to design bibliographic services applicable to their Library and Information Centers.

One major bibliographic information source in India is

INFLIBNET, which is building up the union catalogue of holdings of Indian academic libraries. The databases are now available online at INFLIBNET web site. Basically INFLIBENT is established to provide catalogue-based services, access to databases and document supply services and facilities over computer based network. It has launched union database services for different type of documents having online access facilities to them. Financial assistance is provided to universities to expedite the process of producing their database and putting them to INFLIBNET database.

At International level there are many web pages that provide bibliographic services. Some of the important bibliographic services on the Net for LIS professionals are the following.

* Uncover : URL: http://uncweb. carl. org/uncover/complete. Html. Uncover provides document delivery services and users may browse through the bibliographic information and order articles of journals and documents if required.
* BUBL Information Service URL: http://bubl.ac.uk/. It provides national information service for the higher education community in UK.
* National Academic Press. URL: http://www.nap.edu/readingroom/reader .cgi?auth-free&1abel-book.03090058317. Provides bibliographic description of the document, some of them is full text documents. The documents are classified according to subject. It also provides an index search.
* AALL Online Bibliographic Services Special Interest Section. RL: http://pappas-ntl.bll.edll/obs/obs.htm. The Online Bibliographic Services Special Interest Section (OBS/SIS) of AALL (American Association of Law Libraries) focuses on all aspects of the various national and local bibliographic utilities. These include public access to bibliographic data online, acquisitions subsystems, mail message systems, and integration of circulation systems with the online bibliographic data.

To know more about the features and services provided by these websites, it is necessary to learn about these bibliographic services in detail. For example browse the web page of CARL corporation and its databases, and in particular the Uncover database. We can access the CARL Corporation by accessing the CARL website at URL: http://www.carl.org/carlweb/. The web site at hilp:// www.carl.org,/car.lweb/ provides access to the following databases.

* The Uncover Database
* Library and Information Databases
* Multiple Database Search .CARL Corp's home page

Uncover is an online periodical article delivery service and a current awareness alerting service. The Uncover database contains records describing journals and their contents from 17,000 multidisciplinary journals, which have appeared since Fall 1988. Over 4000 current citations are added daily. Uncover offers us the opportunity to order fax copies of the articles from this database. Uncover is easy to use, with keyword access to article titles and summaries. For example, open the web page of Uncover at the URL:http://llncweb.carl.org/ This opens the home page of UnCover web welcoming us to the current Awareness and Document Delivery services. Uncover provides many services of which some are listed below.

* Uncover desktop Image Delivery
* Searching the Uncover database
* Uncover ravel (an automated document alerting service)
* CarlWeb (provides search of other databases other than the Uncover database)

Now we can click on "Search the Uncover database" link. It presents a screen to enter and search the Uncover database with login and password, this is required only if we need to order the articles. We can still search the database without logging in, by just clicking on the "Search Uncover NOW" button to search for our query. This opens the query form and the screen gives the following options.

* Choose your UnCover database: from
  * UnCover
  * UnCover Express (1 hour delivery)
* Enter search terms:

* Choose search type: (" Keyword Name or author r Journal title Browse)
* Choose number of records to display:

We can enter our search term. For example, Enter the search term "Ranganathan, S.R", click on 'Name of the Author' option to search in the Author field, and press on the enter button. This retrieves all the journal articles with the author name 'Ranganathan, S.R'. We can select any record required. The records provide the author's name, title of the article and title of the journal. The article is hyperlinked and provides more information. When the Journal title is clicked it provides a list of issues, which are further linked to the contents page of that Issue. The result retrieved and presented on the screen.

We can select any articles of the author from this list. This gives details about ordering information, like the price of the service etc. for familiarization we can select one record from the list we have now got, this retrieves information about the record and details to acquire it, if required we can order for the article online by paying the required charges. It provides the pricing information as below.

Fax surcharges apply to orders sent outside the U.S. and Canada. To see a list of country codes with associated fax surcharges, we can press the concerned button.

Pricing.

This article may be available in your library, at no cost to you. To have it faxed from UnCover, the following charges apply:

Service Charge:	$ 15.00
Fax Surcharge:	$ 00.00
Copyright Fee:	$ 29.00
Total Fax Delivery Charge-	$ 44.00

We can click on the title of the journal, to get more information of that journal; this retrieves information about published Volumes and Numbers. Here we can click on any of the issues to get the contents page of that issue. In the contents page all the articles are highlighted and details about each can be found by clicking on them. Enter the term "library cataloguing" to be searched as a keyword. This query retrieves all the articles with the keyword. We can select one of the titles to view the details of ordering it. We can try out using this site by searching any article from the Uncover database as well as searching for the same in the other bibliographic service.

Uncover database and thousands of similar databases on the Net provide good bibliographic services. Here we have explored the bibliographic service of Uncover database in a simple way. We can learn more about the search features of these services by browsing the Net and thus use the required information.

8. INFLBNET

INFLIBNET is an autonomous Inter-University Center of the University Grants Commission (UGC) of India. It is a major National Programme initiated by the UGC in 1991 with its Head Quarters at Gujarat University Campus, Ahmedabad. Initially started as a project under the IUCAA, it became an independent Inter University Center in 1996. INFLIBNET is involved in modernizing university libraries in India and connecting them as well as information centers in the country through a nationwide high-speed data network using the state-of-art technologies for the optimum utilization of information. INFLIBNET is set out to be a major player in promoting scholarly communication among academicians and researchers in India.

Objectives of INFLIBNET as envisaged in Memorandum of Association are:

* To promote and establish communication facilities to improve capability in information transfer and access, that provide support to scholarship, learning, research and academic pursuit through cooperation and involvement of agencies concerned;
* To establish Information And Library Network "INFLIBNET" - a computer communication network for linking libraries and information centers in universities, deemed to be universities, colleges, UGC information centers, institutions of national importance and R&D institutions, etc. avoiding duplication of efforts.

In order to fulfill the broad objectives, INFLIBNET will

* Promote and implement computerization of operations and services in the libraries and information centers of the country, following a uniform standard
* Evolve standards and uniform guidelines in techniques, methods, procedures, computer hardware and software, services and promote their adoption in actual practice by all libraries, in order to facilitate pooling, sharing and exchange of information towards optimal use of resources and facilities
* Evolve a national network interconnecting various libraries and information centers in the country and to improve capability in information handling and service
* Provide reliable access to document collection of libraries by creating on-line union catalogue of serials, theses/dissertations, books, monographs and non-book materials (manuscripts, audio-visuals, computer data, multimedia, etc.) in various libraries in India.
* Provide access to bibliographic information sources with citations, abstracts etc. through indigenously created databases of the Sect oral Information Centers of NISSAT, UGC Information Centers, City Networks and such others and by establishing gateways for on-line accessing of national and international databases held by national and international information networks and centers respectively
* Develop new methods and techniques for archiving of valuable information available as manuscripts and information documents in different Indian Languages, in the form of digital images using high density storage media
* Optimize information resource utilization through shared cataloguing, inter-library loan service, catalogue production, collection development and thus avoiding duplication in acquisition to the extent possible.
* Enable the users dispersed all over the country, irrespective of location and distance, to have access to information regarding serials, theses/dissertations, books, monographs

and non-book materials by locating the sources wherefrom available and to obtain it through the facilities of INFLIBNET and union catalogue of documents.

* Create databases of projects, institutions, specialists, etc. for providing on-line information service.
* Encourage co-operation among libraries, documentation centers and information centers in the country, so that the resources can be pooled for the benefit of helping the weaker resource centers by stronger ones.

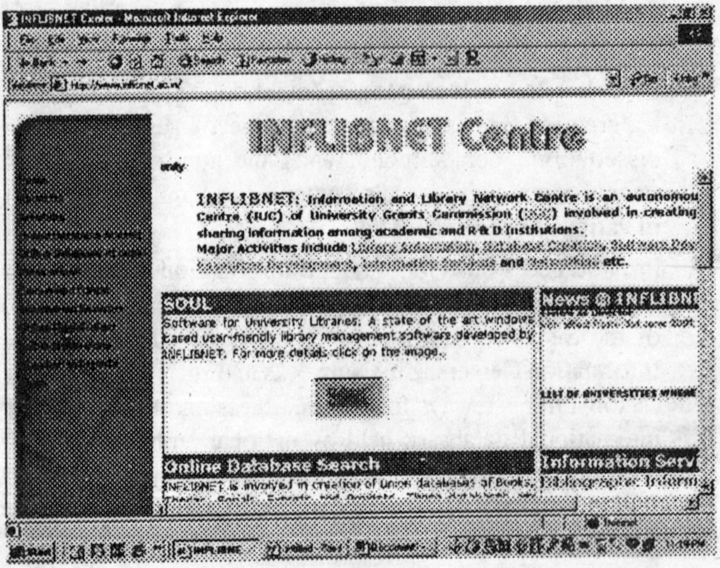

* Train and develop human resources in the field of computerized library operations and networking to establish, manage and sustain INFLIBNET.
* Facilitate academic communication amongst scientists, engineers, social scientists, academics, faculties, researchers and students through electronic mail, file transfer, computer/audio/video conferencing, etc.
* Undertake system design and studies in the field of communications, computer networking, and information handling and data management.

* Establish appropriate control and monitoring system for the communication network and organize maintenance.
* Collaborate with institutions, libraries, information centers and other organizations in India and abroad in the field relevant to the objectives of the Center.
* Create and promote R&D and other facilities and technical positions for realizing the objectives of the Center.
* Generate revenue by providing consultancies and information services.
* Do all other such things as may be necessary, incidental or conducive to the attainment of all or any of the above objectives.

To Access INFLIBNET we can get Connected to the Internet and open the web browser.

* Find the address box, and click in it once.
* Type the URL: http://www.inflibnet.ac.in.
* Press Enter. the INFLIBNET web site appears
* Then we can check various asoectes at the library,

9. Access to Whole Universe of Knowledge

As the digital library system intends to provide a new format to library and information services, the professionals must be aware about its all components to accept this challenge of changing environment. And they should be able to acquire the skills and knowledge of professional tools and techniques in the new environment to fulfill the goal. New developments are taking place every day in the areas of communication and Internet technologies. More powerful and versatile browsers like Microsoft Internet Explorer Release 5 have come. An exclusive net-Internet 2 is starting operation for sophisticated academicians who are presently hampered by the slow speed of all and sundry users of present Internet. The Internet 2, the special Internet, is planned to operate at high speed with the half of a new routing and switching technologies called Gigapops built on ATM switching system. The spread of Internet 2 facility across the continents cannot be far behind. This is exactly the place where the other recent development in communication called FLAG

(Fiber-optic Link Around Globe) will fit it. The project FLAG when completed will be the world's longest cable link measuring about 28,000 km and will provide data transmission speed of 5.3 gaps (gigabytes per second) comparable to futuristic low flying satellite constellations like Iridium and Tele disk. All these developments are going to have direct and indirect impact on the digital library functions accessing them through Internet and their popularity.

14

Putting Library in Internet

Most of the live libraries are presently having web presence. Millions of sites are added to the web every year. No other arena seems to he expanding and changing as quickly as the web. It seems that every day there is something new that can he done on, with, or to the Web. This presents a significant hurdle for those who want to do web pages. If we are relatively new to the web, we might need some sink time,' or time for the information to take root. The webmaster usually is the person who creates, develops, and maintains a web site, but as we will see there is often more things involved than just creating pages and posting them to a web site. Because web mastering is based on technology, its definition can vary from institution to institution or from person to person. Most often the webmaster is classified as someone who can create web pages, but in most instances, the job requires much more than knowledge of posting pages to a site.

Web designers have various roles to play. This does not mean that in every library or institution or in every situation a single individual will be ultimately responsible for al! these tasks. In large corporate settings there often are several individuals involved in web development, but there will always he a coordinating leader for the group. This leader, the lead web designer, will undoubtedly have knowledge in all these areas and be able, to guide, direct, and coach the other individuals in their tasks. If we have to act as a web designer or webmaster for a small library with no other individuals involved with this process, we are the lead webmasters already.

1. Knowledge of Internet

First and foremost, the webmaster is an Internet specialist. An Internet specialist is one who understands what the Net is, from where it came, and where it might be going. The Internet specialist also understands how to connect to the Internet and how to utilize it. We should know that the web did not develop overnight, although current newspaper and broadcast media would like to suggest otherwise.

We have to understand that the future of the web is still relatively unclear. Today the Net is a mass of computing power connected together, enabling many different types of communication to occur. Libraries, corporations, businesses, and institutions all are scrambling to establish their presence on the web. This gives us many opportunities to get involved with institutions that are beginning to establish their web presence. But the future of the web is unclear due to advancements we have yet to discover, not to mention an extremely accelerated period of growth. As the hardware and software advance, so will the capabilities of the web. Much like a business that is bursting at the seams, the web is growing so fast that it is difficult to determine what effect the growth has on performance. Will performance break down as the user base expands? Will it create new advancements in technology? Will the hardware naturally expand to enable growth or will the infrastructure collapse under the increasing load?

Many libraries are rushing headlong to throw their information on the web, working from a paradigm in which the fear of being left behind is greater than the fear of losing money in a web investment. Yet, most have sincere concerns about the longevity and commercial validity of the web. We have to educate our self on the latest technologies so that we can present logical and technological answers to these types of questions and concerns.

Additionally, the webmaster must know how to use the web and how to connect to it. What are the best resources on the web? Where the heck are they, and how do we get connected? From machines to cables to software, we must know how to get our self and our library latched on to this world. When we are surfing the

Web, how do we do it with efficiency? In other words, how do we know a good wave?

2. Information Science

The main purpose of the web is to entertain, inform, or persuade our audience; it is a new way of communicating. To effectively communicate in each of these ways, we must know how to put together several different elements in a logical and effective manner. Most often the webmaster is given content, such as information that describes a library, its services or information on an organization, to put on the web. This makes the task a little easier. Sometimes he or she will need to develop the content or coordinate content development among a group of individuals. In either case, the main purpose behind providing content is to communicate.

An information design specialist is an individual who understands the communication process and how to design products that inform, persuade, educate, or entertain efficiently and effectively. As most developers know that, rule number one in multimedia and hypermedia development is that content is king. Poorly designed content can never be masked. No matter how many slick graphics, dancing bullets, or animated elements are added, poor content is still poor. It is like dressing up the exterior or interior of a house that has a cracked foundation with the intent of selling it. It won't sell because the footing on which everything else rests is unstable. The same is true of poor content. The content is the foundation from which communication occurs and to which all supporting elements enhance and clarify.

In web communication, noise is something with which we should be most concerned for noise disrupts communication. Noise is comprised of those things that distract the receiver and inhibit the reception of the message. Noise can occur from the sender in the form of poor content. It can occur in the communication channel in the form of a hefty page that takes an eternity to download. It also can occur on the receiver's end in the form of an incompatible browser. You see a lot of this on the web. Many people on the Web have things to say; however, due to noise, their messages are not received. In the information age, we must understand that people are inundated with information. When a message is blocked or surrounded with noise, it can he misunderstood, misinterpreted, or ignored outright. A site must communicate clearly, effectively, and precisely for maximum impact.

3. Power to Communicate

Creating a product that communicates effectively, like a web site, requires the use of careful planning so that the product itself is successful. The success of such a work is determined by how well the message is received and interpreted by the audience. So how do we ensure that a product, communicates well? For this we can look for a product that has been deemed successful and see how it was developed.

Creating a good web site can be summed up in one word: planning. Most sites fail because issues arise that were not considered during the site's conception. People instantly jump behind a computer and start pushing pixels and spewing code, inevitably creating, in most cases, a horrid site. Problems with browsers, platforms, fonts, down loading, and so on will make results worse in this quick method of creating a web site. There is no replacement for time spent on planning a site.

When we develop a site, we must he concerned with providing good content. We also must ascertain whether we can adequately provide what our audience wants. Can our equipment support the number of people or hits made to our site? Do we have the resources in-house to support a site, or should we look for outside vendors for help? There are many questions, but they are ones that need to he considered. A hit occurs when a browser from a remote location requests information from a web server. Each time a new or different page is loaded from the site, a hit is recorded.

4. Technical Issues

Most of the things with which the webmaster deals are technical issues such as connecting to the Net, finding resources, and using those resources. However, to some extent the webmaster must have some inclination as to the whole purpose of the web communication. The criterion for a good web site is its communicative value and how efficiently and effectively communication occurs.

The biggest inhibitors of web communication are poorly designed graphics, animations, and multimedia elements. To he an effective web master we must develop an artistic eye, an understanding of the communicative power of graphics, and a designer's imagination. The hypermedia world is filled with many different additive elements that can he used to help a site or page communicate. We should use graphical elements to help communicate more effectively; this is their goal and, purpose. One of the first steps is to develop an understanding of page layout and composition and how it affects readability and visual appeal. Web documents become much better communication tools when they are formatted and include graphics, they also become more interesting.

A technical designer should first understand the technology behind the web. This includes having an understanding of the hardware-networks, machines, and connections-and the client and server software. Fortunately, today's Net is somewhat more standardized than in days gone by. However, there are many standards. The various parts of the web use several terms for which the webmaster must have definitions and understanding. This is the first step in being technically "web adept."

Now, the role of the webmaster is continually changing and evolving. This is natural because the item on which the webmaster's livelihood depends-the web-also is evolving. In days gone by, a single individual was designated as webmaster, but in many organizations today there is often a team of people working to assist and support the tasks of the webmaster. The webmaster still must manage and maintain hardware and software, but often managerial skills extend beyond these two items to one of the hardest things to manage that is people involved.

To master the technology, we must put into practice what we learn. Reading about web brings theoretical knowledge, doing it brings applied and practical knowledge. We can read many books, on subjects well beyond what we learn here, but until we actually start tinkering with the technology it's only head knowledge. Hopefully, we will have the opportunity to put into action what we learn by trying examples, looking at the technology we currently have, or even to the ultimate, setting up our web system using some guide. Regardless, we will have to put into action the things we read for it to actually take root and becomes applied knowledge. The best teacher is the technology.

To develop a technique or style in web development, we must take action and begin developing our own pages and sites. The predominate knowledge base on techniques comes both in page design and information design. To help us develop the eye for design and the understanding of good content, we hopefully already have one of the best applied teachers right at our fingertips: our web connection. One of the best ways to see what is mentioned here is to spend time surfing. In this book we can see examples, and even the web addresses, but we will have to link to the Web ourself-somehow. So we have to be prepared to do a lot of surfing.

5. Developing Simple Site

If our library has some interesting and unique services to offer, if we want to offer our experiences or expertise to the world, there is no better way to do that than by creating and publishing our library's own web page. Building a web page is easier than we might think. If we know how to surf the web and to use any word processing program, we already possess the prerequisite skills for web authoring. Here we will see several ways to create attractive web pages. The basic skills we will learn here will form a foundation upon which we can build later, on our own, to add scripts, multimedia, and other advanced techniques to our skill set. We will also learn to create fancy, formatted email and newsgroup messages. Before we can dive into creating a web page, we need to pick up a more detailed understanding of how a web page works.

5.1. Web Page Constituents

Web page is actually a file in a format called HTML. An HTML file contains nothing but text. The actual text we will see online, and instructions for how that text is to appear. The following is a sample which shows the html text of a web page I have prepared in 1998 for the Kerala Agricultural University's Digital Library in Agriculture.

```
<html><head><title>KAU</title></head>

<body background="http://mypage.com/images/backgrounds/backg5.jpg" text=#000000 link=#0000ff vlink=#ff0000><font face="Arial">

<blockquote><blockquote><blockquote>

<center>

<p><font face="Arial, Geneva" size=+7>KAU</font></p>

</center>

<center>

<img src="http://mypage.com/images/pictures/pict2.gif">

<p><font face="Arial, Geneva" size=+2><b>Digital Library in Agriculture</b></font>

</center>

<center><img src="http://mypage.com/images/lines/line_33.gif"></center><P>

<center>

<br><font face="Arial, Geneva" size=3>KAULIS Digital Library contains digitised full text collections on agricultural research recorded in documents including key books, serials, conference proceedings, reports, maps, graphs and photographs produced by research centres worldwide on practical problem solving research in key areas like productivity, management of natural resources, improving policy environment, institution building, germplasm conservation and building linkages in agricultural system.The databases covers agricultural engineering, animal breeding, animal diseases, arid lands, diary sciences, forestry, forest products, horticulture, nutrition, veterinary science, entomology, plant breeding, plant pathology, soils and fertilizers, weeds and world agricultural economics is also available in the electronic library. </font>

</center><center>

<p><table border=1 cellspacing=3 cellpadding=3></table></center><center>
```

```
<p><i><font face="Arial, Geneva" size=4><b>Other Places to go:</i></b></font></p>

<p><font face="Arial, Geneva" size=3><a href="http://msnhomepages.talkcity.com.NonProfitBlvd/kaulis/index.html">Kerala Agricultural University Library and Information System</a><br>

<a href="http://"></a><br>

<a href="http://"></a></font></p>

</center>

<center><img src="http://mypage.vsnl.com/images/lines/line_33.gif"></center>

<p><center><a href="mailto:kaulis@ hotmail.com"> Restrcted Access. Contact</a></font></center></p>

</blockquote></blockquote></blockquote>

</center></body></html>
```

The text in an HTML file also includes the URLs where any links in the page lead, and the filenames, locations, and page positions of any pictures or other multimedia files, which are stored in their own, separate files. When an HTML file is viewed through a browser, the browser interprets the instructions in the file. The browser formats the text onscreen as ordered, locates the picture files and displays them in their specified positions. The browser also reads and remembers the URLs the links point in so to take a visitor who clicks one. The following figure shows the same html file we have discussed here and shown in the above figure but now the file is interpreted by a web browser that is how we will see the page when accessing it through Internet.

In general, the formatting instructions contained in an HTML file do not precisely control how the page will appear. Rather, the file provides a general idea of how the page is to appear, and each browser realizes those instructions slightly differently. That is why the same web page often looks different in two different browsers. For example, the HTML file may specify that a particular line of text is to be displayed as a "heading." One browser follows that

Html file interpreted by Web Browser

instruction by making the text big and bold, although another may follow it by underlining the text. This idea is often difficult to get used to for new authors are accustomed to word processors that enable precise formatting control.

Today, advanced web authoring techniques that give us greater control are available. But for most authors and certainly all beginners, formatting a web page is not about controlling exactly how the page will look, but rather about designating the role each element plays in the page: a heading, a normal paragraph, and so on. A web page can be made up of many different parts, but most web pages contain most or all of the following core elements.

Tide: Browsers typically display titles in the title bar of the window in which the page appears. Note that the actual title does not appear within the layout of the page, although many authors repeat the title in a big heading near the top of the page layout.

Headings: Browsers typically display headings in large, bold, or otherwise emphasized type. A web page can have many headings, and headings can be nested up to six levels deep; that is, there can be subheadings, and sub subheadings and so on. In HTML, there are six levels of headings, beginning with Heading 1 the biggest and boldest, usually reserved for creating an online page title and going down to Heading 6 a very small, minor heading, indistinguishable from Normal text in many browsers.

Normal Text: Makes up the basic, general-purpose text of the page.

Horizontal Lines: They are sometimes called rules and they dress up the page and separate it into logical sections.

Hyperlinks: Which are simply links and they link to many different things like other web pages, multimedia files like external images, animation, sound, video, document files, email addresses, and files or programs on other types of servers such as Telnet, FTP, and Gopher. Links may also lead to specific spots within the current page.

Lists: Lists may be bulleted or numbered.

***Inline Images*:** Pictures that are incorporated into the layout of the page to jazz it up or make it more informative.

Background: An inline image that, unlike a regular image, covers the entire background of the page so that the text and other images can be seen on top of it. Instead of an image, we can use a solid background color.

Tables: Text and inline images organized in neat rows and columns.

6. Tools for Writing Web Pages

If we are skilled in HTML code, we could write a web page by typing the correct code in a text file, in any word processor or text editing program such as Windows Notepad, WordPad, MSWord, WordPerfect and the like. Some people do it that way, but doing so makes it hard to see what we are creating. We will discuss in detail about HTML in another chapter. But a better choice is a WYSIWYG web-authoring program. A WYSIWYG web authoring program shows us the page, as it will look online, while we are working on it.

WYSIWYG meaning What You See Is What You Get. The

word describes a program that shows us as we create something, exactly how it will look in its finished form, on paper or online. For Windows and the Mac, most word processors, presentation programs, desktop publishers, and web authoring programs are WYSIWYG.

If we are careful to select and install the complete suite, we get a WYSIWYG editor with Explorer and navigator. The full Communicator suite includes Page Composer, which we open from within Navigator by choosing Communicator > Page Composer. The full Internet Explorer suite includes FrontPage Express, which we can open from the same menu where we can open the browser in Windows 98, choose Programs > Internet Explorer > FrontPage Express. We can learn about other web authoring programs at www.yahoo.com/Computers_and_Internet/ Software/ Internet/ World_ Wide_Web/ HTML_Editors/

Even when using a WYSIWYG editor, pages we create will look different when seen through different browsers: WYS is not always WYG. While Even when working in a WYSIWYG editor, it is a good idea to display the document in a browser now and then, to check its appearance. Composer and FrontPage Express each include a button for viewing the page we are editing in Navigator and Internet Explorer.

6.1 Getting Pictures

The pictures we will use in our web pages can come from anywhere. We can draw them in a paint program such as CorelDraw or Windows 98's Paint accessory, scan them from our own photos, or even use images captured by a digital camera.

What matters is not the source of the pictures, but the image file format in which they are stored. The pictures we may include in a web page either as inline images or as background images must be in either the GIF (.gif) or JPEG (.jpg) file format. GIF is usually preferable, because it is supported by all graphical browsers, although JPEG is also supported by most browsers and often produces better looking results with photographs. If the program we use to create images will not save in GIF or JPEG format, many paint programs and some web authoring programs can convert our files to GIF or JPEG.

If we want to use pictures, but do not want to create them, we can find libraries of commercial, shareware, and free clip art files in GIF and JPEG format at the software store and online. Good online starting places for getting clip art and other media, such as sounds include

Yahoo!'s Clip Art Directory: www .yahoo. com/ Computers_and_Internet/Multimedia/ Pictures/ Clip-Art

Index to Multimedia Information Sources: viswiz.gmd.de/ Multimedialnfo/

Microsoft Site Builder Network Home: www.microsoft.com/gallery

Netscape Page Starter Site: home .netscape .com/ assist / net_sites / starter / index.html

Free graphics: www.jgpublish .com/free. htm

6.2. Page Wizards

Fastest way to build a page is by running a page wizard. Both Composer and Front Page Express have one of these wizards, which lead us through filling in a few quick dialog boxes and choosing some options. When we finish, the wizard we get a finished page, ready for publishing. A wizard does not give us as much control as composing the page in a web-authoring program. Using a wizard is faster, however, and if the results are not exactly what we want, we can always open our wizard built page in our web-authoring program and change it. Here we will see how to use Page Composer's wizard, which is unusual because we must use it while online. In FrontPage Express's wizard which works offline we can choose File > New to open a list of options for starting a new page, then choose Personal Home Page from the list. We can create a page easily with Page Composer's wizard, by following the steps given below.

* First we have to open Navigator not Composer and connect to the Internet.
* In Navigator, choose File > New > Page From Wizard. This instructs the browser to connect to the Page Wizard page at

home.netscape.com/home/gold4.0_ wizard.html. We can also simply point the browser to that URL, although going through the menus is easier.

* In the active frame at upper right scroll down past Netscape's cheery introductory copy to display the Start button.
* Click the Start button in the upper right frame. The page appears. The Wizard page is split into three frames.
    * The upper left frame, Instructions, describes each element we will create. Within each description are links that, when clicked, display a form or list of choices in the bottom.
    * The bottom frame, Choices, is where we will type text in forms to create page content or choose aspects of the look of our page from lists of choices.
    * The upper right frame, Preview, shows a preview of our page as we develop it.
* Scroll the Instructions frame until we see the link "give your page a title," and click that link. A form appears in the Choices frame.
* Delete the descriptive text that appears in the form and then we can type a title for our page. The Page Wizard uses this as the HTML document title and as a large, bold heading at the top of the page itself.
* Click Apply. The new title appears in the Preview frame upper right, centered at the top of the page.
* Scroll down the Instructions until we see another link to a page element we can create. Click it, and then follow the instructions to complete the form in the bottom frame. We can continue defining page elements until the Preview frame shows a page to our liking. Note that we can scroll the Instructions backward at any time to make changes.
* When done, we have to scroll to the bottom of the Instructions frame, where we will see buttons labeled Build and Start Over.
* Click Build. The finished page opens in Navigator.

* From Navigator's menu bar, choose File > Edit Page Composer opens, displaying our new home page.
* Click the Save button on Composer's toolbar or choose File > Save; select a folder and filename for our page, and save it. The page is given a default filename of Yourpage. html. We can change this name to anything we like, but make sure the file extension remains. htm or. html.
* Click OK to save the file. Our page is ready to be published or to be edited furtherr in our web-authoring program.

6.3 WYSIWYG Editor

Composing a web page in a WYSIWYG editor is much like composing and formatting a document in any word processor. We type our text, then format it by selecting it with our mouse and applying formatting such as bold, fonts, and so on from toolbar buttons or menu items. If we look at the toolbars in FrontPage Express or Composer, we will probably recognize many of the tools, such as a drop down list for choosing a font or a big B for applying Bold. Although the web authoring programs present us with lots of formatting tools, the precise formatting we apply such as font selections may not be the application of styles, which we choose in either Composer or FrontPage Express from a drop down list on the toolbar.

Besides using a web authoring program or a wizard, there is one more way to create a page. That is in our word processor. Increasingly, word processors have the capability to save files in HTML format. The latest versions of both Microsoft Word and WordPerfect can save file in HTML format. A word processor is not as good for authoring as a real authoring Program. But it makes it easy for us to convert existing documents into web page files. For example, we can open our resume in Word and then save it as an HTML file. This makes it for the web.

7. FrontPage Express

We can design a page in FrontPage Express, by following the steps given below. For this first we have to open FrontPage Express. Opening FrontPage Express automatically starts a new page, but we can also start one by choosing File > New > Normal Page.

* From the menu bar, choose File > Page Properties. The Page Properties dialog box opens.
* Click the General tab, if it is not already selected, then click in the Title box.
* Delete the automatic title, and then we can type one of our own. Then click OK to close the dialog box.
* After giving our page a title is a good time to save it for the first time. Click the Save button in the toolbar or choose File > Save. A special Save dialog box opens.
* In the dialog box, click the As File button.
* Choose a location for the page file, and type a name for the file in the File name box. Then click the Save button to save the file. From now on, we can save the file at any time in one step, just by clicking the Save button on the toolbar.
* Now we can type and edit the text of our page, just as we would in any word processor. We need not worry about formatting that text. We have to just enter the words.
* After our text is typed, we may format the text. Begin by selecting a paragraph to format.
* Drop down the Change Style list from the toolbar, and choose a style like Normal, a heading, and so on to apply to the selected text. ,
* Now add a picture, if we are having an image file we want to use the file should be in GIF or JPEG format, but if it is not, we can use it anyway. FrontPage Express can probably convert it for us.
* In the page, click at the general spot within the text where we want the picture to go. Then click the Insert Image button on the toolbar to open the Image dialog box.
* Click Browse, to browse for and selected the image file. After the file appears in our page, we can reposition the picture by pointing to it, clicking and holding, and dragging to where

we want the picture to appear. Note that we cannot precisely position a picture. Positioning a web page picture means choosing its rough position within the text, and which side of the page it is to be positioned.

When we next save the page file, we may see a dialog box on which we click Yes to accomplish either or both of two important things; Convert the picture file to GIF format if it was not already a GIF file and save the picture file in the same folder as the HTML file if it was originally stored elsewhere. It is always best to store all files that make up a web page the HTML file, the image files, and so on in the same folder or directory on our computer.

* Now add a background. Open the Page Properties dialog box >File > Page Properties and click the Background tab.
* To create an image background, check the check box next to Background Image, and then click Browse to browse for and select a GIF image file, just as we would when inserting a picture.
* To create a color background, choose a color from the Background drop down list.
* Finally, add a link. We can feature links that take our visitors to our favorite places on the web, or we can include a link to another page we have created. So our page can actually be made up of several pages linked together. Begin by selecting the text or picture that will serve as the link. If we use a picture as a link, always we have to provide the same link elsewhere on the page usually at the bottom for use by visitors whose browsers do not display pictures.
* Click the Create or Edit Hyperlink button on the toolbar. The Create Hyperlink dialog box opens. When we are creating a link to another web page, the Hyperlink Type box should read http://. If it does not, drop down the list and choose http:// which is the required type for a web page. We have to remember that the list lets us create links to resources other than web pages.
* In the URL box, type the URL of the web page to which this

link should lead when clicked by a visitor. Be sure to leave the http:// prefix on the URL. Click OK to create the URL.

* Save our page one last time. Now it's ready for publishing, or further editing and refinement.

7.1 Publishing Web Pages

After our web page is finished, we must upload it to a web server so others on the Internet can see it. First, we need space on somebody's web server enough to hold all the files that make up our page. A typical web page with a picture or two usually requires less than 100KB {kilobytes) of space on a server. The larger and more picture filled our page, the more server space we will require.

If our page is related to our library we may be able to get permission to publish it on our institutions server if it is having one. We have to talk to our organization's network administrator or web master. Most colleges and universities have web servers now; which were acquired with support from UGC's INFLIBNET Program and will publish the library page on it as well as allow students and faculty to publish on them their personal web pages. If our institution is not having its own server which is prohibitively expensive and technical for small institutions we need to acquire space on somebody else's web server, usually our ISP's web server. After we know whose server will hold our web page files, we must upload the files from our computer to the server. The exact procedures for doing this differ by ISP. We must get complete uploading instructions directly from the company whose server we will use. In particular, we need to know the following for this.

* The server's address: For example, http: //www .server. com
* The uploading protocol used by the server: For example, HTTP or FTP
* Any username and password that we are required to use to gain access to the server.
* The posting command, which we give the server to gain access for uploading files
* The particular directory in which our files will be stored; For example, http://www.server.com/net/

7.2 Using a Publishing Utility

After our ISP provides us with instructions for uploading our files, we can make uploading easier by supplying those instructions to a web-publishing program like those built into FrontPage Express and Composer. To use either of these utilities, first we have to open in the editor the page we want to publish. Then, we have to complete the following:

* In Composer, click the Publish button and follow the prompts.
* In Front Page Express, choose File. Save As to open the Save dialog box.
* In Page Location, type the complete URL the page will have on the web. Then click OK: and follow the prompts.

The first time when we use one of these publishing utilities, we need to spend a few minutes supplying information about the web server we will use. After we have done that, our uploads from then on will be quick and easy. These utilities remember all our server information so that after we enter the information once, we do not need to exercise in it again. We have to simply start the publishing procedure as before, and most of the steps happen automatically.

8. Formatted Email /Newsgroup Messages

We have earlier discussed email messages containing nothing but text. But we can also put in an email message the same kinds of content and formatting we use in a web page. We can send messages containing all kinds of fonts, colors, pictures, links and the like. If all these can be put in a web page, they can be put in our email message also. But there is one problem in sending fancy messages with multimedia content etc. That is our recipient may not be able to display them. Like a web page, a fancy message must be created in HTML format. To read the message, our recipient must use an email program such as Messenger or Outlook Express capable of displaying HTML based messages in addition to regular email messages.

In Outlook Express and Messenger, it is not necessary to send an HTML message just to send links. Anytime we type a

URL or email address in the body of a message, the email program detects it and formats it as a link. While reading our message, our recipient can click the link to go where it leads, and we can click the links in messages from others.

The majority of those using Internet email today cannot display HTML messages. Hence unless we happen to know that our intended recipient has an email program that can show HTML messages, it is best to stick with plain text messages.

To create an HTML message we can do like this. In Outlook Express we have to open a new message window as we usually would. From the message window's menu bar, choose Format > Rich Text (HTML). In Messenger or Collabra we must change the Preferences to send HTML messages. Choose Edit > Preferences, then choose the Messages subcategory under the Mail & Groups category. Check the By Default, Send HTML Messages check box near the top. Then close the Preferences dialog box and start a new message as usual.

When composing an HTML message in either program, we will notice that the toolbar and menu bar show most of the tools and options available in the suite's web authoring program. We compose and format an HTML message in Outlook Express exactly as we do a web page in FrontPage Express, and we compose and format an HTML message in Messenger exactly as we do a web page in Composer. By default, most programs that can send HTML messages automatically send replies in the same format in which the message was received. In other words, if someone sends us an HTML message, which means the sender's email program can display HTML, and we click Reply to respond to it, the message we create is automatically in HTML format.

9. Web Authoring and Purpose

We do not have to create our own web page without purpose. If we really do have something to say, however, we will find creating and publishing a page fairly easy, especially if we rely on the tools in an Internet suite. Web authoring is a big topic. We have discussed it in a small chapter. There are many voluminous books devoted to the subject, and even a thousand pages cannot cover all about web authoring. Besides practicing and sharpening the skills we have already discussed, our next step should be to learn more about online multimedia specifically, how to do more with pictures, and how to add sound, video, and animation to our pages. We have to carefully study the design and layout of pages we see that impress us and learn from what others are doing. After multimedia, the next hurdle is scripting, and probably doing so with Java. Most people after getting introduced to Java suddenly decide that they already know enough about web authoring. Just about anybody can learn to create web pages and add multimedia to them, but learning Java takes thinking like a programmer, and that is a specialized talent. We can also learn a lot about authoring online. A good way to start is by reading one of the web authoring books.

Over the last decade, Internet communication and services have greatly improved and developed into more useful tools; ones that work the way we do. The Internet has had several major contributors that have helped to make possible what we call the World Wide Web. In addition, the services and things we can do all have become easier to use and more efficient. The various services including the Web, Email, FTP, and Telnet make us more efficient and effective communicators.

15

Basics of HTML

HTML documents are plain text, which are also known as ASCII files that can be created using any text editors like Notepad on a Windows machine. We can also use word processing software if we remember to save our document as text only with line breaks. Some WYSIWYG editors are also available examples are Claris Home Page or Adobe Page Mill, for Windows. WYSIWYG is an acronym for what you see is what you get. As told earlier it means that we design our HTML document visually, as if we were using a word processor, instead of writing the markup tags in a plain-text file and imagining what the resulting page will look like. It is useful to know enough HTML to code a document before we determine the usefulness of a WYSIWYG editor, in case we want to add HTML features that our editor doesn't support.

If we have access to a Web server at our institution we can contact our Webmaster that is the individual who maintains the server to see how we can get our files on the Web. If we do not have access to a server at our organization we can contact a local Internet Service Provider that will post our files on a server for a fee.

In HTML an element is a fundamental component of the structure of a text document. Some examples of elements are heads, tables, paragraphs, and lists. We use HTML tags to mark the elements of a file for our browser. Elements can contain plain text, other elements, or both. To denote the various elements in an HTML document, we use tags. HTML tags consist of a left angle bracket

(<), a tag name, and a right angle bracket (>). Tags are usually paired (e.g., <H1> and </H1>) to start and end the tag instruction. The end tag looks just like the start tag except a slash (/) precedes the text within the brackets. HTML tags are listed below. Some elements may include an attribute, which is additional information that is included inside the start tag. For example, we can specify the alignment of images that is top, middle, or bottom by including the appropriate attribute with the image source HTML code. Tags that have optional attributes are noted below. HTML is not case sensitive. <title> is equivalent to <TITLE> or <Title>. But there are some exceptions also. All World Wide Web browsers support not all tags. If a browser does not support a tag, it will simply ignore it. But any text placed between a pair of unknown tags will still be displayed.

1. Simple HTML Document

Every HTML document should contain certain standard HTML tags. Each document consists of head and body text. The head contains the title, and the body contains the actual text that is made up of paragraphs, lists, and other elements. Browsers expect specific information because they are programmed according to HTML and SGML specifications. Required elements are shown in this sample bare-bones document:

```
<html>
<head>
<TITLE>Internet for LIS</TITLE>
</head>
<body>
<H1>Uses of Internet</H1>
<P>Internet is a Network of Networks.
This is the first paragraph.
While short it is
still a paragraph!</P>
<P>And this is the second paragraph. </P>
</body>
```

</html>

The required elements are the <html>, <head>, <title>, and <body> tags and their corresponding end tags. Because we should include these tags in each file, we might want to create a template file with them. Some browsers will format our HTML file correctly even if these tags are not included. But some will not. So we have to include them.

To see a copy of the file that our browser reads to generate the information in the web page display on our screen, we can select View > Source or the equivalent from the browser menu. Most browsers have a "View" menu under which this command is listed. The file contents, with all the HTML tags, are displayed in a new window. This is an excellent way to see how HTML is used and to learn tips and construct pages. Of course, the HTML might not be technically correct. Once we become familiar with HTML and check the many online and hard copy references on the subject, we will learn to distinguish between "good" and "bad" HTML. We have to remember that we can save a source file with the HTML codes and use it as a template for one of our Web pages or modify the format to suit our purposes.

2. Markup Tags

HTML element tells our browser that the file contains HTML-coded information. The file extension .html also indicates this as an HTML document and it must be used. If we are restricted to 8.3 filenames e.g., LeeHome.htm, we have to use only .htm for our extension.

The head element identifies the first part of our HTML-coded document that contains the title. The title is shown as part of our browser's window.

The title element contains our document title and identifies its content in a global context. The title is typically displayed in the title bar at the top of the browser window, but not inside the window itself. The title is also what is displayed on someone's hotlist or bookmark list and so we have to choose something descriptive, unique, and relatively short. A title is also used to identify our page for search engines such as HotBot or Infoseek. Generally we should keep our titles to 64 characters or fewer.

The second and largest part of our HTML document is the body, which contains the content of our document displayed within the text area of our browser window. The tags explained below are used within the body of our HTML document.

HTML has six levels of headings, numbered 1 through 6, with 1 being the largest. Headings are typically displayed in larger and/or bolder fonts than normal body text. The first heading in each document should be tagged <H1>. The syntax of the heading element is: <Hy>Text of heading </Hy> where y is a number between 1 and 6 specifying the level of the heading. We should not skip levels of headings in our document. For example, we should not start with a level-one heading (<H1>) and then next use a level-three (<H3>) heading.

Unlike documents in most word processors, carriage returns in HTML files are not significant. In fact, any amount of white space including spaces, linefeeds, and carriage returns are automatically compressed into a single space when our HTML document is displayed in a browser. So we do not have to worry about how long our lines of text are. Word wrapping can occur at any point in our source file without affecting how the page will be displayed. In the earlier example shown in the Minimal HTML Document the first paragraph is coded as

<P>Internet is a network of networks.

This is the first paragraph. While short it is

still a paragraph! </P>

In the source file there is a line break between the sentences. A Web browser ignores this line break and starts a new paragraph only when it encounters another <P> tag.

It is important that we should indicate paragraphs with <P> elements. A browser ignores any indentations or blank lines in the source text. Without <P> elements, the document becomes one large paragraph. One exception is text tagged as "preformatted," which is explained below. For example, the following would produce identical output as the first HTML example:

<H1>Level-one heading</H1>

<P>Internet is a network of networks. This is the

first paragraph. While short it is still a

paragraph! </P> <P>And this is the second paragraph. </P>

To preserve readability in HTML files, we have to put headings on separate lines, use a blank line or two where it helps identify the start of a new section, and separate paragraphs with blank lines in addition to the <P> tags. These extra spaces will help us when we edit our files but our browser will ignore the extra spaces because it has its own set of rules on spacing that do not depend on the spaces we put in our source file. The </P> closing tag may be omitted. This is because browsers understand that when they encounter a <P> tag, it means that the previous paragraph has ended. However, since HTML now allows certain attributes to be assigned to the <P> tag, it is generally a good idea to include it. Using the <P> and </P> as a paragraph container means that we can center a paragraph by including the ALIGN=alignment attribute in our source file.

<P ALIGN=CENTER>

Internet for LIS

</P>

The formatted version is

Internet for LIS

It is also possible to align a paragraph to the right instead, by including the ALIGN=RIGHT attribute. ALIGN=LEFT is the default alignment; if no ALIGN attribute is included, the paragraph will be left aligned.

3. Lists

HTML supports unnumbered, numbered, and definition lists. We can nest lists too, but use this feature sparingly because too many nested items can make it difficult to follow. To make an unnumbered, bulleted list, we have to start with an opening list <UL> for unnumbered list tag and then enter the <LI> (list item) tag followed by the individual item; no closing </LI> tag is needed and thenend the entire list with a closing list </UL> tag. Below is a sample three-item list:

<UL>

<LI> apples

<LI> bananas

<LI> grapefruit

</UL>

The output is:

* apples
* bananas
* grapefruit

The <LI> items can contain multiple paragraphs. We have to indicate the paragraphs with the <P> paragraph tags.

A numbered list also called an ordered list, from which the tag name derives, is identical to an unnumbered list, except it uses <OL> instead of <UL>. The items are tagged using the same <LI> tag. The following HTML code:

<OL>

<LI> oranges

<LI> peaches

<LI> grapes

</OL>

produces this formatted output:

1. oranges
2. peaches
3. grapes

A definition list coded as <DL> usually consists of alternating a definition term coded as <DT> and a definition description coded as <DD>. Web browsers generally format the definition on a new line and indent it. The following is an example of a definition list:

<DL>

<DT> Domain Name

<DD> Human-language name of a computer on the Internet, as opposed to its more computer friendly numeric IP address.

<DT> Email

<DD> Electronic mail known by its short form Email is a system whereby a computer user can exchange messages with other computer users via a communications network.

</DL>

The output looks like:

Domain Name

Human-language name of a computer on the Internet, as opposed to its computer friendly numeric IP address.

Email

Electronic mail known by its short form Email is a system whereby a computer user can exchange messages with other computer users via a communications network.

The <DT> and <DD> entries can contain multiple paragraphs indicated by <P> paragraph tags, lists, or other definition information. The COMPACT attribute can be used routinely in case our definition terms are very short. If, for example, we are showing some computer options, the options may fit on the same line as the start of the definition.

<DL COMPACT>

<DT> -i

<DD>invokes NCSA Mosaic for Microsoft Windows using the initialization file defined in the path

<DT> -k

<DD>invokes NCSA Mosaic for Microsoft Windows in kiosk mode

</DL>

The output looks like:

-i

invokes NCSA Mosaic for Microsoft Windows using the initialization file defined in the path.

-k

invokes NCSA Mosaic for Microsoft Windows in kiosk mode.

Lists can be nested. We can also have a number of paragraphs, each containing a nested list, in a single list item. Here is a sample nested list:

```
<UL>
<LI> Earlier States of Kerala:
<UL>
<LI> Travancore
<LI> Cochin
<LI> Kerala
</UL>
<LI> Ancient South Indian Kingdoms:
<UL>
<LI> Chera
<LI> Chola
</UL>
</UL>
```

The nested list is displayed as

* Earlier States of Kerala:
    * Travancore
    * Cochin
    * Kerala
* Ancient South Indian Kingdoms:
    * Chera
    * Chola

Extended Quotations

We have to use the <BLOCKQUOTE> tag to include lengthy quotations in a separate block on the screen. Most browsers generally change the margins for the quotation to separate it from surrounding text. In the example:

<P>Bill Gates on Internet</P>

<BLOCKQUOTE>

<P> Internet is a tidal wave. It will wash over the computer industry and many others, drowning those who do not learn to swim in its waves.

</P>

<P>—Quoted by Raman Nair in Internet for LIS </P>

</BLOCKQUOTE>

the result is:

Bill Gates on Internet.

Internet is a tidal wave. It will wash over the computer industry and many others, drowning those who do not learn to swim in its waves.

—Quoted by Raman Nair in Internet for LIS

The <BR> tag forces a line break with no extra white space between lines. Using <P> elements for short lines of text such as postal addresses results in unwanted additional white space. For example, with:

Center for Informatics Research and Development

Kudappanakunnu

Trivandrum, Kerala 695005

The output is:

Centre for Informatics Research and Development

Kudappanakunnu

Trivandrum, Kerala 695005

The <HR> tag produces a horizontal line having the width of the browser window. A horizontal rule is useful to separate major sections of our document. We can vary a rule's size (thickness) and width (the percentage of the window covered by the rule). Experiment with the settings until we are satisfied with the presentation. For example:

<HR SIZE=4 WIDTH="50%">

4. Character Formatting

HTML has two types of styles for individual words or sentences: logical and physical. Logical styles tag text according to its meaning, while physical styles indicate the specific appearance of a section. For example, in the preceding sentence, the words "logical styles" was tagged as "emphasis." The same effect (formatting those words in italics) could have been achieved via a different tag that tells our browser to "put these words in italics." The following is the HTML file of the Home Page of College for Women Trivandrums.

```
<html>
<head>
<title>H.H. The Maharaja's Government College for Women </title>
<meta http-equiv="Content-Type" content="text/html; charset=ISO-8859-
1">
<meta name="generator" content="Created Using Yahoo! PageWizards
2.6/2.60.14/">
</head>
<body bgcolor="#CCCC99" link="#3333FF" vlink=" #666633"
text="#000000"
>
<table border=0 cellspacing=0 cellpadding=0 width=626>
<tr valign="top" align="left">
<td><img src="http://www.geocities.com/clipart/pbi/c.gif' height=1
width=20></td>
<td><img src="http://www.geocities.com/clipart/pbi/c.gif' height=1
width=13></td>
</tr>
<tr valign="top">
<td colspan=32 height=15></td>
</tr>
<tr valign="top">
<td colspan=1 height=12></td>
<td colspan=8 rowspan=5 width=39 align="center" valign="middle"><img
height=37 width=39 src="http://www.geocities.com/clipart/pbi/bullets/Templates/
aboutme_classic_bullets.gif' border=0 ></td>
```

```
<td colspan=23 height=12></td>
</tr>
<tr valign="top">
<td colspan=1 height=4></td>
<td colspan=20 height=4></td>
<td colspan=2 rowspan=3 width=13 align="center" valign="middle"><img
height=13 width=13 src="http://www.geocities.com/clipart/pbi/bullets/Templates/
aboutme_classic_grnbullet.gif" border=0 ></td>
<td colspan=1 height=4></td>
</tr>
<tr valign="top">
<td colspan=1 height=4></td>
<td colspan=1 height=4></td>
<td colspan=17 rowspan=1 width=538 align="center"
valign="middle"><img height=4 width=538 src="http://www.geocities.com/clipart/
pbi/hrules/Templates/aboutme_classic_horzline.gif" border=0 ></td>
<td colspan=2 height=4></td>
<td colspan=1 height=4></td>
</tr>
<tr valign="top">
<td colspan=1 height=5></td>
<td colspan=20 height=5></td>
<td colspan=1 height=5></td>
</tr>
<tr valign="top">
<td colspan=1 height=12></td>
<td colspan=23 height=12></td>
</tr>
<tr valign="top">
<td colspan=6 height=11></td>
<td valign="middle" align="center" colspan=13 rowspan=5
width=266><b><font color="#006600" face="TimesRoman" size="+3"><span
style="font-size:36">H.H. The Maharaja's Government College for Women </
span></font></b></td>
<td colspan=13 height=11></td>
</tr>
<tr valign="top">
```

```
<td colspan=3 height=13></td>
<td colspan=1 rowspan=27 width=4 align="center" valign="middle"><img height=665 width=4 src="http://www.geocities.com/clipart/pbi/vrules/Templates/aboutme_classic_vertline.gif" border=0 ></td>
<td colspan=2 height=13></td>
<td colspan=1 height=13></td>
<td colspan=3 rowspan=1 width=13 align="center" valign="middle"><img height=13 width=13 src="http://www.geocities.com/clipart/pbi/bullets/Templates/aboutme_classic_grnbullet.gif" border=0 ></td>
<td colspan=9 height=13></td>
</tr>
<tr valign="top">
<td colspan=3 height=16></td>
<td colspan=2 height=16></td>
<td colspan=13 height=16></td>
</tr>
<tr valign="top">
<td colspan=3 height=31></td>
<td colspan=2 height=31></td>
<td colspan=2 height=31></td>
<td colspan=1 rowspan=22 width=4 align="center" valign="middle"><img height=612 width=4 src="http://www.geocities.com/clipart/pbi/vrules/Templates/aboutme_classic_vertline.gif" border=0 ></td>
<td colspan=10 height=31></td>
</tr>
<tr valign="top">
<td colspan=3 height=141></td>
<td colspan=2 height=141></td>
<td colspan=2 height=141></td>
<td colspan=2 height=141></td>
<td colspan=1 rowspan=19 width=237><font size="-1"><span style="font-size:12">The College, originally a school for Christian girls, was taken over, by the Travancore Government during the reign of H.H.Sri Avittam Thirunal Maharaja of Travancore and was recognized as a High School by the Madras University in 1890. In 1897 it become the Maharaja's College for Girls and in 1920 the college got its present name H.H.The Maharajas College for Women. In 1928 it became a First Grade College today with 22 subject departments, more than 1200 teachers and 3000 students it is the biggest college in the State offering  Degree, Post Graduate and MPhil courses and providing facilities for research leading to
```

```
Phd of Kerala University. In 1993 the college was declared as a Centre of Excellence
by the Government.  <br></span></font></td>
        <td colspan=7 height=141></td>
        </tr>
        <tr valign="top">
        <td colspan=3 height=23></td>
        <td colspan=17 height=23></td>
        <td colspan=2 height=23></td>
        <td colspan=7 height=23></td>
        </tr>
        <tr valign="top">
        <td colspan=3 height=125></td>
        <td colspan=8 height=125></td>
        <td colspan=4 rowspan=1 width=180 align="center" valign="middle"><img
height=125 width=180 src="collegeview photo 12.jpg" border=0 ></td>
        <td colspan=5 height=125></td>
        <td colspan=2 height=125></td>
        <td colspan=7 height=125></td>
        </tr>
        <tr valign="top">
        <td colspan=3 height=5></td>
        <td colspan=17 height=5></td>
        <td colspan=2 height=5></td>
        <td colspan=7 height=5></td>
        </tr>
        <tr valign="top">
        <td colspan=3 height=24></td>
        <td colspan=7 height=24></td>
        <td align="center" colspan=6 rowspan=1 width=213><b><i><font size="-
2"><span style="font-size:10">A view of the college building</span></font></
b></i></td>
        <td colspan=4 height=24></td>
        <td colspan=2 height=24></td>
        <td colspan=7 height=24></td>
        </tr>
        <tr valign="top">
        <td colspan=3 height=28></td>
```

```
<td colspan=17 height=28></td>
<td colspan=2 height=28></td>
<td colspan=7 height=28></td>
</tr>
<tr valign="top">
<td colspan=3 height=18></td>
<td colspan=3 height=18></td>
<td colspan=11 rowspan=1 width=243><b><u><font color="#336600"><span style="font-size:14">College Library Services</span></font></b></u></td>
<td colspan=3 height=18></td>
<td colspan=2 height=18></td>
<td colspan=7 height=18></td>
</tr>
<tr valign="top">
<td colspan=3 height=10></td>
<td colspan=17 height=10></td>
<td colspan=2 height=10></td>
<td colspan=7 height=10></td>
</tr>
<tr valign="top">
<td colspan=3 height=22></td>
<td colspan=3 height=22></td>
<td colspan=11 rowspan=1 width=243><a href="http://hindu.com"><span style="font-size:14">Read Hindu Daily</span></a></td>
<td colspan=3 height=22></td>
<td colspan=2 height=22></td>
<td colspan=7 height=22></td>
</tr>
<tr valign="top">
<td colspan=3 height=4></td>
<td colspan=17 height=4></td>
<td colspan=2 height=4></td>
<td colspan=7 height=4></td>
</tr>
<tr valign="top">
<td colspan=3 height=22></td>
```

```
<td colspan=3 height=22></td>
<td colspan=11 rowspan=1 width=243><a href="http://deshabhimani.com"><span style="font-size:14">Read Deshabimani</span></a></td>
<td colspan=3 height=22></td>
<td colspan=2 height=22></td>
<td colspan=7 height=22></td>
</tr>
<tr valign="top">
<td colspan=3 height=4></td>
<td colspan=17 height=4></td>
<td colspan=2 height=4></td>
<td colspan=7 height=4></td>
</tr>
<tr valign="top">
<td colspan=3 height=22></td>
<td colspan=3 height=22></td>
<td colspan=11 rowspan=1 width=243><a href="http://www.mathrubhumi.com/"><span style="font-size:14">Read Mathrubhoomi</span></a></td>
<td colspan=3 height=22></td>
<td colspan=2 height=22></td>
<td colspan=7 height=22></td>
</tr>
<tr valign="top">
<td colspan=3 height=4></td>
<td colspan=17 height=4></td>
<td colspan=2 height=4></td>
<td colspan=7 height=4></td>
</tr>
<tr valign="top">
<td colspan=3 height=34></td>
<td colspan=3 height=34></td>
<td colspan=11 rowspan=1 width=243><a href="http://www.ipl.org"><span style="font-size:14">Use Worldwide Libraires through College Library</span></a></td>
<td colspan=3 height=34></td>
```

```
<td colspan=2 height=34></td>
<td colspan=7 height=34></td>
</tr>
<tr valign="top">
<td colspan=3 height=28></td>
<td colspan=17 height=28></td>
<td colspan=2 height=28></td>
<td colspan=7 height=28></td>
</tr>
<tr valign="top">
<td colspan=3 height=18></td>
<td colspan=3 height=18></td>
<td colspan=11 rowspan=1 width=243><b><u><font color="#336600"><span style="font-size:14">To Contact</span></font></b></u></td>
<td colspan=3 height=18></td>
<td colspan=2 height=18></td>
<td colspan=7 height=18></td>
</tr>
<tr valign="top">
<td colspan=3 height=6></td>
<td colspan=17 height=6></td>
<td colspan=2 height=6></td>
<td colspan=7 height=6></td>
</tr>
<tr valign="top">
<td colspan=3 height=19></td>
<td colspan=3 height=19></td>
<td colspan=6 rowspan=2 width=59><b><font size="-1"><span style="font-size:12">Name:</span></font></b></td>
<td colspan=1 height=19></td>
<td colspan=4 rowspan=4 width=173><b><font size="-1"><span style="font-size:12">H.H. The Maharajas Government College for Women, Trivandrum -695014. Telephone: 91 0471 324986, 337 30.7</span></font></b></td>
<td colspan=3 height=19></td>
<td colspan=2 height=19></td>
```

```
<td colspan=7 height=19></td>
</tr>
<tr valign="top">
<td colspan=3 height=2></td>
<td colspan=3 height=2></td>
<td colspan=1 height=2></td>
<td colspan=3 height=2></td>
<td colspan=10 height=2></td>
</tr>
<tr valign="top">
<td colspan=3 height=22></td>
<td colspan=10 height=22></td>
<td colspan=3 height=22></td>
<td colspan=10 height=22></td>
</tr>
<tr valign="top">
<td colspan=3 height=16></td>
<td colspan=10 height=16></td>
<td colspan=14 height=16></td>
</tr>
<tr valign="top">
<td colspan=3 height=2></td>
<td colspan=28 height=2></td>
</tr>
<tr valign="top">
<td colspan=3 height=6></td>
<td colspan=3 height=6></td>
<td colspan=6 rowspan=2 width=59><b><font size="-1"><span
style="font-size:12">Email:</span></font></b></td>
<td colspan=1 height=6></td>
<td colspan=4 rowspan=2 width=173><a
href="mailto:womenscollege@yahoo.com"><b><font size="-1"><span style="font-
size:12">womenscollege@yahoo.com</span></font></b></a></td>
<td colspan=14 height=6></td>
</tr>
<tr valign="top">
```

```
<td colspan=7 height=15></td>
<td colspan=1 height=15></td>
<td colspan=14 height=15></td>
</tr>
<tr valign="top">
<td colspan=32 height=28></td>
</tr>
<tr valign="top">
<td colspan=7 height=25></td>
        <td colspan=8 rowspan=1 width=125><!– Yahoo! Presence ->
<ahref="http://edit.yahoo.com/config/send_webmesg?.target
=womenscollege&.src=pg">
<img border=0 src="http://opi.yahoo.com/online?u=
womenscollege&m=g&t=2"></a></td>
<td colspan=17 height=25></td>
</tr>
<tr valign="top">
<td colspan=32 height=10></td>
</tr>
<tr valign="top">
<td colspan=2 height=4></td>
<td colspan=3 rowspan=3 width=13 align="center" valign="middle"><img
height=13 width=13 src="http://www.geocities.com/clipart/pbi/bullets/Templates/
aboutme_classic_grnbullet.gif' border=0 ></td>
<td colspan=23 height=4></td>
<td colspan=2 rowspan=3 width=13 align="center" valign="middle"><img
height=13 width=13 src="http://www.geocities.com/clipart/pbi/bullets/Templates/
aboutme_classic_grnbullet.gif' border=0 ></td>
<td colspan=2 height=4></td>
</tr>
<tr valign="top">
<td colspan=2 height=4></td>
<td colspan=3 height=4></td>
<td colspan=18 rowspan=1 width=538 align="center"
valign="middle"><img height=4 width=538 src="http://www.geocities.com/clipart/
pbi/hrules/Templates/aboutme_classic_horzline.gif' border=0 ></td>
<td colspan=2 height=4></td>
<td colspan=2 height=4></td>
```

```
</tr>
<tr valign="top">
<td colspan=2 height=5></td>
<td colspan=23 height=5></td>
<td colspan=2 height=5></td>
</tr>
</table>
</body>
</html>
```

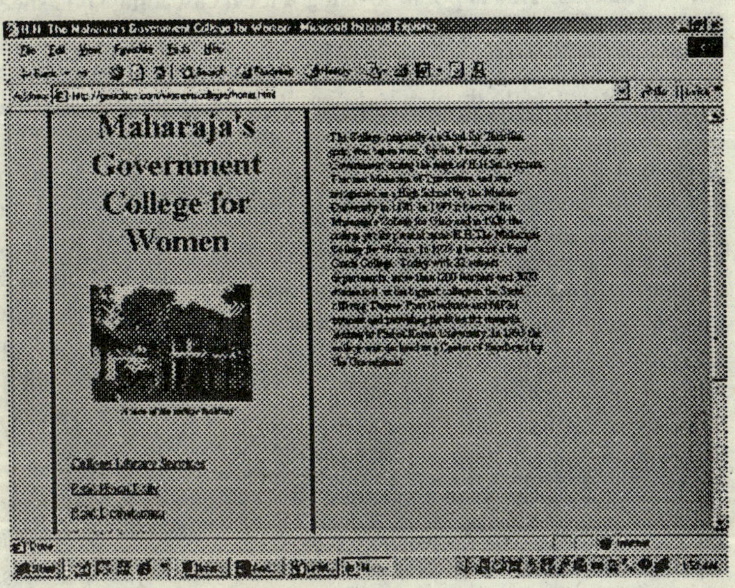

If physical and logical styles produce the same result on the screen in the ideal SGML universe, content is divorced from presentation. Thus SGML tags a level-one heading as a level-one heading, but does not specify that the level-one heading should be, for instance, 24 point bold Times centered. The advantage of this approach, which is similar in concept to style sheets in many word processors, is that if we decide to change level-one headings to be 20-point left-justified Helvetica, all we have to do is change the definition of the level-one heading in our Web browser. Indeed, many browsers today let us define how we want the various HTML tags rendered on-screen using what are called cascading style sheets, or CSS. CSS is more advanced than HTML, though, and will not be covered in this Primer. Another advantage of logical tags is that they help enforce consistency in our documents. It is easier to tag something as <H1> than to remember that level-one headings are 24-point bold Times centered or whatever. For example, consider the <STRONG> tag. Most browsers render it in bold text. However, it is possible that a reader would prefer that these sections be displayed in red instead. This is possible using a local cascading style sheet on the reader's own computer. Logical styles offer this flexibility. If we want something to be displayed in italics and do not want a browser's setting to display it differently, we should use physical styles. Physical styles, therefore, offer consistency in that something we tag a certain way will always be displayed that way for readers of our document. We have to try to be consistent about which type of style we use. If we tag with physical styles, we have to do so throughout a document. If we use logical styles, we have to stick with them within a document. We save to keep in mind that future releases of HTML might not support certain logical styles, which could mean that browsers will not display our logical style coding. For example, the <DFN> tag short for definition, and typically displayed in italics is not widely supported and will be ignored if the reader's browser does not understand it.

4.1. Logical Styles

<DFN>for a word being defined. Typically displayed in italics. (NCSA Mosaic is a World Wide Web browser.)

<EM>for emphasis. Typically displayed in italics. (Consultants cannot reset password unless we call the help line.)

<CITE>for titles of books, films, etc. Typically displayed in italics.

<CODE>for computer code. Displayed in a fixed-width font. (The <stdio.h> header file)

<KBD>for user keyboard entry. Typically displayed in plain fixed-width font. (Enter passwd to change our password.)

<SAMP>for a sequence of literal characters. Displayed in a fixed-width font. (Segmentation fault: Core dumped.)

<STRONG>for strong emphasis. Typically displayed in bold. (NOTE: Always check our links.)

<VAR>for a variable, where we will replace the variable with specific information. Typically displayed in italics. (rm filename deletes the file.)

4.2. Physical Styles

<B> bold text

<I>italic text

<TT>typewriter text, e.g. fixed-width font.

Escape Sequences (a.k.a. Character Entities)

Character entities have two functions, escaping special characters and displaying other characters not available in the plain ASCII character set that is primarily characters with diacritical marks. Three ASCII characters; the left angle bracket (<), the right angle bracket (>), and the ampersand (&)—have special meanings in HTML and therefore cannot be used "as is" in text. The angle brackets are used to indicate the beginning and end of HTML tags, and the ampersand is used to indicate the beginning of an escape sequence. Double quote marks may be used as-is but a character entity may also be used (").

To use one of the three characters in an HTML document, we must enter its escape sequence instead:

< the escape sequence for <

> the escape sequence for >

&the escape sequence for &

Additional escape sequences support accented characters, such as:

ö a lowercase o with an umlaut: ö

ñ a lowercase n with a tilde: ñ

È an uppercase E with a grave accent: È

We can substitute other letters for the o, n, and E shown

above. Unlike the rest of HTML, the escape sequences are case sensitive. We cannot, for instance, use < instead of <.

5. Linking

The chief power of HTML comes from its ability to link text and/or an image to another document or section of a document. A browser highlights the identified text or image with color and/or underlines to indicate that it is a hypertext link often shortened to hyperlink or just link. HTML's single hypertext-related tag is <A>, which stands for anchor. To include an anchor in our document;

* we have to start the anchor with <A (include a space after the A)
* and then specify the document you're linking to by entering the parameter HREF="filename" followed by a closing right angle bracket (>)
* enter the text that will serve as the hypertext link in the current document
* enter the ending anchor tag: </A> (no space is needed before the end anchor tag)

Here is a sample hypertext reference in a file called US.html:

<A HREF="MaineStats.html">Maine</A>

This entry makes the word Maine the hyperlink to the document MaineStats.html, which is in the same directory as the first document.

5.1 Relative Versus Absolute Pathnames

We can link to documents in other directories by specifying the relative path from the current document to the linked document. For example, a link to a file NYStats.html located in the subdirectory Atlantic States would be: <A HREF="Atlantic States/ NY Stats .html"> New York</A>. These are called relative links because we are specifying the path to the linked file relative to the location of the current file. We can also use the absolute pathname (the complete URL) of the file, but relative links are more efficient in accessing a server. They also have the advantage of making our documents more "portable" for instance, we can create several web pages in a single folder on our local computer, using relative links to hyperlink one page to another, and then upload the entire folder of web pages to our web server. The pages on the server will then link to other pages on the server, and the copies on our hard drive will still point to the other pages stored there. It is important to point out that UNIX is a case sensitive operating system where filenames are concerned, while DOS and the MacOS are not. For instance, on a Macintosh, "DOCUMENT.HTML", "Document.HTML", and "document.html" are all the same names. If we make a relative hyperlink to "DOCUMENT.HTML", and the file is actually named "document.html", the link will still be valid. But if you upload all your pages to a UNIX web server, the link will no longer work. Be sure to check your filenames before uploading. Pathnames use the standard UNIX syntax. The UNIX syntax for the parent directory (the directory that contains the current directory) is "..".

If we were in the NYStats.html file and were referring to the original document US.html, our link would look like this: <A HREF="./US.html">United States</A>. In general, we should use relative links whenever possible because; it is easier to move a group of documents to another location for because the relative path names will still be valid, it is more efficient connecting to the server and then there is less to type. However, we have to use absolute pathnames when linking to documents that are not directly related. For example, consider a group of documents that comprise a user manual. Links within this group should be relative links. Links to other documents perhaps a reference to related software should use absolute pathnames instead. This way if we move the user manual to a different directory, none of the links would have to be updated.

5.2 URL

As we have discussed earlier the World Wide Web uses Uniform Resource Locators (URLs) to specify the location of files on other servers. A URL includes the type of resource being accessed e.g., Web, gopher, FTP, the address of the server, and the location of the file. The syntax is:

scheme://host.domain [:port]/path/ filename

where scheme is one

file: a file on our local system

ftp: a file on an anonymous FTP server

http: a file on a World Wide Web server

gopher: a file on a Gopher server

WAIS: a file on a WAIS server

News: a Usenet newsgroup

telnet: a connection to a Telnet-based service

The port number can generally be omitted. That means that unless someone tells us otherwise, we have to leave it out. For example, to include a link to this primer in our document, we have to enter: <A REF="http://www college for women.org > college for women </A>. This entry makes the Home page of college for women a hyperlink to this document. There is also a mailto scheme, used to hyperlink email addresses, but this scheme is unique in that it uses only a colon (:) instead of :// between the scheme and the address.

5.3 Links to Specific Sections Inside

Anchors can also be used to move a reader to a particular section in a document either the same or a different document rather than to the top, which is the default. This type of an anchor is commonly called a named anchor because to create the links, we insert HTML names within the document. But for long document, it can be time consuming to move through when all we really want to know about is one bit of information. Internal hyperlinks are used to create a "table of contents" at the top a document. These hyperlinks move us from one location in the document to another location in the same document.

We can also link to a specific section in another document.

5.4 Links Between Sections of Different Documents

Suppose we want to set a link from document A (documentA.html) to a specific section in another document (MaineStats.html). Enter the HTML coding for a link to a named anchor:

documentA.html:

In addition to the many state parks, Maine is also home to

<a href="MaineStats.html#ANP">Acadia National Park</a>.

Think of the characters after the hash (#) mark as a tab within the MaineStats.html file. This tab tells our browser what should be displayed at the top of the window when the link is activated. In other words, the first line in our browser window should be the Acadia National Park heading. Next, we have to create the named anchor (in this example "ANP") in MaineStats.html:

<H2><A NAME="ANP">Acadia National Park</a></H2>

With both of these elements in place, we can bring a reader directly to the Acadia reference in MaineStats.html. We cannot make links to specific sections within a different document unless either we have write permission to the coded source of that document or that document already contains in document named anchors. For example, we could include named anchors in a document we are writing. But if that document did not have named anchors, we could not make a link to a specific section because we cannot edit the original file on another's server.

5.6 Links to Specific Sections within

The technique is the same except the filename is omitted. For example, to link to the ANP anchor from within MaineStats, enter:

...More information about

<A HREF="#ANP">Acadia National Park</a>

is available elsewhere in this document.

We have to be sure to include the <A NAME=> tag at the place in our document where we want the link to jump to (<A NAME="ANP">Acadia National Park</a>). Named anchors are particularly useful when we think readers will print a document in its entirety or when we have a lot of short information we want to place online in one file.

5.7 Mailto

We can make it easy for a reader to send electronic mail to a specific person or mail alias by including the mailto attribute in a hyperlink. The format is:

<A HREF="mailto:emailinfo@host">Name</a>

For we can example, enter:

<A HREF="mailto:ramannair_r@yahoo.com">

R. Raman Nair</a>

to create a mail window that is already configured to open a mail window.

6. Inline Images

Most Web browsers can display inline images that is, images next to text that are in X Bitmap (XBM), GIF, or JPEG format.

Other image formats are also being incorporated into Web browsers. Each image takes additional time to download and slows down the initial display of a document. We have to carefully select our images and the number of images in a document. To include an inline image, we have to enter:

<IMG SRC=ImageName>

where ImageName is the URL of the image file.

The syntax for <IMG SRC> URLs is identical to that used in an anchor HREF. If the image file is a GIF file, then the filename part of ImageName must end with .gif. Filenames of X Bitmap images must end with .xbm; JPEG image files must end with .jpg or .jpeg; and Portable Network Graphic files must end with .png.

6.1 Image Size Attributes

We should include two other attributes on <IMG> tags to tell our browser the size of the images it is downloading with the text.

The HEIGHT and WIDTH attributes lets our browser set aside the appropriate space (in pixels) for the images as it downloads the rest of the file. We can get the pixel size from our image processing software, such as Adobe Photoshop. Some browsers will also display the dimensions of an image file in the title bar if the image is viewed by itself without an enclosing HTML document. For example, to include a self portrait image in a file along with the portrait's dimensions, we have to enter: <IMG SRC=SelfPortrait.gif HEIGHT=100 WIDTH=65>. Some browsers use the HEIGHT and WIDTH attributes to stretch or shrink an image to fit into the allotted space when the image does not exactly match the attribute numbers. Not all browser developers think stretching/shrinking is a good idea. So we should not plan on our users having access to this feature. Check your dimensions and use the correct ones.

6.2 Aligning Images

We have some flexibility when displaying images. We can have images separated from text and aligned to the left or right or centered. Or we can have an image aligned with text. We have to try several possibilities to see how our information looks best.

By default the bottom of an image is aligned with the following text, as shown in this paragraph. We can align images to the top or center of a paragraph using the ALIGN= attributes TOP and CENTER.

To align with the top of the image (<IMG SRC = "BarHotlist.gif" ALT="[HOTLIST]" ALIGN=TOP

To center text on the image (<IMG SRC = "BarHotlist.gif" ALT="[HOTLIST]" ALIGN=CENTER>).

To display an image without any associated text (e.g., our organization's logo), we can make it a separate paragraph. We have to use the paragraph ALIGN= attribute to center the image or adjust it to the right side of the window.

```
<p ALIGN=CENTER>
<IMG SRC = "BarHotlist.gif' ALT="[HOTLIST]">
</p>
```

The result is that the image is centered; and the text paragraph starts below it and left justified.

6.3 Alternate Text for Images

Some World Wide Web browsers primarily the text only browsers such as Lynx cannot display images. Some users turn off image loading even if their software can display images especially if they are using a modem or have a slow connection. HTML provides a mechanism to tell readers what they are missing us specify text to be displayed instead of an image. For example: <IMG SRC="UpArrow.gif" ALT="Up"> where UpArrow.gif is the picture of an upward pointing arrow. With graphics-capable viewers that have image loading turned on, we see the up arrow graphic. With a text-only browser or if image loading is turned off, the word Up is shown in our window in place of the image. We should try to include alternate text for each image we use in our document, which is a courtesy for our readers or, for users who might be visually impaired, a necessity.

7. Background Graphics

Newer versions of Web browsers can load an image and use it as a background when displaying a page. Some people like background images and some don't. In general, if we want to include a background, we have to make sure our text can be read easily when displayed on top of the image. Background images can be a texture (linen finished paper, for example) or an image of an object (a logo possibly). We create the background image as we do any image. However we only have to create a small piece of the image. Using a feature called tiling, a browser takes the image and repeats it across and down to fill our browser window. In sum we generate one image, and the browser replicates it enough times to fill our window. This action is automatic when we use the background tag shown below. The tag to include a background image in the <BODY> statement as an attribute: <BODY BACKGROUND="filename .gif">

7.1 Background Color

By default browsers display text in black on a gray background. However, we can change both elements if we want. Some HTML authors select a background color and coordinate it with a change in the color of the text. Always preview changes like this to make sure our pages are readable. For example, many people find red text on a black background difficult to read. In general, we have to try to avoid using high-contrast images or images that use the color of our text anywhere within the graphic. We change the color of text, links, visited links, and active links using further attributes of the <BODY> tag. For example: <BODY BGCOLOR="#000000" TEXT="#FFFFFF" LINK="#9690CC">

This creates a window with a black background (BGCOLOR), white text (TEXT), and silvery hyperlinks (LINK). The six-digit number and letter combinations represent colors by giving their RGB (red, green, blue) value. The six digits are actually three two-digit numbers in sequence, representing the amount of red, green, or blue as a hexadecimal value in the range 00-FF. For example, 000000 is black (no color at all), FF0000 is bright red, 0000FF is bright blue, and FFFFFF is white (fully saturated with all three colors). These number and letter combinations are generally rather cryptic.

For some basic colors typically those in the standard sixteen color Windows palette we can also use the name of the color instead of the corresponding RGB value. For example, "black", "red", "blue", and "cyan" are all valid for use in place of RGB values. However, while not all browsers will understand all color names, any browser that can display colors will understand RGB values, so use them whenever possible.

8. External Images, Sounds, and Animations

We may want to have an image open as a separate document when a user activates a link on either a word or a smaller, inline version of the image included in our document. This is called an external image, and it is useful if we do not wish to slow down the loading of the main document with large inline images. To include a reference to an external image, enter: <A HREF="MyImage.gif">link anchor</A>. We can also use a smaller image as a link to a larger image. Enter: <A HREF="LargerImage.gif"><IMG SRC="SmallImage .gif"></A>. The reader sees the SmallImage.gif image and clicks on it to open the largerImage .gif file. Use the same syntax for links to external animations and sounds. The only difference is the file extension of the linked file. For example, <A HREF="AdamsRib.mov">link anchor</A> specifies a link to a QuickTime movie. Some common file types and their extensions are:

plain text	.txt
HTML document	.html
GIF image	.gif
TIFF image	.tiff
X Bitmap image	.xbm
JPEG image	.jpg or .jpeg
PostScript file	.ps
AIFF sound file	.aiff
AU sound file	.au
WAV sound file	.wav
QuickTime movie	.mov
MPEG movie	.mpeg or .mpg

We have to keep in mind our intended audience and their access to software. Most UNIX workstations, for instance, cannot view QuickTime movies.

9. Fill-out Forms

Web forms let a reader return information to a Web server for some action. For example, suppose we collect names and email addresses so we can email some information to people who request it. For each person who enters his or her name and address, we need some information to be sent and the respondent's particulars added to a database. This processing of incoming data is usually handled by a script or program written in Perl or another language that manipulates text, files, and information. If we cannot write a program or script for our incoming information, we need to find someone who can do this for us. The forms themselves are not hard to code. They follow the same constructs as other HTML tags. What could be difficult is, the program or script that takes the information submitted in a form and processes it. Because of the need for specialized scripts to handle the incoming form information, fill-out forms are not discussed in this primer.

16

Internet Tomorrow

To some extent we can predict how Internet will evolve over the next few years. The most important change the merging of web content and local content has already begun, and will affect not just the way we use the Internet, but the way we use our computer overall. We should follow up what net surfing is becoming, so that we can anticipate and quickly exploit new developments as they arrive. We should also know the optional changes Internet Explorer can make to our computer; changes that offer a preview of the way all computers will work tomorrow.

1. WEB INTEGRATION

Although we may not think of it this way, what we do on the web is not that different from what we do on our computer or Local Area Network. The following table shows how online activities and local activities are really much the same.

On a Computer (Local Activities)	*On the Web (Online Activities)*
We navigate to programs and files by clicking folders or clicking through a directory.	We navigate to programs and files by clicking links in web pages and in directories of links.
At times, we navigate to a file by specifying its location, for example, by entering a disk letter and path {such as c: \ file. txt.	At times, we navigate to a file by specifying its location, for example, by entering a URL such as www .web. com/file. htm.

We open programs and files by double clicking their file icons or names.	We open programs and files by clicking links, which may be pictures {icons) or text {names).

In light of this comparison, developers have wondered on the reasons for treating online resources and local resources differently. So the attempt for retooling our computers to enable us to do everything the same way had begun. The present thought is that there is no need to learn two different ways to perform the same basic task, just because one file is on our computer and the other is on a web site in Washington. A file is a file and location should be irrelevant. That is the idea behind web integration. On a web-integrated system, we navigate among files and folders, and open files and programs, the same way whether the file is local or on the web. We need not learn two different ways of getting around, and in many cases, we will not even have to think about whether the file or program we want to use is on the web or on our computer.

The basic thing about web integration today is the assignment of default programs for accessing online content. When we install most browsers in Windows, the browser is automatically assigned in the file Registry as the default program for displaying HTML files and dealing with URLs. Anytime an HTML file icon is opened, or URL entered, the browser opens, automatically to display it. On most systems, the browser also determines whether the requested file is online or offline, and connects to the Internet automatically, if necessary.

2. Benefits of Web Integration

Once we get accustomed to web integration, we might find that we use our computer more productively and more intuitively. Whenever our brain must jump back and forth between two skill sets which is an activity called code switching, our productivity suffers. When we can do all things with one set of skills, our brain can focus on the task at hand, not on the techniques that accomplish it. On a web-integrated computer, we will deal with all files and programs the same way, whether they are online or local. This streamlined way of working may also make us more comfortable working with online resources, so that we will get more out of the web.

3. Forms of Web Integration

Web integration is already here in a primitive form in Internet Explorer. Very soon, however, a similar level of web integration will emerge as a standard feature of all personal computer operating systems, including any new versions of Windows, Mac OS, or Unix to come along from now on. Each time we buy a new computer or upgrade our present computer to a new operating system, we will probably notice a tighter level of web integration and more built in Internet software than before. Within two or three years from now, seamless web integration will be taken for granted on a personal computer. But even sooner now, actually, we will see web integration manifesting itself in a variety of ways beyond the operating system. Here we will see the ways in which the online and offline worlds merge now and in the near future. A growing list of programs and file types are already designed to incorporate web-based content or integrate with web based services.

4. Net-Smart Programs

Some items on the Help menu and items within the help files of Internet Explorer, Navigator, and other programs lead to online content. For example, choose Help > Member Services in Navigator, and Navigator connects to the Internet and opens a Member Services page on Netscape's web site. The interesting thing is that these menu items look just like any other menu item and it takes us online until we choose it. As far as the program is concerned, there is no difference between local and online resources.

It makes sense for a browser to assume that we have an Internet connection, but what about other kinds of programs, such as word processors or money managers. They also are beginning to incorporate online content, particularly in their Help menus and in menu items that lead to web pages for registering with the program's developer or downloading upgrades and accessories.

Many Microsoft products even some unrelated to the Internet have a Microsoft on the Web item on their Help menus. That item opens a submenu of choices, each of which leads to online content. Microsoft's Cinemania that is a movie reference CDROM includes a Go Online button we can click to download the latest movie reviews and add them to our copy of Cinemania. Also, many programs unrelated to the Internet are nonetheless built to integrate with related web based services.

When purchasing a program based on its capability to interact with the Internet, we have to check the printed literature available along with it or details printed in the pack. Some programs are designed to interact with the net only through a particular ISP or online service. We have to use that provider to take advantage of any online features offered by that product. In such cases, the program developer is not really providing the benefit of web integration; rather, the developer is acting as a salesperson for an Internet provider. As non-Internet related programs rely increasingly on online content, users without Internet accounts may begin feeling a little left out. For others this approach makes good sense. Online content saves disk space on our computer. More importantly, it enables a program's developer to ensure that we can always get the latest, most complete information. For example, as users discover flaws called bugs in a program, instructions for dealing with the bugs can be added to the online help text, or a file for fixing the bug called a patch and they can be made available from a link in the help text.

5. Net-Smart Files

Recent versions of many document-producing programs enable us to put live, active links to online content within a document. For example, in Microsoft's Office 97 and 2000 programs like Word, Excel, PowerPoint, Access, and Outlook when we type an URL in any document that URL is automatically formatted as an actual, functioning link. We can enable or disable this feature from each program's AutoCorrect dialog box. On paper, of course, the link is useless. Suppose we give someone that document as a file, however, either on a disk or attached to an email message, while reading the document on his or her computer, the reader can activate the link to access online content, if the reader's computer is Internet connected.

When creating a document that will be distributed and read in this way, we can add links that the reader may optionally click to access online content that expands upon, reinforces, or supports the content in our document. For example, when mentioning a particular library, we might insert a link to that library's web page. In fact, if we are provided with this book as a set of MSword files, we could click any web page we have seen to go straight to it.

6. Net-Smart Machines

The Net PC concept takes web integration one-step further than a web integrated operating system. A Net PC is a computer with a sealed case and no floppy drive or CD ROM drive. Files get into or out of a Net PC only through a network it is connected to, such as the Internet. In some Net PC scenarios of several that are evolving, the programs we use would run on servers; in others, programs are downloaded to our computer as needed. In either case, a Net PC can be a smaller, cheaper box than the typical Mac or PC of today, and could be used effectively to browse the Internet. A team of heavy hitters including Microsoft, Intel, Compaq, and IBM is developing Net PCs. The early models are aimed at corporate

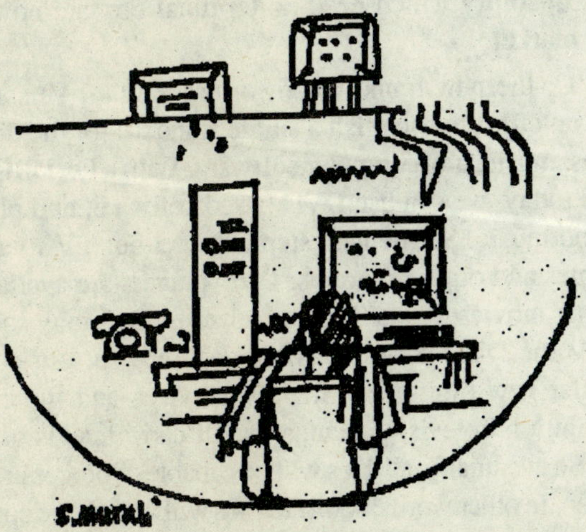

Figure 16.1

sales, but some foresee the Net PC as an affordable home Internet terminal. Most experts today, however, do not see the Net PC in homes. The cost of a Net PC is so close to that of a budget PC that a home user would always opt for a more flexible, full function computer.

Screens are needed for both computers and televisions. So attempts were made to make TVs that are also PCs, to save the cost of having two screens. That is the basic idea behind what some people call PCTVs, televisions that are also computers and maybe videophones, too. The PCTV has also started to arrive but given the popularity of the Internet, any true PCTV is to be fully web integrated if it is to catch the market. Many experts believe that the PCTV idea will not catch on, because watching TV and computing are fundamentally different activities. One is a big screen, group activity in the living room, the other is mostly a solitary, reading intensive activity best done close to the screen, at a desk. Still, many high tech companies that believe in PCTV now have started to offer products that could pave the road to PCTV. The Web TV terminal box turns our TV into an Internet terminal although not a full computer we may use for other applications. TVs with built in Web TV capability which need no terminal box are now getting ready for market.

DVD; the new home video format, Digital Versatile Disc (DVD) is an effort to establish a single standard for the discs used for movies, music, and computer software. With a DVDROM drive in our PC today, we can use DVD based software, and play DVD movies and music. So the next step is to get our TV to use DVD based games and other programs. DVD players are available now for showing movies on our TV, but newer models may soon show on our TV the DVD based software designed for our computer. The popular new digital satellite TV services and the emerging High Definition Television standards; all carry television signals digitally. So eventually, all TVs will be capable of processing digital information. In other words, soon all TV s will already be computers, probably adaptable to other computing and communications tasks, such as the Internet.

7. Internet Explorer

Earlier versions of Internet Explorer were only web browsers. It is still a browser, of course. But at our option, Internet Explorer can add to Windows a feature called the Active Desktop, sometimes also called Web Integrated Desktop or Windows Desktop Update.

The Active Desktop changes Windows 98 or Windows ME/NT/2000 in a way in which accessing and opening files and programs on our own computer or local network is just like accessing and opening a web page on the Internet. In effect, Internet Explorer makes all of Windows 98 and its later versions behave a lot like the web, and it provides a preview of the way all computer systems will probably behave tomorrow.

7.1 File Icon

The Active Desktop makes every file icon, program icon, or folder icon in a Windows folder, in Windows Explorer, and on the desktop into a link. The icon labels are underlined just the way a link is underlined in a web page, and the pointer turns into a pointing finger when on the icon, just as it does on link. Because of this link formatting, we do not have to double click the icon to open a file, folder, or program, as we have always had to do in Windows. Instead, we point to the link like file icon and click once, just as we do to activate a link online. Also, we no longer have to click at all to select a file icon when moving, copying, or performing another such operation on it. We have to just point to the icon and wait a second, and the icon is selected

7.2 Channel Bar

As we have seen earlier Internet Explorer puts the Channel bar on our desktop when the Active Desk top is installed. By putting one click access to Internet resources right on the desktop, the Channel bar is both an important tool for, and symbol of, web integration.

7.3 Folders

The appearance and behavior of all our Windows folders changes on the Active Desktop. As mentioned earlier, file and folder icons become links, but there is even more webbiness than that.

We can now get from place to place in a folder just as we get around the web, by using the browser like toolbars on every folder window. Folders on the Active Desktop also work like a web page in other ways. They may show inline images or have backgrounds. When we point to an icon that is selecting it, information about that icon is displayed on the left side of the window. Sometimes, a preview may appear automatically; point to an image file, and a rough view of the image appears automatically on the left side of the folder window.

7.4 Windows Explorer

Windows Explorer is the file management system built into Windows 98, ME, 2000 etc. This is different from Internet Explorer, which is the browser. Perhaps in part to eliminate the confusion Microsoft has more or less merged Internet Explorer with Windows Explorer. We now use a browser like window to do all the stuff we used to do in Windows Explorer: display and navigate among disks, folders, and file lists; create, copy, move, and delete files; and open files and programs.

If we install the Active Desktop, and later decide we do not like it, we can easily remove it, whole or in part. To turn on or off the display of the Channel bar and Active Desktop wallpaper, from the Start menu we can choose Settings > Active Desktop > View as web page. To customize the way we click and other ways the Active Desktop works, we have to choose Settings > Folders & Icons. To completely delete the Active Desktop, open Control Panel, choose Add/Remove Programs, select Internet Explorer from the list, and click the Add/Remove button. On the dialog box that appears, choose Remove the Windows Desktop Update component, but keep the Internet Explorer web browser.

7.5 Programs Menu

The Active Desktop puts our Favorites that are our list of pages we like to visit, right into our Windows Start menu. Choose a Favorite, and Internet Explorer opens automatically to take us there. Besides opening the Favorites list from the Programs menu, we can open it in any folder window or in Windows Explorer, just by choosing Favorites from the menu bar.

8. The Powerful Library Tool

The Internet is no more an abstract concept for library and information service community. We have no choice other than using Internet as a tool to provide cost-effective information service. In Indian context, there are many problems in using Internet -availability of Telecom infrastructure, power supply, a good Local Area Network in university environment, etc. One has to pool and manage the resources in order to access the Internet. Library schools must prepare the students to handle different search engines as well as to tackle the regulatory issues. The knowledge and skills required to retrieve information on the Internet are:

* an awareness of the basic concepts of the Internet such as hypertext, Internet addressing, browser software, etc.,
* online searching skills -the skills required for interaction, searching joining a mailing list, locating information using search engines etc.

8.1. Internet and Future Society

In the Plenary talk given to 49nth FID Conference and Congress Prof. T. Viswanathan, the world renowned scientist from India has given a glimpse of the life in the coming days and the unique role Internet and networks are going to play. The future of the Internet and the ways of life cannot be explained in a better way. Let me quote him from the notes I have taken while listening to his magical talk.

'Rapid advances in information technology have unleashed forces, which are shaping and affecting the basic structure of our society. New perceptions on how to organize work, how to produce and trade, how to manage and how to create wealth have placed knowledge, information and connectivity at the center-stage of human endeavor. In the networked society that is evolving the homes rather than the offices are likely to be the activity centers. Networked society would result in less-travel society. Physical location may become irrelevant for being able to receive or deliver services. This would bring about radical changes in work culture. Enhanced productivity is promised by flexi hours of working coupled with innovative management of resources and manpower. It is estimated that on an average, the working persons in the world spend over 20% of the active time in a day on travel. With travel time saved, home-centered activities would lead to better creativity, innovation and productivity. Telecommuting culture with home-centered activities would eventually lead to a home-centered economy. The present society is characterized by community formation based on work centers. Persons who work in the same office or factory tend to form a bond of such as association, union or a. club. Social activities are usually centered on such formations. In a home-centered environment, the communities will comprise of groups from among people pursuing different jobs and professions in life. Under those circumstances, a true social community is likely to emerge.

'The last few centuries have been characterized by mass production with large industrial houses being set up. This has led to power brokering between work force and the management characterized by strikes, lock outs etc. In a networked society, small community dwellings that are self-contained would emerge. The community needs will be met locally from products available in its natural surroundings. The concept of associations and unions may vanish in the networked society. This would also imply that production would take place locally with a large number of persons engaged in producing goods that are required. This is an interesting scenario for large-scale employment and for overcoming the present problems of unemployment.

Prof. Visvanathan emphasized that Anyone, Anytime, Anywhere, Any information any format will be the feature of coming networked society. A full-fledged networked society implies that every human being on the planet has an access to the network. Network connectivity to home would become an essential infrastructure facility much as electricity or water supply connection. When the networked information society is fully developed, it should be possible for a person from the poorest of the villages in the world to access information resources in the richest of the cities in the world. Network infrastructures which are expected to operate 24 hours a day and 365 days a year would make time zones and holiday patterns irrelevant in the life style of people. Cost of accessing resources across the nations may become independent of time of access or day of the week. What would matter is the need and convenience of the person accessing information. "Any time" facility would foster the growth of "on demand" culture enabling greater flexibility in the life style of individuals and communities." Anywhere" has implication for persons who are accessing information as well as for the information resources being accessed. It should be possible for a person from anywhere in the world to access an information resource located anywhere else in the world. The concept of location independent access would become a reality when a person would be able to access information from anywhere in the world irrespective of his place of residence. Implementation of such a scheme would call for universal identification of individuals, which remains permanent for the lifetime of the individual. In fact, a child may be assigned a universal code as soon as she/he is born and would be identified by that code throughout her/his life on the planet.

'With more and more emphasis towards right to access, any information should become available to any individual on the planet. Some information may be priced whereas some others may be free but access to any information should be a reality. A shift to this scenario is already visible in the information policies of different nations. A networked society should pose no trans border barriers and be able to communicate information in any format that is assimilable by the recipient. Real time machine translation may become a reality.

'There are three communication technologies that are expected to play complementary roles in shaping the networked society of tomorrow. Optical fibers, satellites and short-haul radio. Each is capable of meeting certain important requirements of the networked society: optical fibers provide the bandwidth; satellite communication provides quick remote area connectivity and the short-haul radio links promise to be excellent last-mile links.

'Internet services today represent only the tip of the iceberg that would unfold in a fully developed networked society. Today's Internet services are predominantly text and data oriented with only sprinkles of graphics and still pictures. Tomorrow's services, placed broadly under two categories of Interactive services and Distribution services, would handle full-fledged voice, motion video and all other forms of information. Support of such services call for a broadband infrastructure and the most promising worldwide infrastructure is Broadband Integrated Services Digital Network. Asynchronous Transfer Mode is a set of international standards that define a new method for sending large quantities of voice, data and video information simultaneously over networks. ATM is ideal for a wide range of applications including traditional data communication, imaging, video, and multimedia.

'It is now well-established fact that there has been a continuous generation of information on the earth in the last 20 years. It will continue for years to come. In order to substantiate the viewpoint of information explosion, one tends to quote the annual publication figures such as one million journal issues, hundred thousands monographs, one million patents and tens of thousands of reports and dissertations. Such citations ignore a major source of information in the world today, viz the data from weather and remote sensing satellites, which would form the bulk of information that would be generated in the coming decades. An estimate shows that all the planned remote sensing and weather satellites by the year 2000 would generate one terabyte of data per day. A little reflection will reveal that this is equivalent to about one million books of 300 pages each being published every day. If we compare today's volume with this, what we are generating is only a miniscule.

'Apart from the current information, the world has been accumulating information over millions of years which are stored in different forms in different parts of the world. This information, when digitized would perhaps run into several million terabytes. All these statistics should give us an idea about what is in store for us in the ensuing information society. Perhaps, a large section of the population would spend its time in evolving effective and efficient data, information and knowledge management techniques.

'Current data warehousing software efforts are directed towards corporate data resource, which needs to be managed effectively to maintain leadership in a competitive world. These efforts need to be scaled up by orders of magnitude before even the simple applications of the networked society can be managed effectively. Data mining, also called knowledge discovery in databases, pertains to retrieval techniques used for handling voluminous mass of data. Very Large Database Management Systems require new approaches to handling massive data the future databases would contain. Data mining ensures fast retrieval of specific data items from very large databases. It also attempts to enforce the condition that no stored data remains irretrievable. Today's data mining techniques range from online application processing tools that query multidimensional databases to advanced artificial intelligence techniques like Machine learning, neural network &, rule-based systems and genetic algorithms. To efficiently mine gigabytes and terabytes of data in a timely fashion, use of parallel processing techniques would become inevitable. Data mining today is centered on local databases. For a networked society, data mining has to be implemented in large-scale telecommunication networks. In the networked society, the world would move from mining for coal or gold to mining for data, information and knowledge.

Prof. T. Visvantahan concluded his talk by stating that we are at the threshold of a new world order which may set in within the next one or two decades. A networked society would emerge as the central theme of living with the society's trade, economy, occupation, development, education, culture and leisure all centered around networking.

9. Knowing Further

So we have got a glimpse of things which most people who have to handle Information Services consider as important aspects of Internet. Too advanced and specialized aspects we have not cared to go through now. By this time we have understood everything one requires to smoothly surf the net as well as provide some library services through the net. Net is a world infinite. With the knowledge we have gained now we can surely wander, explore and conquer the realms of knowledge available on the Information Super Highway as well as put some of our information there.

Any book on Internet becomes obsolete even before it gets printed. That is the speed at which developments are occurring in IT and Internet technology. But revising a book in such a short time is not possible and practical. So readers can get additional information and updates of portions of this book which has become obsolete; from the site maintained by CIRD: after the publication of this book.

To visit the web site for further information and for giving suggestions we can follow the steps given below.

* Connect to the Internet and open the web browser.
* Find the address box, and click in it once.
* Type the URL: http://www.cird.india.org That URL will work in any browser, but if we use latest versions of Internet Explorer or Navigator we can optionally omit the http:// prefix.
* Press Enter. The website of CIRD will appear on the computer screen. Double click the item Internet for information management. We can get additional information if any available.

Let us together now prepare and maintain a good guide to the Internet for Librarians. Point out the defects and give the suggestions. Any additional information or corrections readers recommend will be notified in the web site. You can send them by email to cirdindia@yahoo.com or authors address : ramannair_r@yahoo.com and contribute to improve this book.

Let us conclude by saying information will be the most important resource and one of capital importance tomorrow. Internet will be the major tool and system helping its acquisition, and distribution. The role of libraries in these processes as well as storage, organization and management of information or content that is accessible through Internet needs no special mention.

Select Bibliography

Numerous sources on Internet is available. This is a select list of resources that offer practical advice. These information sources have helped to prepare this book and information was freely extracted from them.

Andrew Hammock, Andrew and Kleppinger, Eugene. Online! : Internet guide for students and writers. . New York: St. Martin's Griffin, 1997

Bates, M.E. The Internet: part of a professional searcher's toolkit. *Online,* 21 (1) Jan/Feb, 1997

Bradley, P and Smith, A. World Wide Web: how to design and construct home pages, London, Aslib, 1995.

Cole, C and Carter, S. Interview and online searching for undergraduates doing a social science assignment. , *Information Processing and management,* 32 (6) Nov, 1996

Dawson, A. The Internet for library and information professionals, London, Library Association Publishing. 1997.

Dholakia, N. The Webs and the Webnots: access issues in the information age. *7elematics and Informatics,* 14 (2) May 97,

Don Busche, Don and Satterlee, Angela. Adventures on the Internet: a beginner's guide Boyd & Fraser Pub. Co., 1996.

Dong, L T Su, LT. Search engines on the World Wide Web and information retrieval from the Internet: a review and evaluation. *Online and CD ROM Review,* 21 (2) Apr 97

Drabenstott, M S Weller, M.S. Handling spelling errors in union catalogue searches. *Library Resources and Technical Services,* 40 (2) Apr, 1996

Estrada, Susan. *Connecting to the Internet. An O'Reilly Buyer's Guide.* Sebastopol, CA: O'Reilly & Associates, 1993.

Flangen, Patrick and Charleston, S.C. Telecommunications: today's ten most critical telecommunications technologies with a focus on the Internet. Computer Technology Research Corp.,

Foote, M Harrison, M Watson, M. Electronic library resources: navigating the man. Resource Sharing and Information Networks, 12 (2) 1997, 1997

Garlock, K. L. and Piontek, S. Building the service based library Web step-by-step guide to design and options, Chicago/London, ALA. 1997.

Glister, Paul. The SLIP/PPP connection: the essential guide to graphical Internet access. New York: Wdey, 1995.

Heidenreich, F. Know your search engine: a comparison of 6 popular Web search engines. *Health Care on the Internet. 1* (2) 1997,1997

Iivonen. Factors lowering the consistency in online searching. *Online Information Seminar proceedings.* Oxford and New Jersey, Learned Information (Europe) Ltd, 1996,

Kahin, S. and Wright, C. Internexus: a partnership for Internet instruction, in Kinder, R. (ed.) Libraries on the Internet: impact on reference se New York, Haworth Press, 1994.

Kehoe, Brendan P. *Zen and the Art of the Internet: A Beginner's Guide.* 3d ed. Englewood Cliffs, NJ: PTR Prentice-Hall, 1994.

Kennedy, S.D. The onslaught of Internet resources: strategies for keeping up with information can be applied to the net. *Information Today,* 14 (3) Mar 97, p.52-3. 1991,

Kochmer, Jonathan. *The Internet Passport. Northwest Net's Guide to Our World Online.* 4th ed. Bellevue, WA: NorthWestNet, 1993.

Koutnik, C. The World Wide Web is here: is the end of printed reference sources near? *R_O,* 36 (3) Spring, 1997

Krol, Ed. *The Whole Internet. User's Guide & Catalogue.* Sebastopol, CA: O'Reilly & Associates, 1994.

Marine. April et al. *Internet. Getting Started.* Englewood Cliffs, NJ: PTR Prentice-Hall, 1992.

McMahon. K. Using the BUBL information service as an Internet reference resource', *Managing information*, 2 (4), 1995.

Mooney. G. Intelligent information retrieval from the World Wide Web using fuzzy user modelling. *Library and information Research, Vews,* 21 (67) Winter 1996,

Morphet, John, P. Windows on the Internet: the complete tool chest on CD-ROM. John P. New York: McGraw-Hill, 1995.

Pal, A., Ring, K. and Downes, V. Intranets for business application. London, Ovum Reports.1996.

Poulter, A. The design of World Wide Web search engines: a critical review. *Program,* 31 (2), 1997

Raisch, M.J. The wide world of the World Wide Web. A description of Web browsers and search engines. , 24 (1) Spring, 1996

Raman Nair, R. Computer Application to Library and Information Services. New Delhi, Ess Ess, 1992.

Rusch-Feja, D. Subject oriented collection of information resources from the Internet. *Libri,* 47 (1) Apr, 1997

Spink, A. Multiple search session's model of end-user behaviour: an exploratory study. *Journal of the American Society for Information Science,* 47 (8) Aug, 1996

Still, I. (ed.) The Internet library: case studies of library Internet management and use, Westport, Mecklermedia.1994.

Storey, T and Daryuple, T. On the Web with OCLC First Search and Net First', OCLC newsletter, 220, 1996.

Stout, Rick. The World Wide Web complete reference. Rick Stout. Berkeley: Osbon, McGraw-Hill, 1996.

Tanenbaum, Andrew S. *Computer Networks.* 2d ed. Englewood Cliffs, NJ: Prentice-Hall,1988.

Tedd, L. A. Introduction to sharing resources via the Internet in academic libraries and information centers in Europe', Program, 29 (1), 1995.

Tennant, Roy et al. *Crossing the Internet Threshold: An Instructional*

Handbook. Berkeley, CA: Library Solutions Press, 1993.

Todino, Grace, John Strang, and Jerry Peck. *Learning the UNIX Operating System. Newton*, MA: O'Reilly & Associates, 1993.

Tomaiuolo, N.G and Packer, J.G. An analysis of Internet search engines: assessment of over 200 search queries. *Computers in Libraries,* 16 (6) Jun, 1996

Torok, A.G. Internet search engines: are users ready? *Towards a worldwide library. A ten-year forecast Proceedings ofthe-19th Internnational Sym*posium 23-26-Se*ptember 199&* Edited by Ahmed H. Heal and Joachim W. Weiss. Essen, Germany, Universitatsbibliothek Essen, 1997.

Tseng, G., Pouter, A. and Sergeant, G. The library and information professional's guide to the World Wide Web, London, and Library Association Pub, 1998.

Vishwanathan, T. Connectivity and information Technology. Key note address at IFLA Seminar, (Aalborg) Denmark, 1997.

Vishwanathan, T. Evolving New Information society: an Indian perception. Third Asia pacific Seminar on Research and Development management, Manila, February 1998.

Vishwanathan, T. Networked Society: Vision and Technology Options. Science Reporter, December 1998.

Watson, I. Searching the V~: a quick comparison of Infoseek, Lycos, Yahoo, Info Market, and Webcrawler. *Managing Information,* 3 (1) Jan, 1996

Woodward, I. Cataloguing and classifying information resources Internet, in Williams, M. E. (ed.) Annual review of information scie7 technology, Medford,

Index